LIVING TRADITION IN THE GARDEN

LIVING TRADITION
IN THE GARDEN

RICHARD GORER

DAVID & CHARLES

NEWTON ABBOT   LONDON

NORTH POMFRET (VT)   VANCOUVER

I would like to express my gratitude to John Murray (Publishers) Ltd
for allowing me to quote from the writings of William Robinson

0 7153 6398 0

Library of Congress Catalog Card Number 74-81598

Set in 11 on 13pt Bembo and printed in Great
Britain by Latimer Trend & Company Ltd
Plymouth for David & Charles (Holdings)
Limited South Devon House Newton Abbot
Devon

Published in the United States of America
by David & Charles Inc North Pomfret
Vermont 05053 USA

Published in Canada by Douglas David &
Charles Limited 3645 McKechnie Drive
West Vancouver BC

CONTENTS

LIST OF ILLUSTRATIONS

PART ONE

GARDENS

I

A PICK-ME-UP BEFORE WE START

We might as well start by giving our morale a boost. If I say that the cultivation of plants for ornament is probably the highest point that civilisation has yet reached I have no doubt that a number of eyebrows will be raised. Still the point is at least arguable, even though the ornamentation of a house with works of art may be cited as a rival peak. This may well have been so once, but now that currency tends to suffer from inflation, the assembling of works of art has not only an aesthetic but also a financial significance; it is not necessarily a flower of civilisation, it may be only part of the struggle for survival. The ornaments of civilisation can only come after the basic material needs have been satisfied, and if we buy a picture, not because it gives us pleasure but because we hope to sell it again for more money in the future, we cannot claim any more virtue than the man who fills in the pools or takes a flutter on the stock exchange.

No one yet grows flowers in order to survive. Plants, be they an aspidistra on the window-sill or in a demesne of many acres, are only there for enjoyment. By any practical standards they are quite useless. We cannot eat them; we cannot sell them generally, we can only enjoy them. If the taking of considerable trouble for innocent but useless enjoyment is not a measure of civilisation, I do not know what is. I am assuming that by civilisation we mean the profitable employment of the time left over from the business of survival; the civilised man would not be bored even though no form of entertainment or partial stupefaction (such as may be legally supplied with alcohol and illegally with other drugs) were available. Few of us can be civilised for all the time available, but it is as well to have some idea as to its potentialities and the gardener can probably claim that he realises more of them than most people. The modern tendency is not to do things oneself but to pay other people to do it for you. Many more people watch football than play football, and even gardeners can go to Kew Gardens, London or Wisley in Surrey, rather than grow the plants themselves. However, by and large they don't. There are more private than public gardens in Great Britain.

Although it would appear to be an occupation with no practical value, the growing of plants seems to respond to some basic human need. During the industrial revolution, when mills were quite remarkably black and satanic, many of the artisans were florists, as they were called in those days. Nowadays a florist is a person with a shop selling cut flowers, but in the mid-nineteenth century he was simply a person who grew certain flowers. The Paisley weavers with their laced pinks are perhaps the best known of these artisans, but others grew auriculas, carnations, polyanthus and even ranunculus. Moreover, the modern circumscribed dwelling where no garden may be available has resulted in the enormous boom in house plants. It is a refreshing thought that philodendrons are taken from Panama, and cordylines from the South Pacific islands to decorate high rise flats in South London.

Gardening, so far as anyone can be certain about these matters, seems to have originated in China around 800 BC and reached its zenith there between AD 960 and 1279, during the Sung dynasty. The Greeks do not seem to have gone in for gardening much, although some flowers shown on the Knossos frescoes can surely only have been grown for ornament. The Romans went in for a sort of exterior architecture, in which fountains and shade trees played a part, but the next great flourishing of gardening seems to have been in Persia and Turkey in the early sixteenth century (possibly somewhat earlier). Western Europe does not seem to have done much until the late sixteenth century; the Tudor knot gardens were little more than geometric designs made out of living material. There were, also, cultures of which we know remarkably little. The dahlia would seem to have been well cultivated by the Mexicans long before Humboldt brought them to

Europe in the early nineteenth century, and the early Spanish writers speak of great gardens in Mexico and Peru.

Less likely to have a gardening tradition are the islands of the South Pacific, but nevertheless it would seem that there was one. The popular coleus was brought back from a garden in Java. Since at the time there was a large Dutch colony there, it might be assumed that it was the result of these keen gardeners that this plant was brought into cultivation, but when John Gould Veitch visited New Caledonia in 1864, he was able to collect two other forms (called *Coleus gibsonii* and *C. veitchii*) which were apparently generally cultivated there. This might be thought an isolated instance, but coleus were not the only garden plants he found. I do not know if anyone has ever found a convincing *C. blumei* growing wild; its origins are obscure and it might even be a hybrid, but the wild form of *Cordyline terminalis* is well known. It is a graceful plant with plain, green leaves. When he visited the South Sea Islands (the actual places of origin are never given) J. G. Veitch was able to send back a large number of different cultivars, some with crimson leaves, others variegated with white. From the same expedition came a large number of different crotons (*Codiaeum variegatum*). I have no idea what a wild codiaeum looks like; the plant seems never to have been described nor depicted, but the garden forms are very numerous and diverse and most of these figured in J. G. Veitch's sendings. Generally he seems to have stayed with Wesleyan missionaries when he visited the islands, and they may well have had the plants in their gardens, but they would scarcely have been able to breed them. It seems to me that we must concede a gardening tradition even in so undeveloped a place as the South Sea Islands. It really does seem that having ornamental plants around does fulfil something basic to our make-up.

Not that there is anything particularly surprising in this. The calming effect of natural phenomena, particularly on those employed in extremely artificial conditions, does not require any very recondite explanation. We can well sympathise with the Paisley weavers wishing to turn to something other than bricks and mortar in their scanty spare time. It is noteworthy that doctors, who have to spend so much of their time in the presence of human misery, are remarkably likely to turn to gardening as a relaxation. Moreover, if you spend your life in a monotonous occupation, such as working on a conveyor belt, you may well enjoy an occupation in which there are a lot of different techniques and activities.

2

WHAT WE OUGHT TO SEE

A conveniently loose division could place gardeners into two classes: the landscapists and the plantsmen. The two categories are by no means exclusive and probably the best gardens are those that partake of both categories. It is mainly a matter of emphasis. The landscapist is concerned with the total effect, and he reaches the ultimate in the famous Japanese garden which consists entirely of raked sand and a few well chosen, agreeably shaped and situated rocks. No growing plants are allowed to invade its 'Fearful Symmetry'. The plantsman is more interested in what he grows, rather than where he grows it and his ultimate is perhaps reached in the frame planted with *Oncocyclus* iris, which looks unimaginably beautiful in April and May and is of no other interest for the rest of the year.

There is a variant of the landscapist, which I term—probably unfairly—the exterior upholsterer. This reaches its ultimate in such gardens as Hidcote, Gloucestershire, and Sissinghurst, Kent, where one can pass from the Grey and White Garden to the Pink and Blue Garden with the same ease as, in a furniture store, one passes from the Regency dining-room to the modern Swedish lounge.

If it were not for the fact that the results are so often remarkably pleasing, I would feel inclined to condemn this form of gardening. After all, all you need is a catalogue and a bank balance and the rest is easy. In essence it is the same technique that used to be applied to so many public gardens, and which has been universally condemned. Fill your beds with yellow calceolaria and white alyssum or with scarlet geraniums and blue lobelias. It is true that the grey and white harmonise, while the scarlet and blue do not, but this may well be a matter of contemporary taste and by no means an absolute. Such gardens may be very restful to the eyes, but the inspiration behind them is that of the interior decorator. If one of the exponents of this form of gardening came forward with a novel arrangement, which will seem harmonious to us, of geraniums, calceolarias, alyssum and lobelia, I would be prepared to pay more respect to him. I suppose the main objection to gardening in colour schemes is that it tends to split the garden up into tiny sections, which after a time induce claustrophobia. Of course if you have a very large garden, you can easily have a few isolated compartments, where you can indulge in various forms of gardening without ruining the general effect, but so few of us do have very large gardens.

The founder of modern gardening theory is always thought to be that peculiar—and to me rather distasteful—character, William Robinson, but he built very largely on the writings and theories of a gentleman called Shirley Hibberd, who deserves more honour than he seems to have achieved, and from him we will take an exposition of the landscapist's credo. This comes from a book first published in 1856, subsequently going into many editions, during which it was considerably modified. Here, however, is the 1856 version. It comes from a book with a delightful title of *Rustic Adornments for Homes of Taste*; not, one would have thought, a good selling title, but there one must obviously be wrong as it went from edition to edition. The extract is rather long, but I hope you will agree with me in relishing every word.

'How then should a garden be planned? It should first of all be laid out so that every diversity of surface may be turned to good account to increase its beauty; the hollows should be made deeper, the elevations higher. Near the house the artificial tone should be highly cultivated, for here at least the garden is but an amplification of the house itself—here, if you can, have a terrace to overlook the brightest scenes you have. Along the southern and west sides of the building, if the garden be on that side, construct a terrace half as wide as the house is high. Let this terrace be truly Italian, with balustrades, vases and statuary; with climbing plants of the richest character to scale its most salient angles. From this terrace let a flight of stone steps lead to another terrace, of double the width of the first, and let this terrace be laid out as an elaborate flower garden, on a ground of turf, with stone fountains, statues, vases, and one or two highly-wrought tables and seats of iron or bronze. Here, in the summer, your gaudy parrots will chuckle on their poles, your fountains will splash and sparkle in the sun, above glowing parterres of flowers laid out in Italian patterns, and a few of the choicest shrubs, with perhaps a monster vase or two, loaded with gorgeous flowers, will set off the angles and serve as a framing to the whole.

'From this lower terrace let your paths lead off over lawns sprinkled with evergreens, flower beds, avenues of deciduous trees, for which hornbeam, lime or horse-chestnut, would be best. Converge the paths so that every slope forms a separate scene complete in itself, when so contemplated, and yet forming but a part of the whole . . .

'At every opening point in the shrubberies you will place some object to arrest the eye—a statue, a pile of rock, a fine acacia, an orange or azalea in a tub, a trained pyrus or weeping ash to form a distinct object on the sward or on a border beyond the path; in some places where you would have a shady passage leading to a view of the open country, you will plant an avenue, perhaps a quincunx, and the path here will be of mossy sward *closely shaven*, instead of gravel. Where this moss-walk opens again on the outer path, you will place your rosary, arching the path with the richest of the perpetual bloomers, breaking the sward into elaborate patterns of dwarf roses, *on their own roots*, in masses of separate colours, and bounding the whole with a space of turf, dotted with the finest standards in clumps of threes, each triad being bound into one head of odorous beauty by the copper wire which passes like a cord through their several stems. Beyond the rosary across the lawn is an immense sweeping background of holly or rhododendron, or at least of two sorts of shrubs only, and these are broken here and there to open views of other portions of the garden. From this point the ground rises with lawn on the left hand, and on the right a continuous bank, studded with wild thyme, strawberries, masses of roses, honeysuckle, and here and there grand pyramidal avenues of hollyhocks. As the path ascends we come into view of a dense shrub-bery, before or amidst which here and there arise the tall outlines of some majestic firs, or the red cedar, the cypress, the arbor vitae, the white poplar or the hemlock spruce. When the summit has been gained, the scene that opens is entirely new.

'Below on the left lies the sloping swards, dotted with roses, tree peonies and hollyhocks, and backed by the rich and dark borders of shrubs; above, on the right, is the bank covered with roses and trailing cistuses, and broken here and there by immense clumps or knolls of ivy; and this bank extends round in front of us, so as to cross the path and lead the way to a rustic summer-house perched on a hillock, the front of which towards the lawn is faced with rockwork, and planted with ferns and alpines, and the base of it dips into a mimic lake, not fashioned so as to deceive us as to its size, but neatly margined with aquatic plants and its bosom dotted with a few majestic swans, and some curious water-fowl.

'If you found places on your terraces and near the windows of the house for flowers, in elaborate patterns of mosaic, for noble vases, statuary, fountains, sculptures, and gay climbers to festoon the balu-strades, here is the proper place for such rustic work as you may care to indulge in. You may embellish the lawns with bark baskets of flowers, tree stumps filled with flowers and ferns, masses of rock covered with ivy and wild creepers, with, in suitable spots, a rustic seat, a table, a summer-house, or a thatched bee-shed, each object being so placed as to form the key to a separate scheme, and to have a visible use to sanction its adoption. Wherever your walks wind they should lead to something or somewhere; they should not wind merely to form ovals and parabolas, but to disclose a scene, a view, an object, or a group of objects; where something which you cannot remove requires to be hidden, throw over the path an archway, build a knoll and cover it with ivy, construct a bower, plant a group of shrubs or trees, but let every detail form only a part of the whole, however each may be to a certain extent complete in itself. Here is a resting place umbrageous with branches on one side, open on the other to your own grounds, and if you have a view of a neighbouring church, a distant hill, a coppice, a wood, or a sheep-walk, let some good point be selected for observing it . . .

'From this nook of coolness and verdure four walks may lead back in another direction to your American garden, blushing in its pride of purple blooms, through other lawns covered with fruit . . . Then your kitchen-garden, which you enter through a screen of filberts and raspberries, brings you once more towards the house and you have only to cross the few borders of shrubs that intervene between the lawns and vegetable ground to reach again the Italian garden, where the fountains once more delight you with their musical splashing, the flower pots load the air with fragrance, and the sinking sun gilding the soft edges of the masonry . . . warns you that the dews are increasing and the lights are ready in the drawing room, you take a farewell glance at a scene of which you cannot tire, and join the family circle in the best of tempers for coffee, gossip, books, or kisses and romps with the children.'

We may, perhaps, feel that this scheme, excellent as it may be, is not really very practicable, but the author has forestalled our objections.

'But,' he goes on to write, 'it may not be in the power of every reader of this work to plan a garden on such a scale. Nevertheless, the *idea* of such an arrangement may be carried out in a small plot of a hundred square feet, and no matter what the size, shape or position of a garden, the leading principles of taste must be kept in view at every step to insure success in the end.'

Perhaps to counterbalance this rather formal idea of garden design I might quote an early example of the plantsman's garden. It dates from 1900 and the writer was George Wilson, a name I hope you will not recognise for a few moments.

'On retiring from business . . . in 1878 I had the chance of buying Oakwood . . . a farm of about sixty acres with an old oak wood and many sorts of soil. Rhododendrons and many other such plants grow vigorously and look after themselves. With a mixture of loam lilies are happy, and in beds in full sun the early irises, calochorti, ixias and many bulbs liking hot places flourish. Iris kaempferi having succeeded on the banks of our ponds, and now, having a rather damp six-acre field of good soil, we made a wide winding ditch, planting these irises in damp soil. These were beautiful, so we have made a larger, wider ditch from which we have great hopes for next year. Gardening friends have spoken very kindly of the . . . garden. In a note in the *Gardeners' Chronicle* of 23 June 1883, one of the greatest plant authorities, Canon Ellacombe, wrote: "I saw it first three years ago, and thought it a very pleasant but not a very hopeful experiment. When I saw it last year I was astonished at the progress made, but was still doubtful of its general utility. I had the pleasure of seeing it again last week, and must confess that it is a great success." Another great gardener who has a beautiful and successful garden of her own, on going round with me, said: "I don't know what to call this place, it is not a garden," and on my assenting to this said, "I think it is a place where plants from all parts of the world grow wild." This being what I aimed at, was very comforting.'

You have probably realised that George Wilson is G. F. Wilson and that the garden at Oakwood is now the Royal Horticultural Society's garden at Wisley, Surrey. I would dearly like to know whether the lady who made the very comforting observation was Ellen Willmott or Gertrude Jekyll.

If you are searching for a rather tenuous posthumous survival—we cannot call it immortality as its duration is in the nature of things not very long—you will probably do better as a plantsman than as a landscapist, although I can imagine no more ignoble a reason for making such a choice. In any case, although the name will survive, very few people—unless they are members of the Garden History Society—will be able to tell you what a particular person did. There is an enormous snowdrop known as 'Arnott's Seedling', but who was Arnott? Well, if you can get hold of the periodical known as *The Garden* for the period around the turn of the century, you will scarcely find a number without some contribution by S. Arnott, who lived at Carsethorn near Dumfries. He seems to have grown practically every hardy plant that was available to him, including such improbable plants as *Jankaea heldreichii*, and he seems to have been anxious to share his knowledge with all and sundry. In this he seems to have been very different from James Allen of Shepton Mallet, who raised many famous plants, including the blue *Anemone nemorosa* 'Allenii', but does not seem to have been very articulate. This, however, is by the way. I suppose the ideal garden would combine the scope and panorama of the landscapist, with the contents of the plantsman. You are never going to find this, but it is obviously the ideal at which to aim.

A fact that seems to be only rather slowly impinging on gardeners, is that there are twelve months in the year. Rather too often they seem to have acted on the assumption that there were only two or three. Admittedly this has often been pointed out before. Here is an anonymous writer in the *Floral World* for September 1862: 'I hate the bedding system in private gardens, because it almost makes an end of gardening altogether. I can enjoy the endless repetitions of scarlet and yellow and blue and blue and yellow and scarlet at the Crystal Palace, Regent's Park, Kensington, and other places planned especially for the excitements of holidays, but I get weary of it in private gardens and I see clearly that their possessors barter away solid and substantial pleasures for a momentary glitter, which often disappoints them and certainly leaves the ground a dreary blank during seven or eight months of the year.'

The writer goes on to amplify his point with considerable skill: 'Answer me this question: does the whole pleasure of a garden consist in the spectacle of badly assorted colours during July, August and September; say, for instance, red and yellow in close proximity with dots of white and blue thrown in by accident? You say "no" and you deny that your bedders are "badly assorted", but you will admit this; that the tendency of the bedding system is to circumscribe the pleasures of the garden to mere colour and to a brief season—there, you have admitted quite enough . . . Now, to speak the plain truth I'm an enthusiast about the bedding system, and that makes me touchy when I see it abused, or carried out too extravagantly for the size of the garden and the means of the proprietor. What pleasure is it to me, think you, to ask me to see your garden when I turn my eyes from the beds to the borders and find you are like the King of Bonny, out at heels and elbows, yet decked with tinsel and feathers. I see plainly that all your strength is expended in furnishing those beds and all the rest of your garden is as meagre and miserable as a leg of mutton on the fourth day of its coming to table.'

The author goes on to commend a large assortment of herbaceous flowers with a lushness of language which can only be appreciated in small doses, such as 'six and twenty species of dianthus with their white, rose and ruby blossoms sprinkled about them like favours of the fairies; a dozen arenarias; thirty campanulas which seemed to jingle their bells as the cool breezes of the morning swept amongst them, as if it loved to kiss the edges of their cups that had taken the stain of the blue sky and the drift of the untrod snow. Had I not these endless species of British geranium, some with blooms a thousandfold more beautiful than all your scarlets, for what can surpass *striatum* in the pattern of its lines, like the threads of a spider's web dyed by the sunbeams, and woven into kirtles for the good people that live in the honied shelter of the wild flowers?' The language may be extravagant, but the plants he recommends—*Geranium striatum, Epilobium fleischeri, Dicentra cucullaria, Corydalis nobilis* and *Thalictrum tuberosum* among others—are a surprisingly subtle and recondite list for 1862.

The truth is that we ought to revise our views on gardening in the last century. Admittedly it introduced the bedding that our anonymous author disliked in the wrong place, but this was by no means all geraniums and calceolarias and lobelias. The article from which I have just quoted is followed by one entitled 'The Bedders of the Season', in which Shirley Hibberd gives a list of desirable bedding subjects; the list is long and varied, with occasional asperity. How splendid to be able to write of a comparative novelty, 'that wretched thing Agathea coelestis variegata, which I warned our readers not to speculate in too boldly and now advise them not to touch at all, if they have abstained hitherto and to throw away if they have it. The old Cape aster was worth keeping, but this variety has forgotten how to bloom in donning a new leafage, and neither for its variegation or its flowers is it worth a place in any garden. Not so Scrophularia nodosa variegata . . . there you have a first class subject for edgings, which anyone can keep and propagate.' Silver-leaved plants were much in demand and *Cerastium biebersteinii* was to be preferred to 'our old friend, tomentosum', while others included *Gnaphalium lanatum, Centaurea argentea, C. candidissima* and *C. gymnocarpa*, variegated mint, golden mint (what has happened to this?), variegated-leaved daisies (another plant that seems to have got lost), while some more unusual bedding subjects were *Oenothera fraseri*, *Mimulus cupreus* and a double white pyrethrum. There was also a variegated fuchsia, known as Meteor, which, Mr Hibberd remarks 'makes a superb bed'.

From this it can be seen that the bedding craze did at least introduce a large number of plants, many of which are still prized in our gardens, even though they may have first been introduced to grace a form of gardening that is now condemned. The melancholy fact must be faced that in spite of all their ostentation with public bedding, the Victorians had a much larger selection of plants to choose from than we have nowadays, even allowing for all the accretions from China that have been introduced in the first three decades of this century. We seem to have lost more than we have gained, most notably in greenhouse plants, though this is probably not so in shrubs, where we seem to have a better choice than a century ago. Alpines seem about the same, although there may well now be more plants available than there were then. The lists of such nurseries as Backhouse of York and the Comely Bank nurseries in Edinburgh (where × *Phyllothamnus* was raised as early as 1845) make surprising reading. Herbaceous plants are in the doldrums at the moment and there are very few available to the inquiring gardener compared to what there was a century ago.

Of course, a century and more ago new plants were being introduced by all the leading nurseries, many of whom would finance expeditions for this purpose. Even in those days, plant-hunting expeditions were very expensive—indeed allowing for the devaluation of currency, probably more expensive than they are nowadays—but presumably it paid firms like Veitch and William Bull to finance these expeditions, whereas now it is only by means of a general subscription that an expedition can be got under way. Nurserymen obviously do not do so well financially as they did, and gardeners are certainly far less enterprising than they were. Fortunately there are numerous exceptions to this generalisation and we need not despair.

3

THE PURLIEUS

Before we get into the garden proper it might be worthwhile considering what is going on round the edges. Territorial defence is not confined to wild animals and we will certainly want to designate where our garden ends and someone else's begins. I suppose we have three choices. One could dig a ditch or moat, which would certainly separate our garden from anyone else's fairly effectively. One could have either a wet ditch or a ha-ha. Failing that we are left with a hedge or a fence. The choice will presumably depend mainly on one's needs. If you live in the country and have fields around you, a ha-ha may have much to commend it, as it will enable you to give the impression that your garden is much larger than in point of fact it is. And a wet ditch may enable you to grow aquatic plants, which you might otherwise be unable to do. I cannot see either a dry or a wet ditch being of much use in built-up areas. Children would be liable to fall in and hurt themselves, and it also means that privacy will not be available.

However, there is no need to enclose your garden in the same way from every aspect and you may wish to have one side open to view. I have excluded walls from the choice of surrounds, as they are out of the price range of most of us, but a south-facing wall will furnish protection for many plants that would otherwise prove too tender and should certainly be borne in mind if it is financially possible.

The choice between hedge or fence will again be ruled by local conditions as much as anything else. If you have only a small garden, you will find that hedges occupy a lot more of the garden than their appearance would suggest. The really esurient plant is privet, which will send out its long fibrous roots a good ten feet in every direction, rendering the soil more or less useless in its vicinity. The golden-leafed variety is cheerful during the winter, but if the weather is very severe it is liable to shed all its leaves at worst, and to have them scorched and unsightly-looking at the best. Privet does make a good thick hedge, which is effective as a barrier against wind, but practically any hedge will serve as a wind-break, while privet may also act as a frost trap, preventing the katabatic action which keeps frost on the move.

Of course, if you live in a sheltered hollow at the bottom of a hill, probably nothing will prevent spring frosts from causing damage, but anything that prevents air movement is liable to exacerbate the trouble, and you will probably be better off with a deciduous rather than an evergreen hedge. On the other hand, in particularly exposed and wind-swept situations you might find your evergreen hedges being flattened by equinoctial gales, while the deciduous hedge will escape better. Hedges also have the disadvantage of having to be clipped at regular intervals. With an electric hedge-clipper this is not a very demanding task, but it is time-consuming and it does entail the purchase of an additional piece of equipment; so the arguments against hedges are not negligible. Of course, if they are there when you take the garden over you may have to make the best of them, but if you are starting from scratch I would think twice before planting them. As to the material of which they should be composed, we will come back to that in a minute.

Let us first consider fences. These are not cheap, and if they are made of wood they are usually of a comparatively short life. On the credit side, they can be used to support climbing plants and may thus give more pleasure than any hedge. Most fences are of little use as wind-breaks, unless you indulge in a close fence, which is expensive and liable to collapse in gales, or in the sort of enlarged sheep-hurdles, made from plaited twigs, which may also suffer from the effects of exceptionally strong winds. This does not seem to have been a problem that exercised earlier gardeners much although William Robinson affords a paragraph in *The English Flower Garden*.

'The iron fence destroys the beauty of half the country seats in

England and the evil is growing every day. There are various serious objections to iron fencing, but we will only deal here with its effect on the landscape. Any picture is out of the question with an iron fence in the foreground. Where an open fence is wanted, nothing is so fine in form and colour as a split Oak fence and rails made of heart of Oak with stout posts. A sawn wood fence is not so good. As Oak is so plentiful on most estates, good examples of split Oak post and rail fences should be more often seen. Oak palings are often used and sometimes where a good live fence of Holly, Quick and wild Rose on a good bank would be far better; but Oak paling is often a precious aid in a garden as a dividing line where the colour of brick or other walls would be against their use, or where for various reasons walls would not do.'

This cannot be said to contribute anything other than Mr Robinson's views on the problem, which he does not seem to have considered particularly carefully. Still, I have also managed to track down a reference to wind protection, although it is scarcely one that will commend itself nowadays:

'Few countries are so rich in the means of shelter as our own, owing to the evergreens that grow freely with us and thrive in seashore and wind-swept districts. Shelter may be near flower-beds and distant or wind-breaks across the line of prevailing winds, and the north and east winds, and may be of Yew, Holly, Cedar of Lebanon (never Deodar), native Fir, a few other hardy firs and the ilex.

'Among the kinds of shelter, walls, thickly clad with climbers, evergreens and others, are often the best for close garden work, because they do not rob the ground, as almost any evergreen tree will; and in doing their work, they themselves may bear many of our most beautiful flowers. Half-hardy evergreens, like the common cherry laurel and Portugal laurel, should never be planted to shelter the garden, because they may get cut down in hard winters.' (Incidentally, by ilex, Robinson does not mean holly, but the everygreen oak, *Quercus ilex*.)

For once, the older writers have not helped us much, although we can see a suggestion in Robinson's advice to grow creepers on the sheltering wall. Suppose we can devise a sheltering fence and grow creepers on it. We are not exhausting the soil with hedgerow roots and we can grow something ornamental as well as protecting our boundaries. A possible method was suggested by G. F. Wilson in 1900, although in his case he was concerned in making individual shelters for particular plants. Take the ordinary iron railings and tie laths to them, 'two sets one above the other overlapping about 9 inches, this gives stability . . . One cross piece is put above the railings to stiffen the laths. The laths do not touch each other so air passes between them. The whole shelter, iron, laths and twine is well painted over with black varnish.'

This sounds pretty good to me. The iron foundation would be permanent, while the laths would uphold your climbers until they had become sufficiently woody to support themselves before the laths finally disintegrated. The iron railings—they are the kind often seen in public parks with about two or three horizontals—might be initially expensive, but this would be the whole of your expenditure. Today we would presumably use something like cuprinol, rather than black varnish, to preserve the laths as long as possible. Admittedly the climbers will need training, and occasionally tying in, but you are increasing the attraction of the garden, not taking up part of it with a living wall, which will need nearly as much attention as the garden. I imagine this structure would be sufficiently pervious to strong winds, so that it would not be liable to blow down in gales. This scheme seems to me the most advantageous for the plantsman; but then again many people like hedges and we should perhaps not dismiss them quite so brusquely as we have done so far.

For William Robinson, tall hedges were made of yew or holly, while lower hedges would be made from box. That is to say that they were invariably constructed of evergreens. However, towards the turn of the century, other writers were suggesting rose hedges, advising as their components, such plants as crimson rambler and the hybrids of the sweetbriar with various other roses, bred at the suggestion of Lord Penzance, and still known as Penzance briars. These plants can scarcely be expected to make a hedge in the normal sense of the term and what must have happened is that a fence of some kind was erected and the roses trained along them. This would have looked attractive when the roses were in flower, but rather exiguous at other times; it is really only a limited number of rose species which are suitable for hedging and even these are far from ideal. The best one is the sweet briar, *Rosa rubiginosa*, in which the leaves are always attractively fragrant and the plant, being reasonably compact, will respond quite well to the inevitable clipping, where most roses will tend to get too exuberant. The sweetbriar hedge will even flower and bear heps, provided you do not mind the top looking somewhat ragged. However, with rose hedges it is not usually the top that is the worry, but the bottom, which tends to be bare of leaves, apart from the occasional new growth rising from the roots. By and large, then, the rose hedge is a delightful idea, but not very practicable.

A possible modification is to insert the odd trailing rose among more conventional hedging material. I did this once with the very fragrant 'Zephyrine Drouot', which has the advantage of being thornless, so that the growths can be plaited among the other hedging material without hands and clothes getting lacerated. Other plants that can be used in this way are honeysuckles and the double pink bramble, *Rubus ulmifolius* fl. pl. The trouble is that they tend to come into flower at the same time as the hedge requires clipping and you are left with the alternative of an untidy flower-studded hedge or tidily clipping off all the flower buds. If, like me, you have no strong feeling about tidy hedges, you are all right, otherwise it is probably a mistake to try and have summer-flowering climbers or shrubs in the hedge.

The position is rather different for plants that flower in the early spring and quite floriferous hedges can be made of such subjects as the sloe, *Prunus spinosa*, which you could make more interesting by occasionally putting in a plant of the reddish-leaved 'purpurea'. If you like a purple-leaved hedge (and personally I find too much purple extremely depressing and a bad background, except for very light-coloured foliage or flowers) you could use the attractive *Prunus* × *blireiana*, with double pink flowers, or the white-flowered *Prunus* × *cistena*. Some people even use the old *Prunus* × *pissardii*, but this will not flower as a hedging plant, as it likes to make a sizeable tree. As all these plants flower in March and April, they can be expected to give quite a good account of themselves, although since they tend to flower on the year-old wood they will never be as floriferous as unpruned bushes. The same applies to the American current, *Ribes sanguineum*, and forsythia, both of which make quite adequate hedges, with some few flowers, but again you will have to clip away most of the flower-bearing wood. If you don't mind some untidiness, *Cotoneaster simonsii* will give quite a display of red berries in the autumn, but it will not make a tidy hedge.

If for some reason I had to make a hedge, I think I would use beech. The colour of the young green leaves is one of the glories of the spring landscape; I could diversify it with the odd purple beech if I so desired, and I may well get a fine display of gold in the autumn. Moreover, the leaves in the interior of the hedge remain attached to the twigs for most of the winter, so that the hedge is reasonably opaque at that time, although it will still filter the wind in a very satisfactory manner.

The autumn colour of beech makes me think that instead of searching for hedging subjects that bear flowers, we might do better to search for subjects with good autumn colour. Around where I live the hedges are mainly of hawthorn, which sometimes colours well, and also of the native maple, *Acer campestre*, which is more capricious in its autumnal behaviour. Some plants turn yellow, some turn red and some do not colour at all. It does, however, make a very attractive hedging subject and might well be given consideration. There may be other maples that would be suitable hedging subjects. Either *A. ginnala* or *A. tartaricum* might respond well to being treated in this way. Unfortunately, price would at the moment militate against any experiments. *A. japonicum* might also be experimented with. It is again possible that other *Crataegus* species might supplement the old hawthorn. *Crataegus crus-galli* or *C. macracantha* would make a formidable zareba and they both tend to colour brilliantly in the autumn.

I wonder also how that marvellous tree *Malus tchonoskii* would respond. It has lovely silvery leaves in the spring, which colour brilliantly in the autumn; neither the flowers not the fruits are particularly outstanding and, if it would respond, I can see an absolutely marvellous hedge being made from this crab apple. This is, of course, the wildest fantasy: *M. tchonoskii* is, at the moment, a connoisseur's tree to be found in few gardens, and for a plant to be used as hedging it must be easy to propagate in large quantities. It might be possible with *Liquidambar styraciflua,* but this has few merits apart from its display of autumn colour, and as a general rule it makes a very large tree. If general impenetrability is a requisite, I should like to experiment with the gleditschias, either *Gleditschia caspica* or the popular G. *triacanthos.* They have the most horrific spines, but the fern-like leaves are very attractive. They are, unfortunately, very late in coming into leaf and this might be an argument against their employment.

If we think of evergreens I would like to try some of my favourite eleagnus. Normally, the various evergreen species *EE.* × *ebbingei, macrophylla* and *pungens,* make rather sprawling shrubs and they might not respond well to being trained into a hedge, but I suspect that they would prove excellent subjects, and their leaves are certainly more ornamental than most evergreens. One could scarcely use the beautiful golden-variegated form of *E. pungens* on its own as a hedge; it would be too overwhelming *en masse,* but the odd one could liven up a hedge of—let us say—*E. pungens* 'Simonii'. In the same way I would like to see *Osmanthus ilicifolius* tried, which has attractive silver-backed holly-shaped leaves and is not an exceptionally rapid grower. Both the elaeagnus and this osmanthus come fairly readily from cuttings and so material should be fairly easily obtained. I suppose having made these suggestions I shall be told that these have all been tried in various gardens, and that I am displaying not my imagination but my abysmal ignorance. Well, as they say, there's a lot of it about.

By and large, I would just as soon not have hedges at all. They form a convenient lair for various insect and mammalian pests and birds will nest in them. Not that this later point is necessarily an objection, but those of us who wish to grow either early-flowering prunus or berrying shrubs find ourselves looking at the birds with decidedly ambivalent emotions. If you have bullfinches you are to be condoled with, and these birds do nest in hedges, so if you do not have hedges you may lessen their incidence, although probably not to any significant extent unless all your neighbours follow your example. Berries are eaten by so many different birds that there is not much you can do about it. After all, the plant is producing its seeds in berries for the birds to distribute them, so their eventual disappearance down the birds' throats is only to be expected. We can only hope that the birds do not learn the same trick as the greenfinch, which has now developed a taste for unripe fruits of *Daphne mezereum*, so that you have to take special steps if you want mezereon seed. If the birds would learn a little self-restraint and let all the berries ripen before they eat them, some of us might feel more kindly towards them.

In any case, birds are only one of many pests harboured by hedges. They also give protection to mice, slugs, snails, aphids and various other unwelcome visitors. In addition hedges take a lot of nourishment out of the ground, and if space is limited probably do not justify their existence. The matter is very different in large gardens, where hedges are often essential to separate compartments and to add to the landscape.

Where it is simply a matter of marking out boundaries, I would rather put in good stout posts and stretch either wire-netting or plastic mesh between them and then grow as many climbers as I could. If I wanted an evergreen screen I should concentrate on such things as the evergreen honeysuckles and *Clematis armandii* (provided I was in a district where it can be grown) and holboellia; otherwise I would go in for a large selection from actinidia, through clematis to vines and wistaria. These would need less attention than hedges, and would be more attractive to look at. Moreover, if you are starting from scratch, you will get results sooner. My estimation is that the financial outlay is about the same.

4

LAWNS

Almost everyone wants to grow lawns, but no one wants to look after them. A measure of the influence the British have had on gardening is the prevalence of lawns even in countries where they are practically ungrowable. In North America, for example, the winters are too snowy and cold and the summers too hot and dry for lawns to look respectable, but nevertheless they are still grown. In fact outside the United Kingdom there are very few countries where grass lawns are easy to maintain and they are liable to cause more trouble than any other department in the garden. Sometimes annual re-seeding is necessary.

Perhaps we should start by defining what we require from a lawn. We want an expanse of green, which will serve to rest the eye from the bright colours that we hope will be in other parts of the garden. The lawn should have a level surface and be comfortable to walk upon. It should be easy to maintain and should keep its green colour even during droughts. There is, obviously, no reason why it should be made from grass, but no suitable alternative is immediately available, although, as we shall see, alternatives have been tried. There is really no reason why grass should be the entire component of a lawn, but if other plants are present we may require that they should be evergreen. From the point of view of appearance, in the summer neither clover nor plantains spoil a lawn, but they are herbaceous and will leave blank spaces in the winter. Daisies are evergreen and there can be no real objection to their presence in a lawn. However it appears to be a form of snobbery that would have the lawn composed of grasses and nothing else.

The trouble with grass is that it grows taller than we would like and so at regular intervals out comes the lawn-mower and someone has to trundle around to produce a fine sward; an operation that takes time and energy. Lawns may be restful to the eyes but they are a considerable nuisance, and what we need is a material which will cover the ground and not need mowing. I well recall the remark my brother made when a friend said to him, 'Oh dear! I see you have moss on your lovely lawn.' 'What you mean,' my brother stated, 'is that I have some grass among my lovely moss.' If one could only persuade moss to cover the area given over to grass, we should still have a restful green area, it would still be agreeable to walk upon, and it would not need mowing. Precisely what would happen during droughts I cannot foresee, but I suspect it would look rather brown and desiccated, although since grass suffers in the same way we need not worry about that unduly. Since the efforts of the gardener and the scientist have always been directed upon eradicating moss rather than encouraging it, we do not know if it is possible to cultivate it in quantity, but I would doubt it. Moreover, mowing has one advantage. It does prevent the taller, deep-rooted weeds from establishing themselves. I can see that if you do not mow you will find docks and nettles establishing themselves in the lawn, although I imagine they could be treated with the same hormone herbicides that are already applied to lawns. They would presumably not harm moss, but they might well be lethal where other suggested lawn plants have been put in. Still, we managed to have lawns before we had herbicides and occasional weeding might be less laborious than mowing. However this is visionary at the moment.

The two plants which have been suggested as an alternative to grass are chamomile (*Anthemis nobilis*) and *Sagina pilifera*, which at the time when it was all the rage was called *Spergularia pilifera*. Both these plants are fairly deep-rooted, so that they do not tend to fade during prolonged dry spells. Although they may, notionally, need less upkeep once they are established, they required considerably more work to establish in the first place, as will be seen. As it is in some ways a cautionary tale, and as it seems to have been forgotten, let me recall the story of the spergularia lawn as it unfolded in the pages of the *Floral World*, beginning in March 1859 with an advertisement from Messrs E. G. Henderson. Incidentally Messrs Henderson's nursery was at St John's Wood in London, and when cricket commentators at Lords refer to the nursery end, it is the end where Messrs Henderson's nursery used to be.

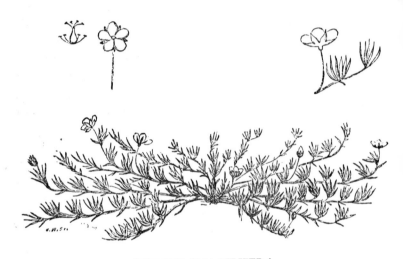

SPERGULARIA PILIFERA

A perfect substitute for grass lawns in villa gardens without mowing

S. pilifera, in its style of growth, is a neat dwarf hardy perennial tufted alpine plant, forming close compact wiry grass-like stems, from a quarter to half an inch in height, at first erect, afterwards decumbent, clothed with closely set green bristle-like leaves, which, by permanent growth and occasional rolling, forms an unbroken level velvet-like surface of the richest conceivable verdure, remaining uninjured in severe drought or intense cold, and assumes the same verdurous tint during the winter months as in summer . . .

'The permanent and uniform condition of dense growth, with the penetrative power of its roots, preserves it from all risks of being parched by extreme exposure in sultry weather; and the progressive accumulation of its moss-like growth gives an elastic pressure to the foot, much softer than the finest Turkey carpet.' The plants were grown from seed, pricked out 'and ultimately transplanted upon the prepared lawn-surface in two or three plants, within one inch or more of each other, and such little plant groups may be formed at a distance of six, nine or twelve inches apart; in such positions the growths will progressively meet and form the rich and beautiful surface now described'.

The actual invention of the spergularia lawn must, it would seem, be attributed either to Mr Mongredien of Forest Hill, near London, or to his gardener Mr Summers, who created a very fine lawn at Forest Hill. Subsequently Mr Summers was lured away from Mr Mongredien by Messrs Carters and put in charge of the propagation and laying of these lawns. The spergularia lawn was big business for a few years.

The tale was taken up in the July number by the editor, Shirley Hibberd, who said that he had determined not to say a single word about it until he could tell the whole story, but that the paper had received so many inquiries that he felt constrained to give an interim report, which consisted chiefly of a description of how he had raised the plants from seeds and put them into new land a foot apart. Hibberd also suggested—a suggestion he had subsequently to recant—that the spergularia was not *S. pilifera* but *S. saginoides*.

Hibberd wrote again in August with considerable enthusiasm: 'As we have a new and distinct form of vegetation offered us in this lawn plant, so I can now see plainly we have in it the best material for a lawn that can possibly be used, because, independent of its close-tufted growth, forming a springy felt under the feet, it holds its own most pertinaciously against all weathers. During the East Indian weather of the first half of July my grass got very much burnt . . . but the *Spergula* was as green at the end of the drought as it was after the rains of June, but it ceased growing to throw up its bloom. Just then the sparrows were bringing their young out . . . what was my mortification to see the old birds by the dozen busy on my *Spergula* plot, tearing it up wholesale, pulling and tugging at the stems and carrying off as large bunches as they could bear on the wing . . . After the sparrows and the drought had done their utmost to reduce the *Spergula* to a minimum, the storms came and set it growing at so rapid a pace, that on this 26th of July [the plants had only been set out on 2 June] my circle is very closely and regularly turfed.'

'The chief point to attend to,' Hibberd wrote later in his article, 'is to have the ground clean and to keep it so by constant weeding.' He worked out that it would cost about six shillings to furnish about five square yards of ground with spergularia plants, which sounds quite expensive.

A year later Hibberd takes up the subject again, and from his article we learn that the original lawn at Mr Mongredien's house had been in existence for six or seven years. Hibberd was certainly pleased with his trial. He suggests that for sour acid soils the common weed *Sagina procumbens* might be used as an alternative or, preferably, *S. saginoides*. Indeed a year later he is writing: 'I see plainly enough that *Pilifera* will be superseded by *Saginoides*. *Pilifera* is not only as good as I have described it but better. My own piece is now exquisite in its close felt of elastic verdure, dense as piled velvet. But *Saginoides* grows twice as fast, and is not so particular about soil, though preferring it sandy; whereas *Pilifera* does best on stiff loams and clays.'

In 1862 the spergula lawn seemed in high esteem: 'J.R., one of our most practical and cautious correspondents, finds it just the thing to carpet narrow verges in a town garden, and a letter now before us from . . . the west part of Suffolk gives the pleasing intelligence that a lawn of half an acre has been formed in two seasons and is now in beautiful condition and that the proprietor of the grounds intends to enlarge it.' On the other hand, a gentleman 'complains that worms and weeds have well nigh killed the patches that were planted last year'. The editor says: 'The real truth is that it requires quite as much care as grass, though in quite another way. It must be frequently weeded, frequently rolled, and worms must be got rid of by the use of lime water. People who are not prepared to give it these attentions should not grow it at all. My circle requires watering with lime water three times every season, especially late in the autumn and early in the spring, at which seasons worm casts kill the plants whenever they are thrown upon it in consequence of the wetness of the soil. So every weed does mischief, grass especially, the roots getting entangled with the spergula; and if not sedulously weeded it neither looks nice nor grows well. Carefully dealt with nothing can surpass the beauty of a *Spergula* lawn.'

By the next year Shirley Hibberd had decided that *S. saginoides* made a better lawn than *S. pilifera*. And to all intents and purposes at this point, the history seems to end. In 1866, in answer to a correspondent, readers were informed that seed of the spergula was no longer offered, but that turfs could be procured from Messrs Carter. Once one had procured turfs, one pulled them to pieces and dibbled the pieces in. The final note can be left to the Royal Horticultural Society's *Dictionary of Gardening*: '*S. pilifera* and *S. procumbens* have been suggested as lawn plants dibbled in 2in apart but in many places they are apt to become patchy.'

What, I hope you are asking, was or is *S. pilifera*? If what they had was *S. pilifera*, and not the similar but more widely distributed *S. glabra*, it is endemic to Corsica and Sardinia, where it grows on rocks in the mountains. *S. glabra* is less densely caespitose, but comes from the Pyrenees, Alps and Appennines, and one would have thought would have been more widely available. However, Mr Mongredien stated that his plant came from Corsica, so it probably was correctly named. It is a sprawling plant with narrow, grassy leaves and small five-petalled white flowers; now that ground-cover plants are becoming in demand, it would obviously repay re-introduction. *S. procumbens* is the common spurry, often such a weed in peat mixture or on acid soil, and is not, I would have thought, a very suitable subject.

The chamomile lawn needs similar treatment, in that plants are inserted about four inches apart and left to coalesce, but it does require mowing from time to time. It maintains a good deep-green colour in dry seasons, but it tends to look rather mucky in the winter. I believe they have now bred a form that flowers very sparingly, but the true chamomile covers itself with large white daisies in the summer, although these could be mown off. Chamomile has a very pungent scent, which not everyone finds agreeable, and this might make mowing a problem to those who find it distasteful. On the other hand this scent has been extolled as a recommendation by its supporters, so it is evidently a case of *de gustibus non est disputandum*. The chamomile lawn would need less frequent mowing than grass, but it does not seem to have achieved much popularity. Probably, as in the case of the spergula, the presence of noxious weeds would soon spoil the appearance.

Two other materials are suggested to give lawns which will not require mowing. One of these is the prostrate thyme, *Thymus serphyllus*, which when well established does tend to smother any weeds that might attempt to penetrate its mass. Still, you might eventually end up with a fairly trouble-free lawn that would not require mowing. It would certainly be rather expensive. Presumably you would put the plants about six inches apart or four to the square foot. The plant comes readily from cuttings and also from seed, so there would not be too much delay or expense in working up the necessary stock, but quite a lot of room would be required to bed the plants out before setting them in their final position. More important, you would have to clear your lawn site of all perennial weeds, as otherwise they would re-establish themselves before the thyme plants had made a complete sward. The final result may be fairly trouble-free, but the preparation would be more laborious than what is normally required when preparing ground for a lawn and I can foresee an interval of two years between the conception and the execution.

Another factor is that once you have your thyme lawn you are faced with the fact that the green of the thyme is not a particularly attractive green, while towards the end of June the lawn is going to turn purple, when the thyme flowers. If you belong to the exterior upholstery school, you may well find that this will clash with your colour schemes. Shirley Hibberd thought that the minute white flowers of *S. pilifera* might interfere with bedding schemes, but the rather scanty flowering of the sagina would not have been unpleasant, while the profusion of purple from your thyme lawn could be either magnificent or disastrous, according to your plans. In any case, for three weeks you would certainly lack a restful spot for the eyes. On the positive side you would have the continual delightful fragrance of the thyme as you walked over it and that might compensate for the rather dull green of its leaves. Thyme lawns do exist, and although a certain amount of occasional hand weeding is necessary, they are comparatively trouble-free once established. I have never seen a very large one and probably this would not be very satisfactory aesthetically.

A more recent suggestion for a lawn is based on the proposition that if you cannot beat them, join them; this is the clover lawn. You sow your surface with a selection of medicks and clovers, which soon prevent anything else from taking over the surface. Since all except a few of these are deciduous I cannot imagine what the lawn would look like in the winter, but I would have thought it would be rather depressing. But as I have never seen one of these, I may be maligning a most acceptable substitute. In any case it sounds as though it would have much to commend it in countries other than Great Britain, where the summers are hot and dry and where perennial grasses soon look sorry for themselves. The clovers would certainly retain a good green colour at this season and this might well compensate for a rather bare appearance in winter. It sounds just the thing for districts like New England, where one does not, in any case, have to worry about the winter appearance of one's lawn as it will certainly be buried under snow for most of the time. Since snow will make grass in the United Kingdom look rather unhappy, one can imagine what the effect would be in districts where prolonged snowfall is the rule rather than the exception. In fact the question of lawns made of material other than grass is one which gardeners in such places as the United States and much of Europe should be considering with more urgency than people in Great Britain, Eire or the Azores.

Of course, if you have a small garden you can do without a lawn altogether. Those of us who were privileged to see the garden that the late R. J. Platt and Aida Foster made at Hawkhurst, Kent, will know that it is possible to have a garden without a lawn and yet one that is both attractive and interesting. So far as I know, lawns are not a feature of either Chinese or Japanese gardens, and yet their designs are highly thought of. The principle of having a deep pool of green to rest the eyes is obviously a sound one, but the idea that the only way of doing this is by closely mown grass has presumably been universally adopted only owing to the fact that the British, as we have already pointed out, seem to be more enthusiastic gardeners than most other nationalities. Any country can produce a keen gardener, but nearly every Britisher, given a patch of ground will tend to attempt a garden, whether he is in his own country or abroad, and since he had a grass lawn in his London suburb, he will attempt to produce one in Sydney or in Katmandu.

I believe that in parts of the United States, where it is extremely difficult to grow grass well, they lay down strips of plastic lawn as though it were linoleum. I can see this raising problems of hygiene and laundering, but at least you have a lawn that is always green, never wants mowing or any attention, and can be rolled up and put away if you go on holiday. It is obviously tempting to replace the most obviously artificial part of the garden with a synthetic reproduction, but I suspect that once we start that we are doomed. Lawns are a pest, but a pest that most of us must learn to live with.

As a matter of fact, the garden I am making at the moment has no lawn; but at the time of writing that is no recommendation. What I am aiming at is a number of shrubs with the intervening spaces filled with wild plants from various parts of the globe, which I hope will eventually supress the less agreeable native wild plants (known to gardeners as weeds). Every now and again a small portion of the garden gives the effect I am trying for and spurs me on, but for the most part it looks a disgracefully unkempt mass and I can never be sure whether I will ever arrive at the result I have in mind. Certainly at the moment it is not an example to follow. I shall be writing more about it later on, but at the moment, if anyone asks me about my garden, honesty compels me to say that I have no garden, only a collection of plants.

5

PATHS

At a pinch we can deprive ourselves ourselves of both hedges and lawns, but paths we must have, and they are worth taking a certain amount of trouble over; when designing your garden therefore, it is imperative to be quite sure where you want the paths to be. It is comparatively easy to alter other features; beds can be grassed over, or parts of the lawn can be taken up without much trouble, but to take up a path and re-lay it somewhere else can be extremely laborious.

If you have doubts about the position it is possible to get some idea by marking out their proposed course with canes, which can be joined by twine. It is probably worth your while to use a rather conspicuous twine, as otherwise it is not easy to see the outline. In plotting out the path, there are a number of points you should bear in mind, such as ease of approach, the amount of space you wish to keep between the paths, and the width you require. Gardens are meant to be walked in, so although you may grudge the ground taken up, particularly if the garden is small, it is as well to make the path wide enough for at least two people to walk abreast, and perhaps even three. Also, you will probably have to wheel a barrow along the path, so do not have too many sharp turns, and if the garden is on a slope the gradients should be made fairly easy. With a very steep site such as Leonardslee, Sussex, it is not easy to supply it with paths that follow these precepts, and to walk around Leonardslee after heavy rain is rather an alarming experience. I doubt, however, if the paths could have been designed much better, although the surfacing could be (and quite possibly now has been) improved.

Having decided on the layout of the paths, the next thing to decide on is their material. Here a number of considerations may apply. In a large shrubbery, mown grass paths are probably the most desirable, as they set off the trees and shrubs and turn the whole area into a forest glade. Gravel paths too have much to commend them, the more so as many plants that would be planted in the scree in the alpine garden will often grow very successfully in gravel. The disadvantage however is that if desirable plants grow in gravel, undesirable ones grow even better, but it is usually possible to stop weeds by putting down a layer of polythene sheeting between the earth and the surfacing material. Weeds will force their way through gravel, through asphalt and, occasionally, even through concrete, but polythene sheeting seems to suppress every growing plant. If, however, you have some six inches of gravel over your polythene, you have enough depth for annual weeds to establish themselves, although you will probably be spared the horrors of deep-rooted weeds. These can, of course, be fairly easily suppressed by various chemicals, of which agricultural salt is probably the cheapest, but it may be an expense you would rather not have. In all probability, it will prove impractical to lay asphalt on polythene, as it is applied hot and will cause the sheeting to melt; anyway too much asphalt does look rather severe and municipal.

Paving stones or coloured tiles have much to recommend them, but they are not cheap. There is much to be said for using them around the house, but elsewhere they may prove excessively expensive. Sometimes broken paving stones are easily obtainable and in that case you can indulge in the crazy paving, so ingeniously devised by Mr M. Kitton and described in his article in the *Journal of the Royal Horticultural Society*, May 1972. Briefly, the stones are laid on polythene sheeting, covered with a dry mortar of two parts of soft sand to one part cement, which is brushed between the pieces and left for the rain to moisten and set. If spaces are required to put plants in between the paving, either stones are subsequently removed or gaps are left which are filled with sand. After a year (or longer if some very persistent weeds were in the soil beforehand) the sand is removed, the polythene sheeting cut out and plants are then inserted in these holes, which can be filled with special compost if the garden soil is not good enough. The result is completely weed-free; the technique can also be used on any surface, which need not necessarily be level, although it should, naturally, not be too undulating.

However, the most effective material for fairly long paths is probably concrete. The path is excavated to a depth of four to six inches, with shuttering along the edges; polythene sheeting is then laid on the bottom and the concrete tipped in and levelled off. You do not want too smooth a surface, as this can become very slippery in wet or frosty weather. If you do not like the normal colour of concrete, both red and green colourants are available to add to the mix, but the ordinary stone colour is not unpleasing after it has weathered. Concrete is not cheap, but it is probably the cheapest path that is permanent, and it will need no further attention. It is also reasonably safe in inclement conditions, although a black frost may turn your path into a skating rink and it will then be a hazard. So, however, will most other paths with a solid foundation and there is not much that can be done about this, except to keep indoors when such (fortunately rare) conditions prevail. In these conditions only grass paths are safe, but they in their turn can become quagmires after heavy rain, while your concrete path enables you to walk dry-shod.

Concrete does look a little severe in the less formal parts of the garden and you then have to decide whether to have access to these parts and mar the appearance, or to avoid such parts in very wet weather. All gardening is to some extent a compromise between what is suitable and what is convenient and the constitution of paths provides an excellent example of this dilemma.

If you want the worst of all possible things, go in for the old-fashioned crazy paving, with the stones loosely buried in the ground and with gaps between which ideally should provide a haven for carpeting plants such as thyme and aubrieta, but which in point of fact so often allowed weeds to infest the paving. Mr Kitton's modification does away with this risk and if you want plants among the paving, follow his example.

Drives are, perhaps, another matter. Here concrete does look rather bleak and asphalt looks very black, but they both give admirable surfaces for wheeled vehicles which is the main object. Gravel well rolled will look more attractive eventually, when it weathers, but it does need more frequent renewal and maintenance. As the purpose of the drive is, in any case, functional rather than decorative, it is probably best to keep this fact in mind. Very severe frosts have been known to crack concrete, particularly if it has been laid comparatively recently, so all in all tarmacadam is probably the best medium for drives. It can, of course, be topped with stone chippings, which disguise the unrelieved blackness, but these also require periodical renewal. Stone chippings do tend to make the surface less slippery during black frosts, which, if the drive is on a slope in any portion, is a consideration. I have seen drives going up a steep bank which were unnegotiable during these periods. They were made of concrete.

Skilful deployment of paths can make a small garden appear much larger than it actually is. This may seem unlikely when you are just starting, and all the plants are immature, but once the shrubs and trees have made enough growth to obscure the course of the paths, you can create an illusion of space by disguising the route of the paths so that the actual limits of the garden are not apparent. Most of us these days have to make do with small gardens, so if we want to grow plants in quantity, we must achieve this illusion of space so as to prevent the feeling of overcrowding.

6

BEDS AND BORDERS

If you are going to grow plants in some quantity, you have to devise compartments in which to place them. In theory these can be any size and any shape, but in practice this is not always feasible. For example, a lawn with a number of cherry trees inserted, each in a small bed, entails far more work than the result would justify. If you put the plants directly in the lawn you are liable to starve them, while if you plant each in a small bed of clean soil, to encourage the roots, you have great trouble in mowing properly. If you want a tree in the lawn—and it is often a most desirable feature—it is simpler to make quite a large bed with the tree in the centre. You can plant the remainder of the bed with shallow-rooting plants, either annuals or ground-cover plants, and when the tree is large enough, you can remove the bed and grass up to the trunk. Eventually, if it is a large tree, it will become too shady for grass to grow properly underneath the branches, but you will have allowed for that in your original plan and if you only have a small lawn will probably have discarded the idea altogether.

At one time in the mid-nineteenth century there was a short-lived craze for what was termed pincushion bedding. Here the lawn was pockmarked with myriads of tiny beds, only one or two feet in diameter and circular in outline. These cannot have looked very nice in any case and must have caused more work than any result could justify. I suppose it is possible that in a very small garden something of the kind could have been worth the trouble it caused, but for even moderately sized gardens it was soon seen to be a lunatic suggestion.

When deciding on compartments in your garden it is as well to be sure what you want to do with them before you start digging. As a rough generalisation, we may say that most trees and shrubs are fairly graceful in isolation, while herbaceous and alpine plants will rely almost entirely either on their flowers or their foliage for their attractions. From this it follows that trees and shrubs should, ideally, be well spaced out, so that they can be viewed from every angle, while herbaceous and alpine plants should be encouraged to grow together into a mass. This is a counsel of perfection, and it needs considerable will-power—particularly if you are a rabid plantsman—not to overcrowd your shrubs, and you may well end up with banks of rhododendrons or viburnums.

The trouble is that these longer-living plants keep on growing. Originally they may have been planted at respectable distances apart, with possibly the gaps filled in with shrubs regarded as being ultimately expendable. It then happens that these smaller shrubs look very effective, and when the time comes to remove them you haven't the heart to do it. But if you have enough strength of character to rip out the cistuses, or the roses, or the berberis or whatever, you will find that the shrubs you wish to preserve have become somewhat leggy and gaunt at the base. If you wait they will probably make up for this on their own, for as soon as the light again reaches the lower levels, they will produce growths from the latent buds. Then you will find that you have miscalculated the distances and put the plants so close that they are growing into each other. You could thin out, but by this time the shrubs are large, and it is quite a labour to remove them; in any case the result is very attractive. So you let well alone, eventually the shrubs grow into an impenetrable tangle, and some twenty years later your successor will be saying harsh things about Victorian shrubberies. In the end almost the whole lot must be cleared out and just one or two plants of greater rarity or beauty left. I don't think there is anything that can be done about this—it is a common occurrence among most of the great gardens around. Probably it does not matter much. You may plant specimen trees, oaks, beeches, cedars or redwoods for posterity, but most of the plants are for your own enjoyment, and *après moi le déluge* is a justifiable attitude. Of course, if you have a will of iron, you can say, 'I have enjoyed all these but this plant and this one have given me the most pleasure, so we will destroy the others so that these can survive happily.' This is an attitude of mind deserving of the greatest respect, but it is not one to which I can lay any claim. There seems to be no doubt that a certain ruthlessness is advantageous in your gardening, but it is not easy to acquire. If there are plants that you dislike it is easy enough to remove them, if they are in the garden when you take it over. But they are not plants that you have brought in because you like them. It is these that are not easy to remove when they get too large or too invasive.

In my own garden, which is mainly devoted to shrubs, I have tried to avoid the necessity for agonising choices by spacing the shrubs and trees out fairly well and filling the intervening spaces with herbaceous plants. My theory is that as the shrubs grow they will eventually drive out the herbaceous plants by the spread of their shade, so that nature herself, the old dame, will decide when the plants should go. Since the garden is barely five years old I am quite unable to say if this is going to work or not. What I can tell you is that some of the shrubs are already too close and some agonising decisions will shortly have to be made.

In most gardens the shrubs and the herbaceous plants are kept separate. The plants used to be in William Robinson's main claim to fame, the herbaceous border, but nowadays we tend to follow the example of Alan Bloom and put our herbaceous plants in beds rather than borders. This is because very few people can now afford a full-time gardener and the herbaceous border took an unconscionable amount of time and labour; the bed is more easily kept in a reasonable condition while giving just as much effect. Moreover, with a bit of landscaping the effect of a border can be given. If the beds are more or less aligned, with a curving outline, interstices of lawn or of some paving material will permit ready access, while not interfering with the visual effect, which can easily be made to represent an unbroken border. Whether you want to represent an unbroken border is quite another matter. Personally I like to be able to walk round plants and view them from several angles and this is not really practicable in a border, unless it is flanked by paths on either side, in which case it can be regarded as a very narrow and long rectangular bed. In my view, both access to the plants and the ability to view them from the most satisfactory angle are best obtained by comparatively small isolated compartments, usually referred to as beds.

Problems can arise when you have walls or hedges as boundaries, as there is a natural inclination to benefit from the wind shelter provided and to put out a border backing on the boundary. This, I feel, is probably a mistake. If you have a wall, by all means use its protection to establish attractive shrubs that would otherwise prove too tender for cultivation, and for this a narrow border may well prove the most satisfactory method, but do not put a lot of plants in front of your wall shrubs, which you would be forced to do if you made a wide border. The wall shrubs will be so interesting in themselves that you do not want to distract from them, and since many will be fragrant you will want to be able to approach them and plunge your nose into the blossoms. With a hedge a border is even more of a liability. The roots from the hedging plants will take most of the goodness from the immediate vicinity, so that heavy applications of fertiliser will be necessary to keep the ground in good heart. In addition you will have to penetrate the border in order to clip the hedge and you are thus liable to damage whatever plants you have in the border.

It is obviously more convenient to have a path, either of grass or paving, between the hedge and whatever flowering plants you have in mind. You cannot even grow climbers up the hedge, as you will find that you are almost certain to clip them, although it is possible, eventually, to get honeysuckles to get well into the hedge, so that they will persist and flower, although less well than they will do if given other conditions. In any case, even if you have a six or ten foot gap between the hedge and your plants you will still enjoy protection from wind, while you will be that much further away from the various pests that the hedge will be sheltering. There is no such thing as trouble-free gardening, but by taking thought you can save yourself unnecessary trouble. If you want to trim your hedge it must be easy of access and if you want to hoe or to dig around plants they must be easily reachable, preferably from a position outside the compartment. Many times in the past I have gone on to a border to clean up the more remote portions, only to find that I have stepped backwards on to some prized plant. If you make your compartments some twelve feet across, and approachable from every side, you can lessen the risk of accidental damage. If you want a wider bed you can always put down a few stepping-stones on which you can stand while wielding the hoe; but there can be no doubt that beds are more easily managed than borders.

I have tended to use the word compartments rather than beds, as the latter calls up a picture of a perfect geometrical figure, usually a circle or a rectangle. This is, of course, pure convention and there is no reason at all why a bed should be regular and symmetrical. Nor, if it comes to that, is there any reason why you cannot have massive effects even though the individual compartments are still of manageable size. If the beds are arranged in a series of triangles, from a small distance they will give the appearance of an unbroken sweep, while when you approach closer you will be able to examine every plant from more than one aspect. If these compartments are set in the lawn you must remember to have sufficient space between them to manoeuvre the mower; indeed this will be the decisive factor in establishing these distances.

As to where you put these beds (or borders if you prefer those), what size they should be, and how many you should have, will depend on a number of factors, all of which are entirely a matter of your personal taste, so that any remarks I make will be very elementary. The main advice I can give anyone planning a garden is not to be in a hurry. Get to feel the lie of the ground and the environs, whatever they may be. After a time it may well come to you that a tree will look at its best in one situation, while an alpine garden will look more satisfactory in another place.

Once the salient features have impressed themselves on you, the more detailed planning can begin. You will want first to decide where the bigger fixtures are going to go. If you contemplate planting a cedar of lebanon or a scarlet oak, or some other ultimately large tree, then if your garden is small this will probably be the focal point, or at least one of the focal points if your garden is more extensive; so you want to make sure you have got it right. It must not, for example, be too near the house. It is not always easy, when you receive a stick six foot tall and nine inches across, to visualise that in the course of years it may reach a hundred feet in height and have a spread of thirty or more feet. What you thought might make a nice view from the lounge window may eventually block this window altogether. By this time it will be too late to take any remedial measures, and since any true gardener would be horrified at taking down a splendid tree, you will be forced to rebuild your house! This sort of mistake can prove expensive. To be slightly less frivolous, if you have a fancy for large willows or poplars, site them well away from any drainpipes, as the roots have a fatal tendency to make their way to these and eventually to crack them in order to reach the water inside. Possibly with the more extensive use of plastic piping this risk is now less than it was, but it is as well to bear it in mind.

Once you have fixed on the salient features of the garden, you can start to get down to more detail. By all means draw a plan, and cut out shapes to represent the beds and play at jigsaws with them, but remember that unless you have a very good visual imagination what looks good on paper may not necessarily look good in fact. In the same way I am a little dubious about those theorists who advocate outlining the potential compartments with canes and twine. The result always looks to me no more than a meaningless jumble of twine and canes, but this is probably due to a defect in me, and if you do not share this defect you may find such a course very helpful. What I find slightly more helpful is to outline the compartments with plastic hose or something similar, as you can easily try other shapes if you find the original one unsatisfactory. This, of course, comes rather expensive. Still, eventually you will have to define the shape of your compartments with something, and probably toilet rolls, weighted down at intervals, will prove the cheapest medium, provided that the weather remains fine during the planning period. This sounds rather stupid, but if you wish to have curves, your twine is not going to be much good, and you do need something that is easy to see and which is durable. One of those machines that mark out the lines on tennis courts and other sports grounds might well be the answer, except that it makes no allowance for second thoughts. Once you have lined out your boundaries, you have little chance of altering them without causing confusion, so some portable material is the obvious answer. Of course if you are going in for regular geometric figures—circles, rectangles or stars—there is no problem; it is only when you start on bays and promontories that these problems arise.

If you are starting from scratch, should you have a planting plan? In theory yes, but in practice . . . All your theories are liable to be swept aside by suddenly seeing a plant that had not occurred to you before and which you obviously must have. If, for example, *Stewartia sinensis* was not known to you, and you see it and decide to plant one in your garden, you can easily make havoc of any plan that has been too carefully assembled. On the whole I think the most practical method with a compartment, as with the whole garden, is to establish the focal points and work round them. You will want to know, of course, the ultimate height of the various subjects as well as with their width and rate of growth, and very hard you will find it to obtain this information, if indeed it can ever be furnished. We should always remember that, in spite of our plans and drawings, plants are living things, each with their own individuality. If you live, for example, on the west coast, *Berberis darwinii* may grow thirty feet high and have a spread of twenty feet; in East Anglia it may only reach twelve feet and spread for nine.

Apart from these wide climatic differences, which you can minimise by seeing how other plants of the kind you are growing fare in your neighbourhood, every garden has its own microclimate which will influence the rate of the plant's growth as well as its ultimate dimensions. We all know how a plant will sulk and fret in one position in the garden, while after being moved—possibly only a few yards—it will decide to thrive, and this behaviour is most likely due to the microclimate. These microclimates are not measurable to the average unscientific gardener, so that gardening becomes a matter of empiricism, of which your planting plan can take no account. It is possible to find out which plants grow rapidly and which grow slowly, and this relative rate of growth will be maintained under all conditions. Even here, though, matters are not completely clearcut. Most berberis species, if grown from seed, grow extremely slowly for the first two or three years and then start to make growth at a very rapid rate. The nurseryman is therefore quite justified in stating that berberis are rapid growers, but if you are growing berberis from seed you may well think that something is wrong. All this knowledge comes from experience but, unfortunately, by the time you have acquired the experience, you may have wrecked your garden.

Colour schemes are delightful in theory but can usually be disregarded in practice. There are a few plants, such as the Kurume azaleas, which so smother themselves with flower as to obscure the leaves, but most plants have their colours cushioned by the green of their leaves, so that the juxtaposition of clashing colours is rarely so painful as might be thought, and it is only with plants that show little green when flowering that much care is needed. On the other hand, there are some obvious rules that can be followed. Light flowers show up best against a dark background while bright flowers are at their best against a light background. I once planted a *Prunus davidiana* with only the sky behind it, with the result that it was practically impossible to see the flowers when they emerged, and the most effective embothrium I have seen is at Sheffield Park, Sussex, where it has a bank of white rhododendrons behind it. At the same place there is another embothrium backed by a purple beech and the result is dire, so some elementary thought must be taken. If your visual sensibility is very great you may find yourself planning in this way.

'Much may also be done by assorting the colouring of the roses and their foliage with that of their groundwork of larger growth. I am now preparing a piece of ground for this kind of well-thought-out planting. It is a small area, roughly circular, among Yew, Holly and Ilex of about twelve years' growth. Near the foot of one Ilex I am planting a group of Cistus laurifolius. The leaves of both are approximately of the same quality of cool dark colouring, and I judge that they will form an admirable ground for the almost blue leaves and milk-white bloom of Rosa brunoniana, while among the Cistus will again be the bluish foliage and white bloom of Rosa alba, a kind that, though scarcely a climber, is excellent for straggling through bushes 7 feet to 8 feet high. This group will lead to Maiden's Blush and the lovely Celeste, still with bluish foliage. On the further side, where the

Yews give place to Bambusa Metake, the Roses are of pale green leafage. Here is already a large bush of Rosa Polyantha (multiflora), more than thirty paces in diameter, whose fresh green nearly matches that of the Bamboos, while through these the Crimson Rambler pushes its bright flower-laden sprays' (*The Garden*, Vol LVIII, p 434). *Bambusa metake* was Siebold's name for *Arundinaria japonica*.

This was written, or to be more accurate spoken, by one of the greatest garden designers, Gertrude Jekyll; but in spite of that august name I doubt that the effect was all that the text suggests. To start with, *Rosa brunonii* (not *brunoniana*) cannot be said to have 'almost blue' leaves. In some forms, presumably the most authentic, they are greyish when they first emerge, but they soon have a darker hue. Similarly the other roses with bluish foliage are, in reality, a green with a suggestion of grey in them, most marked in *R. alba* and barely remarkable in the other two. Nor, I think, would most of us agree that crimson rambler has 'pale green leafage'. The old Latin proverb *De gustibus et coloribus non est disputandum*—there is no arguing about tastes or colours—must be brought into our comments on this carefully thought out plan. Moreover, the *R. alba* that is straggling through the *Cistus laurifolius* will flower at the same time, which seems rather wasteful. I would also not be very enthusiastic about disentangling and cutting out the dead canes of crimson rambler from among the bamboos. I can see that patch becoming an impenetrable jungle, filling up slowly with dead trails of the rambling rose.

Miss Jekyll was no theorist, but carried out her designs under her own supervision, so we would not expect her to make this sort of mistake, and personally I warm to her idea of trailing climbing roses among dark-leaved evergreens, but it is not easy to get even so vigorous a rose as *R. brunonii* to interpenetrate the branches of holly, although the yew and evergreen oak would have been easy enough. In point of fact it looks as though Miss Jekyll's taste was not commensurate with her knowledge of plants. We cannot blame her for not planting *R. soulieana*, with its glaucous leaves, instead of *R. brunonii*, as Soulié's rose was barely in cultivation at the time, but *R. fedtschenkoana*, also with glaucous leaves and a long flowering season, as well as decorative heps, had been in cultivation since 1876 and would have served her purpose far better than *R. alba*.*

It is worthy of note that it was in the foliage that Miss Jekyll was chiefly interested, although the colours of the flowers were chosen to blend according to the artistic tenets of the day. Foliage is, indeed, the main part of the larger garden landscape, with the result that we have people complaining about the rhododendrons that have been inserted among the trees at Stourhead, Wiltshire. The objectors have two points: first, that most rhododendrons were unknown to gardens when Stourhead was designed, and secondly that their garish colours strike a false note in what is basically a design of green trees and water. Still, to be consistent, they ought to encourage beds of regal pelargoniums, as one of the proprietors, Sir Richard Hoare, was a pioneer in breeding these in the beginning of the nineteenth century. Sweet named the genus *Hoarea*, now regarded as a section of *Pelargonium*, in his honour.

The great landscapists of the late eighteenth and early nineteenth centuries—Capability Brown, Repton and Kent—took very little interest in flowers as such. The flower garden was regarded as a small affair, and it was to trees and shrubs that they chiefly resorted for their effects. You may perhaps remember Mr Milestone, the landscapist in Peacock's Headlong Hall.

'This you perceive is the natural state of one part of the grounds. Here is a wood never yet touched by the finger of taste; thick, intricate and gloomy. Here is a little stream dashing from stone to stone, and overshadowed with these untrimmed boughs . . . Now here is the same place corrected—trimmed—polished—decorated—adorned. Here sweeps a plantation, in that beautiful regular curve: there winds a gravel walk: here are parts of the old wood, left in these majestic circular clumps, disposed at equal distances with wonderful symmetry: there are some single shrubs scattered in elegant profusion: here a Portugal laurel, there a juniper; here a larch, there a lilac; here a rhododendron, there an arbutus. The stream, you see, is become a

* I may be doing Miss Jekyll an injustice. Although the rose was introduced into cultivation in 1876, it does not appear to have flowered at Kew before 1900, when it was depicted in the *Botanical Magazine*.

canal: the banks are perfectly smooth and green, sloping to the water's edge: and there is Lord Littlebrain rowing in an elegant boat.'

This was published in 1816 and gives not only the romantic's objections to the actions of the landscapists, but also gives an accurate, even if satirical, picture of the way they worked. If Repton had designed Lord Littlebrain's park, we might well have had a Red Book showing just such a transformation as described above. However, such landscaping is only possible with an extensive acreage and the modern Repton may consider himself lucky if he has an acre to fashion. The classical models will not help us now and the problems must be worked out afresh.

We seem to have moved rather a long way from my query as to the advisability of a planting plan, but the scale of the garden is obviously an operative factor. In a small garden, plants are never far away; we cannot think in terms of vistas, but almost everything must be immediate. Even so there must be some standards that we can apply. With trees and shrubs the type and colour of the foliage may well prove to be our principal object. Flowers are comparatively ephemeral in their appearance, while leaves are permanent in the case of evergreens and present for anything from four to seven months in the case of deciduous trees. Usually it is as well to establish a nice balance between the two. Most, though by no means all, evergreens are somewhat heavy of aspect, and these can be balanced by light-leaved deciduous plants. The colours of the flowers cannot, of course, be disregarded completely, but colours that 'shriek' when juxtaposed are less common in the world of gardens than in the world of upholstery and too much should not be made of this.

With herbaceous plants, the foliage is usually of little importance, except for ferns, and the blending of colours and arranging for them to flower at the same time will be much more a matter for consideration. Not that everyone would disregard foliage even in herbaceous arrangements. I have heard people recommend that the upright sword-shaped leaves of iris can be set off with some ferny foliage, such as ferula or thalictrum. There are, of course, herbaceous plants that are grown solely for their foliage, such as many of the artemisias and other silver-leafed subjects, the purple-leaved fennel and the purple-leaved

Clematis recta, and there are numerous plants with variegated leaves, about which I find it impossible to raise much enthusiasm, but which many people find intriguing. Indeed, on reflection, I think we have been rather unenterprising in our herbaceous arrangements. The 'blaze of colour' from mid-June until September has tended to obscure the fact that a much longer display, even though somewhat less brilliant, is perfectly feasible. The long border at Great Dixter in Sussex is an example of what can be done by imaginative planning, but it must be confessed that it entails a lot of work as well as someone with Mr Lloyd's exhaustive knowledge. He has shared his knowledge with us in *The Well-tempered Garden*, but not everyone can afford the time that he gives to his superlative displays.

There is a tendency, which I feel is basically correct, to separate the herbaceous and the woody subjects, but I suppose it is not really necessary. In the early stages of any shrub- or tree-planting, there should be large gaps between the different plants. These gaps are admirable for various bulbous subjects, whose foliage tends to present rather a coarse appearance in other situations. Such plants as colchicums and the larger narcissus are exquisite when in flower, but do produce extremely bulky and long-lasting foliage, which tends to look unsightly in the herbaceous compartments. They can, of course, be planted in grass, but this entails leaving the grass until it has become hay and eventually needs to be scythed before it can be mown. This is fine if you have an old orchard or a so-called wild garden, but lacking these amenities the spaces between your young shrubs will serve adequately. Some people with a passion for tidiness either cut off the foliage altogether or plait it into neat little cones, neither of which activities will do anything except damage the bulbs. If you want to grow daffodils or colchicums you must be prepared to put up with the unsightly foliage, which in the case of daffodils will probably last until mid-June at least, while the colchicums can go on even longer.

It is also possible, with certain reservations, to fill the inter-shrub lacunae with herbaceous plants. They must be reasonably distant from the shrubs or trees and they must not be too tall. If a small shrub is smothered by a clump of achillea or lupins, it will not be killed but it will tend to grow only at the apex so as to escape from the darkness caused by the stronger growing herbaceous plants, so that the resultant shrubs will be leggy and ill-shaped. With very small shrubs even plants such as *Viola cornuta* could cause damage and with these tiny plants it is certainly best to either leave the gaps empty or to use them for spring and autumn bulbs. Plants that would be ideal for these gaps would be the various eremurus, but they are very expensive. They come fairly readily from seed, but take so long to reach flowering size that your shrubs might well have coalesced before the eremurus seedlings flowered. The main trouble with herbaceous plants, once your shrubs are large enough not to be smothered, is that it will probably entail hand-weeding to keep the compartments reasonably clean. With your bulbs you can wield the hoe when the foliage has died down, but the herbaceous plants tend to spread so that the intersties are hard to control without getting down on your hands and knees. If there is not much ground to control, this may be acceptable, but otherwise this problem must be faced.

You may well feel that the problem could be lessened by initially purchasing larger shrubs, but this is not necessarily beneficial in the long run. Young shrubs and trees grow far more vigorously than larger specimens, which may well sulk for several years before re-establishing their natural rhythm of growth. I have only to look out of my window to see a convincing example of this. When I started making this garden I decided to have a number of Crataegus species, as they have always seemed to me a genus that has been unnecessarily neglected by gardeners. They look well in flower and in fruit, some have very attractive foliage, and many colour brilliantly in the autumn. They are also very easy to grow, but large plants hate root disturbance. Among the plants I wanted was the yellow-hawed *C. altaica*, and the only plant the nursery could supply was a so-called 'specimen tree'. I purchased this with some misgivings which proved well-justified. The plant sulked, branches died back and eventually I had to remove almost all the framework that had already been formed and start with a practically bare trunk. The plant is growing away now fairly well, I am glad to say, but it has been overtaken by the younger trees which I was able to obtain for the other species I wanted.

By and large I would mistrust 'instant gardening'. A sizeable container-grown tree at a garden centre may be all right, or it may only have been put in the container quite recently and so have had its roots damaged and its growth checked. Patience is a virtue and like most virtues will bring its rewards. Your horrid little invisible young plant is much more likely, eventually, to make a large vigorous specimen. Even with rhododendrons, which have a close-knit root ball which enables large specimens to be moved without damage, results are finally better with young plants. Your 'specimen rhododendrons' will not show much discomfort, provided they are kept moist throughout their first summer, but they will tend to mark time for the next few years and may well be overtaken by smaller and younger plants.

This being the case, it is best to resign yourself to the thought of your shrub bed looking rather scanty for a few years. Since it should continue looking effective for the next twenty or thirty it is not much of an ordeal, but it does leave the problem of the gaps in the early stages. I think the best solution is spring bulbs followed by a clean cultivation, but you can indulge in low herbaceous plants or in the now popular ground-cover plants, of which I shall have something to say in the second section. I suppose you could put out annuals or bedding plants, but I cannot see them being very effective. If you have a will of iron you could keep the ground clean the whole time and mulch with peat or compost or farmyard manure, which would certainly get your shrubs growing more rapidly than any other course, but it is asking a lot of any gardener to contemplate large areas of bare earth without doing something about it.

7

WATER

If your garden already has a stream running through it, or contains a pond, you must make the best of it. The stream will attract all the spring frosts and conduct them out of your garden along its banks, and it will offer splendid opportunities for waterside plantings, while you can also induce it to form a bog and indulge in the various bog plants that are often so attractive. The pond can also be girdled with those plants that like their toes in water and you can also grow aquatics in the pond itself.

My own feeling, which I gather is not generally shared, is that an expanse of water is beautiful in itself and in the reflections it gives and tends to be spoiled if dotted about with plants, even such beautiful flowers as the various water-lilies. However, if left to itself, water will probably not remain unspoiled. On the contrary, the surface will become covered with algae or with duckweed, so you have to stock the pond with oxygenating plants which remain sub-aquatic and a fauna of water snails and fish to keep matters going smoothly. If you grow water-lilies, you are almost certain to need fish to eat the larvae of the water beetles, which will otherwise chew up the water-lily foliage. If you do like flowers in your water you might well consider the water violet, *Hottonia palustris*, which keeps its leaves under water while sending its flower spike up above the surface, so that you get the best of both worlds. It will not, however, thrive in deep water.

Waterworks are attractive in very hot weather and one can well see that in hot dry countries, such as Spain or Italy, fountains are not only agreeable to look at and to listen to in the heat of the day, but that they also afford a gratifying example of conspicuous waste. Look, they seem to say, we have so much water we can afford to throw it away. In our more temperate climate, when in the summer the sound of plashing water is not such a novelty, I would be a little wary of allowing them in a moderately sized garden. Of course if you are indulging in a period fantasy, recreating an Italian garden or a Victorian terrace, the fountain will give an authentic period touch. I personally have perhaps been conditioned by Jacques Tati's film *Mon Oncle*, in which the family had a garden of the most modern design, which included a fountain that was, presumably, rather expensive to run. Accordingly whenever the front door bell rang there was a wild dash to turn the fountain on before the guest was admitted.

Indeed, in a small garden my instincts are all against any form of water. Ponds I feel should be large, almost enough to be referred to as lakes, and a nasty little oblong of fibreglass says absolutely nothing to me. I can conceive ways in which these enlarged puddles could be effective—in, for example, a large alpine garden, where plants could be reflected in its surface. Of course if you yearn to have goldfish or water-lilies you have to do something about it, but I still beg leave to doubt whether the result is ornamental.

One of the gardens that I should most like to have seen was that created by Sir Frank Crisp at Friar Park, Henley-on-Thames. He seems to have shown a somewhat unexpected sense of humour for a serious gardener, which he apparently was, in spite of arguments to the contrary. In the gardens were 'two lakes, the upper and the lower, separated by a concrete dam some six foot high, ending in a knife edge at water level. Thus, seen from the lawn, the two sheets of water seemed continuous, and it was a favourite amusement after lunch, when the guests were drinking coffee on the lawn, to despatch the patient head gardener down to a boat at the lower end of the lower lake. He would row up towards them till, at a given and carefully calculated moment, he would catch a crab and fall over backwards, the sculls doing a realistic windmill act. Owing to the construction of the two lakes and the point chosen for the catastrophe the crab was fully visible to those on the lawn, but immediately after all was hidden by the invisible dam and boat and rower seemed to sink beneath the surface, and the more nervous were in some need of reassurance' (*Alpine Garden Society Bulletin*, Vol 17, p 173).

One can imagine rather glazed smiles being frozen to the faces of those who were fortunate enough to be regular luncheon guests of Sir Frank's, but the conceit is pleasant enough for an occasional airing. It is unlikely that this Edwardian sense of fun could be indulged in nowadays by many of us (presumably it was not common even in Edwardian times) and for most of us any water must be of rather modest dimensions. If your garden is not large and you want a pond, this must be made the central feature and the rest of the garden must be arranged around it. With any water there are a few elementary precautions that need to be taken. Owing to the beauty of the reflections, there is a great temptation to plant some weeping tree (and there are pendulous forms of a large number of trees) to overhang the water. This temptation must be resisted, as the leaves that fall off in the autumn will fall in the water, where they will ferment and create very disagreeable odours and maybe even kill any fish that you may be encouraging. If you put your tree some little way back you will still enjoy the reflections at a little distance, but this particular horror will be avoided. If your pond is entirely synthetic—made of fibreglass or concrete or just a pit lined with polythene sheeting—you should clean it out once a year. This can be done in the early spring, when most aquatic plants are in a state of quiescence. This is one of the nastiest of garden jobs and there is a great temptation to let everything slide, with the eventual result that the pond becomes silted up and filled with nameless horrors. If the pond is a natural phenomenon this does not happen and, in any case, you cannot empty it at all easily under these conditions, although you can, if you are conscientious, rake up excessive weed and decaying detritus.

If what you yearn for is running water, and this is not naturally available, you can obtain it by a series of electric pumps, which can recycle the water so that the same amount is endlessly circulating. If, in this case, you let your stream broaden out at some stage into a small pond, this will probably remain reasonably clean, although a certain amount of dead leaves and other unwanted materials is bound to accumulate whatever you do. With artificial bottoms to your water, you will have to put your aquatics (unless they are naturally floating) into baskets or some porous container, which they will not be long outgrowing and will after two years need dividing or moving into larger containers. Since I am not particularly fond of water-lilies, I feel that the trouble involved is not commensurate with the result achieved and I would not personally bother with water, unless it were already there. On the other hand, if you live in town and have only a small yard, there are obvious arguments in favour of a small Spanish-type patio, with the surface paved or tiled, a few specimen shrubs and an ornamental basin, as I believe the trade term is for a small pond and fountain. Being a plantsman it is not the sort of garden that I would like for myself, but I would hate to live in a town in any case. If you do have to (or maybe if you want to) then the patio garden is arguably your best answer.

We associate the patio with Spain, but it is really an Arabian invention and is only found in the south of Spain. In the north, where the climate is not unlike ours, you will not find the patio, which is essentially a garden for hot, dry climates. This suggests to me that we should not copy it too faithfully. The main object of the Spanish patio, as of the Italian pergola, is that one can get out into the open air, but in a cool shady position. In Britain we tend to want to sit in the sun, and the plashing fountain that gives an impression of coolth (is there such an antonym of warmth?) in the southern Mediterranean may just echo the raindrops falling on your head further north. The fountain, then, is not an essential feature of the northern patio and can be regarded as an optional extra. Fountains do have a fascination of their own, apart from any impression of freshness that they impart, and if you want a sheet of water in your courtyard it is probably better that it should be continually on the move, rather than static and collecting urban pollution as well as possibly breeding mosquitoes. We have to call such exterior extensions of the house, gardens, as there is no word for what is essentially an outside room, but it is not what I mean by a garden and probably not what you mean either. This does not mean that it cannot be altogether delightful; it can be, but essentially it is to be regarded as a room with a few floral arrangements of a permanent nature. The plants have to conform with the other decorations and the basin takes on the same central importance as a dining-room table.

If you read many gardening books, my last remarks will probably have set up certain echoes in your mind. I seem to be approaching the attitude of those who, in the words of Dean Hole, were 'resolved to maintain against all comers the superiority of the Natural to the Artificial System, of the English to the Italian style of garden'. Why the Dean thought that bedding was particularly Italian in style we shall never know. But it is worth inquiring into what the English style was considered to be.

8

LAUDATOR TEMPORIS ACTI

I suppose the best seller of all garden books is *The English Flower Garden* by William Robinson, which went into fifteen editions, besides a few reprints between 1883 and 1933; a feat of which other horticultural writers can only feel jealous. The author is a mysterious figure, who was born in Ireland in 1838 and received employment as a gardening lad until 1861, when he let out all the fires heating his employer's glasshouses and went first to Dublin and then to London. The story of the neglect of his employer's glasshouses is presumably to be traced to Robinson himself, which does not suggest a great love of plants and may, perhaps, be completely untrue. In London he was employed at the Royal Botanic Society's garden in Regent's Park, London (the present Queen Mary's Garden) and was also befriended by Shirley Hibberd, who encouraged him to write. In 1867 he spent a year in France and the next year his first book about the gardens around Paris appeared. In some manner he acquired enough money, possibly with the aid of a backer whose name has been lost, to start the journal *The Garden* in 1872. He also wrote books in the 1870s on alpine gardening and the wild garden, while the first edition of *The English Flower Garden* appeared in 1883. The following year Robinson purchased Gravetye Manor in Sussex, where he lived until his death in 1935.

Robinson was not a natural writer like Shirley Hibberd, although he had a certain ease of vituperation which is enviable. Here is a quotation which gives, I think, his quintessence: 'Of all the things made by man for his pleasure a flower garden has the least business to be ugly,

Page 65 (*above*) The best thing to do with water is absolutely nothing. Leonardslee in Sussex; (*below*) Victorian bedding after geraniums with the emphasis on foliage. The Wall Garden at Wisley, Surrey

Page 66 (*left*) The Phillip Island Glory Pea. Once in cultivation, but now extinct; (*right*) *Thermopsis barbata*. A plant that should be reintroduced

barren, or stereotyped, because in it we may have the fairest of the earth's children in a living ever-changeful state, and not, as in other arts, mere representations of them. And yet we find in nearly every country place, pattern plans, conventional design, and the garden robbed of all life and grace by setting out flowers in geometric ways. A recent writer on garden design tells us that the gardener's knowledge is of no account, and that gardens "should never have been allowed to fall into the hands of the gardener or out of those of the architect; that it is an architectural matter, and should have been schemed at the same time and by the same hand as the house itself."

'The chief error he makes is in saying that people, whom he calls "landscapists" destroyed all the formal gardens in England and that they had their ruthless way until his coming. An extravagant statement, as must be clear to anyone who takes the trouble to look into the thing itself, which many of these writers will not do or regard the elementary facts of what they write about. Many of the most formal gardens in England were made within the past century, when this writer says all his ideal gardens were cleared away . . . During the whole of that period there was hardly a country seat laid out that was not marred by the idea of a garden as a conventional and patterned thing. With Castle Howards, Trenthams, and Chatsworths staring at him, it is ludicrous to see a young architect weeping over their loss. Even if there is no money to waste in gigantic water-squirts, the idea of a terrace is still carried out often in level plains. There are hundreds of such gardens about the country, and the ugliest gardens ever made in England have been made in Victorian days.

'It cannot be too clearly remembered that geometrical gardens of a deplorable type are things of our own time, and it is only in our own time the common idea that there is only one way of making a garden was spread. Hence, in all the newer houses we see the stereotyped garden often made in spite of all the needs of the ground, whereas in really old times it was not so. Berkely is not the same as Sutton, and Sutton is quite different from Haddon.

'Moreover, on top of all this formality of design of our own day were grafted the most formal and inartistic ways of arranging flowers that ever came into the head of man, ways that were happily unknown to the Italians or the makers of the earliest terraced gardens. The true Italian gardens were often beautiful . . . but "bedding out" or mar-shalling the flowers in geometrical patterns, is a thing of our own precious time, and "carpet" gardening is simply a further remove in ugliness. The painted gravel gardens of Nesfield and Barry and other broken-brick gardens were also an attempt to get rid of flowers and get rigid patterns instead. Part of the garden architect's scheme was to forbid the growth of plants on walls, as at Shrubland, where for many years, there were strict orders that the walls were not to have a flower or creeper of any kind upon them. As these pattern gardens were made by persons often ignorant of gardening, and if planted in any human way with flowers would all "go to pieces", hence the idea of setting them out as they appeared on the drawing-board, some of the beds not more than a foot in diameter, blue and yellow paints being used where the broken brick and stone did not give the desired colour!

'Side by side with the adoption in most large and show places of the patterned garden, both in design and planting, disappeared almost everywhere the old English garden, that is, one with a variety of form of shrub and flower and even low trees; so that now we only find this kind of garden here and there in Cornwall, Ireland and Scotland, and on the outskirts of country towns. All true plant form was banished because it did not fit into the bad carpet pattern. I am only speaking of what everyone must know who cares the least about the subject, and of what can be seen today in all the public gardens round London and Paris. But we shall never see beautiful flower gardens again until natural ways of grouping flowers and variety of true form come back to us in the flower garden.'

And so he goes bumbling on, with dubious syntax and profound historical ignorance, but evidently with his heart in the right place. But what was 'the old English garden . . . with a variety of form of shrub and flower and even low trees' to which he points as to a lost Paradise? It seems to me that we know very little of any garden that seems to fit this description and it can only have been about 1850 that Robinson himself started to take much notice of gardens. Nothing in the descrip-tions of the earlier gardens suggest that he was correct in his views. In the *Floral World* of 1859 a Mr William Harris gives a description of one of the more famous eighteenth-century gardens. Here is what he has to say.

'Prior to about the middle of the last century, the gardens of our nobility were laid out geometrically, according to strict rules of art. [You may well feel that this is where you came in, but the article was written in 1859 so he is referring to 1750 or thereabouts.] A rigid stiffness everywhere prevailed. Even the trees and shrubs were carved into the most fantastic shapes, in imitation of beasts, birds, and dragons; although we cannot say that in so doing our fathers greatly violated the second commandment, so ludicrous were their imitations.

'It is remarkable that the authors of what is now called English Landscape Gardening are names which shine conspicuously in the galaxy of our Standard British Poets—Addison, Pope and Shenstone. These gifted "sons of song", not only by their writings inculcated a purer taste; but each one by himself, following precept by example, laid out his estate with freedom and beauty. Whilst Addison was shaping out his walks . . . at Bilton near Rugby, Pope was equally assiduous in forming his garden at Twickenham and Shenstone in cutting through his dingles and copses at the Leasowes, near Birmingham. In order that the readers of the *Floral World* may form some idea of the beauties of the Leasowes . . . we shall give a description of one scene in this Elysium, remarking that every part exhibited corresponding charms.

VIRGIL'S GROVE

This calm recess formed a fairy scene of surpassing loveliness. A plain obelisk adorned its solitudes . . . Near this obelisk, opposite a dashing fall of water was a seat addressed to the poet Thomson, author of *The Seasons* . . .

'Every object combined its force to delight the eye and bewilder the imagination. On the left was seen the distant prospect of a foaming cascade, throwing its silver sheets of water over craggy rocks; beneath was a rustic bridge, of simple construction, and on an opposite bank to the right appeared a dropping fountain, creeping through the mossy veins of a wild stony mass and stealing down the shelving bounds into the opaque glen, charmingly interwoven with stately trees and brushing underwood . . . The path from hence approached a secluded spot whereon was a bench overhung with these lines . . .

'Returning to the obelisk, a winding path led through a beauteous glen to the cascade, which bursting at once fully on the view, arrested the spectator with sudden admiration. At the bottom of the fall, in a rocky excavation, was a stone seat and recess, and on the other side of the stream a figure of Venus appeared as if rising out of the white foaming surge of the cascade . . .

'Pursuing our way on the left of the cascade was a small stream highly impregnated with mineral particles; it issued from under a square stone . . . A gloomy path led to a root-house, concealed in a secluded nook. The following beauteous lines by Shenstone were inscribed within . . .

> Here in cool grot and mossy cell
>   We rural fays and fairies dwell;
>   Though rarely seen by mortal eye,
>   When the pale moon, ascending high,
> Darts through yon limes her quivering beams
> We frisk it near these crystal streams.

It does not sound the sort of garden that Robinson had in mind, delightful though it doubtless was.

We know a little more of the great plantsmen of the middle and later eighteenth century, the quakers Peter Collinson and John Fothergill. The actual design of their gardens is not clear, but their main interest was in obtaining and growing new plants. Collinson is best known for his championship of the great American collector-botanist John Bartram, but he also had correspondents in China, Russia, Siberia and Aleppo. He certainly had his ideas about garden design, which have a strangely modern sound about them.

'Everyone that would beautifully imitate nature should well consider the diversity and growth of trees, the size and shapes of leaves and the many shades of green. To know how properly to mix them in planting is another manner of painting with living pencils, for greens properly disposed, throw in a mixture and contrast of lights and shades, which wonderfully enliven the pictures and which insensibly strike the senses with wonder and delight. The effects must be charming to see the dark green elm with the lighter shades of the lime and beech, or the yellowish green planes with the silver-leafed abele; the chestnuts, the poplar, the acacia, the horse chestnut, *cum multis aliis*; when fanned by a gentle breeze then how beautiful the contrast how delightfully the lights and shades fall in to diversify the sylvan scene.'

Dr Fothergill not only followed Collinson in getting plants in from numerous correspondents, but also, with others, subsidised collectors. Perhaps the most remarkable of these was Thomas Blaikie, who was sent to the Alps and who brought back a large number of alpine plants, which entered cultivation for the first time; this was in 1775–6. Listed among these is *Gentiana ciliata*, and one would like to know whether Fothergill had any luck with this intractable plant, that has been the despair of all gardeners of whom I have any knowledge. One of Fothergill's American correspondents was Humphrey Marshall and in a letter to him we have a description of Fothergill's method with the plants he received from the United States.

'Under a north wall I have a good border made up of that kind of rich black turf-like soil, mixed with some sand, in which I find most of the American plants thrive best. It has a few hours of the morning and evening sun, and is quite sheltered from the mid-day heats. It is well supplied with water during the summer and the little shrubs and herbaceous plants have a good warm covering of dried fern thrown over them when the frosts set in. This is gradually removed when the spring advances, so that, as the plants are never frozen in the ground while they are young and tender, I do not lose any that come to me with any degree of life in them . . . My garden is well sheltered; the soil is good and I endeavour to mend it as occasion requires. I have a little wilderness, which, when I bought the premises was full of old yew trees, laurels and weeds. I had it cleared, well dug, and took up many trees, but left others standing for shelter. Among these I have planted Kalmias, Azaleas, all the Magnolias and most other hardy American shrubs. It is not quite eight years since I made a beginning [the letter dates from 1772], so that my plants must be considered but young ones. They are, however, extremely flourishing. I have an Umbrella tree [*Magnolia tripetala*] about twenty feet high, that flowers with me abundantly every spring; but the great Magnolia [*M. grandiflora*] has not yet flowered; it grows exceedingly fast. I shelter his top in the winter; he gains from half a yard to two feet in height every summer, and will ere long, I doubt not, repay my care with his fragrance and beauty.'

In the eighteenth and early nineteenth century gardening literature one quite often finds references to laurels, as in Fothergill's letter, and probably most people have followed my example and taken it for granted as a common evergreen. But what, in fact, was the laurel? According to Aiton's *Hortus Kewensis* the common laurel was *Prunus laurocerasus*, known nowadays as the cherry laurel. This had been received from the eastern Mediterranean in 1697 (possibly introduced by Sir George Wheler) and being very easy of increase had become a common evergreen fifty years after its first introduction.

It is safe to assume that most gardeners were not of the calibre of Collinson and Fothergill, and these two may well have started a trend. Collinson's last years were embittered by numerous thefts from his garden, and people do not commit thefts for no reason; so the interest in unusual plants must have been growing—indeed, thriving nursery businesses were starting up around London. Most notable among these in the mid-eighteenth century were Christopher Gray at Kensington and James Gordon at Mile End, both of whom specialised in the new plants coming from America. Indeed for his skill in raising the seeds of ericaceous plants James Gordon has been immortalised in the genus *Gordonia*. By the end of the century there were many more nurserymen, some of whom sent out collectors to foreign parts. Chief among these were Lee and Kennedy at the Vineyard Nursery, Hammersmith and Conrad Loddiges at Hackney.

I have in front of me, as I write, a rather faded and illegible copy of Messrs Loddiges's catalogue for 1823. This consists of forty-eight pages of triple columns, of which the last twelve pages are confined to hardy herbaceous and bulbous plants. So from this we can get some idea of which plants were available to gardeners at that time. Perhaps it is as well to mention that it was printed long before Douglas had visited California, or before Fortune had gone to China and equally before plants such as verbenas and petunias had come from South

America. The list starts with acaena and continues with 28 species of achillea, 53 aconites (including *Aconite volubile*), 47 alliums, 22 anemones (among which is the double form of *Anemonella thalictroides*), only 8 aquilegia, but including *Aquilegia viridiflora*, 13 arenarias, 11 artemisia, 8 asclepias and no less than 44 aster. Sixteen astragalus suggests a skill in cultivation that has since been lost. That intractable marsh orchid *Calopogon pulchellus* was available and there were no less than 60 campanulas. One always thinks of ornamental thistles as being of this century, but here were 10 carduus and 3 carlina. Among the 29 centaureas are some that would scarcely find admittance to gardens nowadays. The main source of exotics at that time had been eastern North America, as we have seen from the number of aster species, the ancestors of our modern Michaelmas daisies, but there were also 9 coreopsis. Among the 4 species of cypripedium offered was *Cypripedium spectabile*. There were no less than 24 delphiniums of which 1, *Delphinium intermedium* was offered in 3 different forms and was probably an early hybrid (there was also a *D. hybridum*). Too detailed a list is apt to prove tedious reading, but we should note that there were 25 dianthus, 16 euphorbias, 19 gentians (including *Gentiana aurea* and *G. incarnata*); 17 galiums represent a genus that is not now used in gardens, as do 4 equisetum, those pestilential horsetails which were so highly thought of as foliage plants until about 1880. Two North American habenarias are a further indication of the popularity of these terrestial orchids and among 7 helonias, *Zigadenus elegans* appears. There were no less than 20 different lilies available (including, however, *Fritillaria camschatica*). The list also contains 40 hieracium and 52 iris. Among the peonies are 12 species, 8 cultivars of *Paeonia albiflora*, 7 of *P. officinalis*, 1 with variegated foliage and 2 of *P. paradoxa* (whatever that was in 1823; one of the cultivars had fringed petals), 18 phlox, 48 potentillas (which must, I feel, have included a number of pretty weedy species), 13 primulas (including *Primula cortusoides*), 23 ranunculus (including such intractable subjects as *RR. glacialis* and *parnassifolius*), 5 rheums, 64 saxifragas, 21 scabiosas, 28 solidagos, 37 thalictrum, 49 veronicas and 33 violas. The catalogue ends with the following paragraph.

'In an establishment of this nature there of course must exist an ardent and continual desire of extending, as well as diffusing the collection. Persons in foreign countries, who are animated by a similar passion, are respectfully invited to a Correspondence, which can hardly fail to become mutually advantageous. A liberal price is at all times ready to be given for fresh seeds or living plants, if new or rare, from whatever quarter of the globe they may have been brought.'

During the late eighteenth and early nineteenth centuries a very large number of plants owed their introduction to cultivation to these anonymous correspondents of the nurserymen. From the early numbers of the Botanical Register we know the name of a few people who sent plants to Kennedy and Lee, but we do not know how they got *Buddleia globosa* from Peru as early as 1774, while Messrs Loddiges who amassed the largest catalogue in the early years of the nineteenth century seem to have depended almost entirely on their correspondents, most of whom, if tradition is to be accepted, were missionaries.

It is perhaps worth turning aside for a moment to assess from what a comparatively limited area this enormous list was drawn. In 1823 the eastern half of North America had been fairly thoroughly explored, but practically no collection had been done on the Pacific side. Possibly a few plants had got to Europe via Russia, but these would mainly have been trees. At the end of the eighteenth century Loddiges had subscribed to Bieberstein's exploration of the Caucasus and he had probably also shared in the sendings of Peter Pallas from many parts of Russia and Siberia. South Africa had been well collected, but there would be little that was hardy from there, and similarly, although there had been a certain amount of collecting in South America, nothing hardy would have emerged. Very little had been brought from China and even less from Japan. Plants could have been sent from the Himalayas, but in point of fact none had yet arrived in cultivation. Plenty of plants were coming in from Australia, but again these were not hardy, so the hardy-plant grower was confined mainly to Europe, northern Asia, the Levant and eastern North America. As time went on many more plants were introduced, but the selection nowadays is so much less than in 1823 that one wonders how much actual progress has been made. Incidentally, in view of the often repeated claims by writers from 1860 onwards that alpine plants had never been properly grown in this country hitherto, it is interesting to note the number of intractable subjects, such as *Anemone baldensis, Arenaria laricifolia, Campanula excisa, Phyteuma comosa, Primula minima, Saxifraga caesia, mutata,* and *stellaris, Soldanella minima, Hedysarum obscurum, Viola palmata* and *pedata,* as well as the ranunculus already mentioned, that Loddiges had on offer.

These then were the flowers that Robinson's perhaps mythical old borders contained and, really, there are very few novelties that have accrued in the intervening years. Most notable of the absentees are, I suppose, the lupins. Loddiges could only offer *Lupin nootkatensis,* although it would not be long before *L. polyphyllus* would arrive among Douglas's sendings. Another absentee in the 1823 list is Kniphofia. *Kniphofia uvaria* had actually been in cultivation since 1707 and three other species *K. burchellii, media* and *pumila,* had subsequently been introduced, but the main flow of species did not come until the second half of the century. Otherwise the main advance in border plants has been in various hybrids of such plants as aster, lupin and delphinium. People who disagreed with Robinson in his admiration of the old-fashioned garden were apt to say that these borders were never consistently attractive. In *The Garden* for December 1872, a Mr C. P. Peach writes:

'I again affirm, if it had not been for such half-hardy plants as Geraniums, Verbenas, Ageratums, Petunias, Lobelias, etc. very few of the small greenhouses which can now be seen in such numbers against villas and country houses, would have been built, and the usual stamp of mixed herbaceous border, which one saw in villa gardens twenty years ago, would have been stereotyped—borders put under the care of an ignorant labourer, dug over every autumn or winter, and then left to take care of themselves. I know some of these borders that still exist in their pristine ugliness, never looking gay at any one period of the year, and, with the exception of a few withered leaves, looking just as bare in the winter as a bedded-out geometrical garden, and certainly more untidy. I do not deny for one minute that herbaceous borders in the hands of skilled artists like the Rev. Mr Ellacombe and the Rev. Harper Crewe may be made both beautiful and interesting, but there are very few gardeners who have the botanic knowledge or cultural skill which is required for such collections.'

This is a reply to a series of articles by Robinson attacking a speech Mr Peach had made in defence of bedding gardens.

Although few people seem to have realised it at the time, the controversy was an early example of the dichotomy I mentioned earlier between the plantsman and the exterior upholsterer. Here are Robinson's final instructions: 'Mixed borders may be made in various ways; but it may be well to bear in mind the following points: select only good plants; throw away weedy kinds, there is no scarcity of the best. See good collections. Put, at first, rare kinds in lines across four-feet nursery beds, so that a stock of plants may be at hand. Make the choicest borders where they cannot be robbed by the roots of trees; see that the ground is good, and that it is at least two and a half feet deep, so deep that, in a dry season, the roots can seek their supplies far below the surface. Plant in naturally disposed groups, never repeating the same plant at intervals along the border, as is so often done with favourites. Do not graduate the plants in height from the front to the back, as is generally done, but sometimes let a bold plant come to the edge; and, on the other hand, let a little carpet of a dwarf plant pass in here and there to the back, so as to give a varied instead of a monotonous surface. Have no patience with bare ground, and cover the border with dwarf plants; do not put them along the front of the border only. Let Hepaticas and double and other Primroses and Rockfoils, and Golden Moneywort and Stonecrops and Forget-me-nots, and dwarf Phloxes and many similar plants cover the ground among the tall plants betimes, at the back as well as the front. Let the little ground plants form broad patches and colonies by themselves occasionally, and let them pass into and under other plants . . .

'The plants of the older kind of mixed border were, like the grasses of the meadows of the northern world, stricken to the earth by winter, and the border was not nearly so pretty then as the withered grass of the plain or copse. But since the revival of interest in hardy and Alpine flowers, and the many introductions of recent years, we have a great number of beautiful plants that are evergreen in winter and that enable us to make evergreen borders . . . Along with these rock and herbaceous plants we may group a great many dwarf shrubs that come almost between the true shrub and the Alpine flower—little woody evergreen creeping things like the dwarf Partridge Berry, Canadian Cornel, hardy Heaths and Sand Myrtles, often good in colour when grouped. Among these various plants we have plenty for evergreen borders, and this is important, as, while many might object to the bare earth of the ordinary border of herbaceous plants near the house or in other favourite spots, it is different with borders of evergreen plants, which may be charming and natural in effect throughout the year.'

It seems fantastic that this rather pedestrian mixture of good sense and misinformation should have been regarded as a clarion call to arms. But this was what did happen; chiefly, I suppose, because Robinson not only wrote books, but had at various times a number of gardening journals under his editorship. The actual work was done by the great plantsmen of the time: Ellacombe, Harper Crew, Archer-Hind, Gumbleton, Ewbank and many others. The curious thing is that Robinson seems to have established the myth that every garden from 1850 until the Robinson revelations in the 1870s was given over entirely to formal bedding.

Now, as I shall be explaining later, there were good historical reasons for the sudden effulgence of bedding plants, and like so many novelties it had its rise and fall. For a time bedding was a 'craze' but, as we have seen, even at its zenith many people were complaining that the old favourites among herbaceous plants were being lost. I doubt if they ever were lost, the more especially as many famous alpine and herbaceous nurseries were either started or already flourishing during this period. James Backhouse of York, for long regarded as the greatest grower of alpines, managed to maintain his position all through the nineteenth century. A reaction was bound to come from the prevalence of bedding and Robinson could have done just as well without any vituperation. Here we may as well return to Shirley Hibberd and 1857.

'As to borders, there is no doing without them; they fringe walls, fences and grass plots, and beautify the walks everywhere. In suburban gardens, and in the gardens attached to town villas, the borders often present the most attractive features, owing to the limited capacity of the garden precluding geometric arrangements and pincushion beds. Borders should never be wider than can be conveniently reached across; in fact a very broad border under a wall or fence does not look well. Borders on grass and in open grounds frequently take the form and arrangement of detached beds, and when they are planted with shrubs, care should be taken to break them here and there into sweeping outlines, so as to open an occasional space for the eye to escape, as well also to increase the means of transit from one part of the garden to another.'

Again he writes: 'To arrange borders so as to have them at all times gay and symmetrically arranged as to colours, demands not only vigilance in preparing a regular succession of varieties, but a nice taste in disposing them, so that each plant or patch of plants shall fully exhibit its beauties and enhance those of its neighbours. Colours, heights and habits must be carefully attended to, and though a formal disposition is essential, there are certain ways of breaking a rigid formality, which, to a tasteful eye, gives much pleasure. It is not a great profusion or a vast variety that will suffice to produce a good effect; indeed a spareness of plants and *a repetition of the same plant* at intervals will generally prove more successful than the most lavish enamelling of confused colours. Then along the lines of various heights how gladly the eye rests upon large masses of shrubs, or grand groups of plants of large growth, or specimen plants from the greenhouse, such as huge geraniums, Dielytra spectabilis, myrtle, andromeda, calceolaria, fuchsia, and others that form objects in themselves, placed far apart and breaking the linear formality by their shrubby masses and their brave powdering of colour. The geometric garden does not well admit of this, except as centres for beds; but mixed borders, when extensive, are greatly improved by an occasional breaking of the whole arrangement, by means of groups and specimens of larger growth, not set back in the row appropriated to the taller kinds, but rising from the midway line from a broad patch of some close-growing gems that clear a space for them and make a carpet round their feet. If the borders are broken by mounds, the effect is still finer, and the same kind of planting is suitable for their summits.'

This does not sound very different from Robinson's border, although he insisted on all his plants being hardy and would not have tolerated 'specimen plants from the greenhouse', nor, I hope, would he have encouraged mounds in the border. Hibberd was by no means insistent on all the plants being hardy. 'What,' he asks, 'will you put in your borders? If they are not to be in ribbons, but in the old style of mixed plants, there will be very little difficulty in making them gay, but the cold pit, the forcing pit, and the greenhouse must be carefully managed to keep up a succession; and now we may say, not a week in the whole year need pass without offering to the ladies something from the borders for a bright boquet [*sic*]. But in the absence of such aids as pits and houses afford, any extent of borders may be kept beautiful, owing to the immense variety of high-class hardy plants we have suitable for beds and borders.'

If we had an immense amount of high-class hardy plants suitable in 1857, we cannot claim that Robinson's precepts were particularly new. In point of fact, of course, bedding never has been superseded, but the breeding of the hybrid tea rose gave us a hardy plant with as long a flowering season as the tender subjects that were used before, and nowadays most bedding in private gardens is devoted to roses. We only deceive ourselves, however, if we think that there is any essential difference between the modern rose garden and Victorian bedding. Indeed, with some recent developments in the rose we are even getting some of the strident colours which modern taste deplores. The object of bedding was to obtain plants with a very long season of flowering, so that the beds remain attractive for a matter of months rather than a week or so. Such plants were not available before about 1840 so that bedding could not have come into existence before that date.

The best Victorian bedding had its subtlety, and a very large selection of plants from which to choose. It was elaborate, and needed ample labour as well as the backing of hothouses, so that it is not surprising that it has tended to be less practised than formerly; still it does survive in most municipal gardens to a certain extent, although rarely with the wide choice that the Victorians could offer.

The most important point that both Hibberd and Robinson made in their writings was never acted upon in their lifetime and is not always followed even today. That was their protest against grafting or budding plants on unsuitable stocks. We have already seen Hibberd using italics to emphasise the importance of having roses on their own roots, and this is echoed by Robinson and other writers. However, unless you strike cuttings yourself, you are not likely even nowadays to get roses on their own roots, though you will probably achieve this with lilacs, rhododendrons, and clematis, which is a somewhat belated triumph. I understand there is some controversy—as indeed there always was—as to the reliability of modern hybrid roses on their own roots, but I suspect that it is often unjustified and the fact that one can get many more roses by budding than by rooting cuttings is the operative factor.

Whether hybrid roses really are better on their own roots is a matter which one would have thought could have been easily demonstrated in test plots, and the fact that this has not (so far as I know) been done seems to suggest that they probably do do rather better. The main argument used by its advocates was that in very severe winters, if the top got killed by frost, the plant would send up more growths from the roots, and the correspondence columns of *The Garden* were able to print letters from American growers testifying to this. In addition, Robinson claimed that roses on their own roots lived longer. 'The dog Rose stock makes a strong growth for a few years, but then it gradually dies and leaves us with a very poor Rose garden and prickly suckers. A good Rose on its own root may live as long as the average man, or longer.' On the other hand, he says that 'the plant on its own root is more fragile than on the Dog Brier. That being so, it is a wise plan to put the cuttings where we want the plant to grow.' I have not seen this fact stated by other writers and do not know if roses on their own roots are more brittle than grafted specimens; *a priori* it sounds unlikely.

Robinson also suggests that roses on their own roots are more floriferous. His habit of interplanting his roses with 'Pansies, Pinks, Carnations, and many of the most valuable annuals we grow', has not been encouraged by later growers. His full list of ground cover plants for his rosebeds reads: 'Evening Primrose, Mignonette, Violas, Silvery Speedwell, Baby Blue Eyes [Nemophila], Encrusted Saxifragas [which he calls Silvery Rockfoils], Blue Anagallis, dwarf Campanulas, Rock Scabious, Phacelia, Our native Geranium [which was this? *G. sanguineum* or *G. pratense*?], Sand Pinks [*Tunica saxifraga*], Dwarf Thyme, Viola gracilis, Linaria pallida, Silvery Gypsophila, The Blue Bindweed and the Shamrock Pea.'

It is probably always a mistake, if one is writing didactically about gardening, to cite oneself as an exemplar, but in the 1926 edition, this is what Robinson did, listing his complete planting scheme as at December 1922. Some read rather curiously, such as a bed of 'Ophelia' rose with an undergrowth of *Platycodon mariesii*; a bed of mixed helianthemum, grey-leaved senecio (what was this? The only grey-leaved senecio he lists is *Senecio greyii*), Rose K. of K. (a red HT), *Lilium szovitzianum* and *Perowskia atriplicifolia*. A mixed bed of bronze-leaved roses and *Gladiolus primulinus*. Edging crocus beneath encrusted saxifragas.

Incidentally, if you want an excuse for using Latin names for plants, *The English Flower Garden* provides it, since Robinson decided to give English names wherever possible. This laudable aim was, however, complicated, by Robinson's admiration for Ruskin, who had invented a number of English names where none existed. This practically entails learning a new language where saxifrages are termed rockfoils and aster species are starworts. Indeed in order to make himself intelligible Robinson usually has to give the Latin name in parenthesis after his English one. We have already seen the explanation of the sand pinks and we can also learn that the silvery speedwell was *Veronica incana*; *Viola gracilis* he termed the Greek viola, and the blue bindweed, as one might have guessed, was *Convolvulus mauritanicus*. Here are a few more for you to try to identify. Tassel tree, grand bellflower, madwort, silver bush, sandwort, Himalayan laurel, purple apple-berry, walking leaf, mountain sweet, tickseed, rockspray, brush bush, New Zealand ribbon-wood, lily tree, borage-worts, etc. Do any of these names mean anything to you? Personally I would want them elucidated. They are, in the order above: albizzia, adenophora, alyssum, anthyllis, arenaria, aucuba, billardiera, camptosorus, ceanothus, coreopsis, cotoneaster, eucryphia, hoheria, magnolia and mertensia.

I would have left the matter here, were it not that I have just discovered the explanation for a sentence that has always puzzled me greatly and I pass this information on for others who may have been similarly puzzled. In the preface to one of the later editions of *The English Flower Garden* Robinson wrote:

'The rose of Sharon, which is beautiful in France and also in our country, I planted a large group of it. It grew well for many years, but never flowered, and seeing it was hopeless, I gave it to a friend in the Thames Valley, where it grew and flowered well.'

The only rose of Sharon with which I am acquainted is that splendid but invasive *Hypericum calycinum*, which will grow and flower everywhere, and I could not imagine what Robinson could mean. I have just found out that at the turn of the century *Hibiscus syriacus* was also known as rose of Sharon and the sentence at last makes sense. It does serve as a warning that vernacular names may be as misleading as Latin ones, which are usually either unintelligible or out of date but which do not lead to this particular confusion.

Page 83 (left) Malus tchonoskii. A marvellous plant with silver leaves in the spring, orange and crimson in the autumn. Excellent as a tree, but how would it do for hedging?; (below) the snake-bark maple is attractive throughout the year

Page 84 Show ranunculus. These have, it would seem, vanished for ever

9

THE MASTER'S MASTER

In 1871 Robinson started *The Garden*, in which the fight against artificial as opposed to 'natural' gardening was opened. In the same year
was published Shirley Hibberd's *The Amateur's Flower Garden* and in
his Chapter 6 we find set out, in rather better English than Robinson
could command, the main credo of this better-known work.

'The hardy herbaceous border is the best feature of the flower garden,
though commonly regarded as the worst. When well made, well
stocked and well managed, it presents us with flowers in abundance
during ten months out of twelve, and in the remaining two blank
months offer some actual entertainment and many agreeable hints of
pleasures to come, to make an ample reward for the comparatively
small amount of labour its proper keeping will necessitate. Given a few
trees and shrubs, a plot of grass, and comfortable walks, the three first
essentials of a garden, and a collection of hardy herbaceous plants is the
fourth essential feature, and may well be the last; for the bedding
system may very well be dispensed with in a homely place, provided
the hardy flowers are admitted, and cared for, according to their
merits. It may be that many a reader of this will be disposed to question
whether geraniums should be swept away to make room for lilies, and
verbenas denied a place because of the superior claims of phloxes, but
such a question we do not propose—our business is to point out that
the bedding system is an embellishment added to the garden: the
herbaceous border is a necessary fundamental feature . . .

'It is an important characteristic of the herbaceous border that its proper tenants are hardy plants that need no aid of glass or fuel for their preservation during the winter . . . In the cultivation of bedding plants we may fairly reckon on a brilliant display for three months, and it may extend to four—say from 1st of June to the 30th of September, but the herbaceous border will be gay from the end of April to the middle of October, a period of six months, and will offer us a few flowers in February, and a few in November and December, and in a mild winter will not be utterly flowerless even in January. It would be an exaggeration to say that the herbaceous border is capable of a display of flowers all the year round, but it is very nearly capable of a consummation so devoutly to be wished. To the advantages of hardiness and continuity of bloom must be added a third and grand qualification of a distinguishing kind—that of variety. It is scarcely an exaggeration to say that the varieties of form, colour, and general character, amongst hardy herbaceous plants is without limit; but as variety may be obtained amongst ugly plants, we are bound to add that the proper occupants of the garden we are considering are all beautiful, and a considerable proportion are well-known favourites. Nevertheless, it must be admitted that with all their good claims to loving regard, the hardy herbaceous plants obtain but scant attention, and tens of thousands of persons who know that verbenas are somewhat showy when in flower, and would like to grow thousands of them, are prepared any day to ignore the whole tribe of herbaceous plants as weedy things that have had their day, and, with the exception of a lily or two, and, perhaps, a hollyhock, deserving of a place only in the unsavoury hole where grass mowings and the sweepings of the poultry house are deposited with a view to a "mixen". It ought to be needless to attempt this vindication, but we feel bound in duty to the reader to urge that every rational development of the hardy garden will prove advantageous to the lover of flowers, as tending both to lessen the expense and labour which the keeping of the garden necessitates, and considerably augment the pleasures that it is capable of affording as the seasons change and the year goes round.'

It is possible that the balanced approach of Hibberd was not so effective as the invective of Robinson, but I doubt it. I think the trend was back to the more labour-saving garden in any case. I do not feel we can leave Hibberd without another quotation, which I suggest that all writers on gardening should blazon above their desks.

'If it is herein stated that roses will not grow like houseleeks on tiled roofs, nor rhododendrons in beds of chalk, those points must be considered settled, for they do not admit of discussion. But when it is further added that beds of roses do not assort tastefully with beds of geraniums, that coniferous trees are out of place in a flower border, there is room for difference of opinion, and the reader is at liberty to quarrel with the author to any extent . . . On matters of practice, the practical man has within certain limits which propriety will point out, the right to dictate. On matters of taste dictation is equally unjust and absurd. When we encounter subjects that divide opinions amongst those who study them, we must be careful to avoid dogmatism, and that spirit of self-satisfaction which would make "I say" a law binding on all the world.'

10

HOW LONG DOES A GARDEN
SURVIVE?

If you are a gardener it is usual to act as though the garden would
survive for all time, as well as that you yourself will. But neither you
nor I will, and gardens also seem to have some sort of life span. If you
plant a cedar of Lebanon, you are justified in assuming that if you come
back two hundred years later it should still be there, but most plants are
not so long-lived. This seems a fairly safe remark to make, but if anyone
asks how long plants do live, I should like to know where I can find the
answer. I have heard of two cases recently of *Acer hersii* var *grosseri*
dying after about twenty years. Whether this is indicative of its
average life-span I do not know, but the matter is of some interest and
I feel some useful work might be done on the average garden life of
woody plants in particular. There still exist some plants from Hooker's
rhododendron seed collected in 1851, but not very many, and the
plants are certainly approaching the end of their lives. At Glasnevin,
the Dublin Botanic Garden, there is an *Abelia triflora* which may well
have come from seeds or plants sent by Madden in the 1850s and at
Garinish, the island off the west coast of Ireland, there is an embothrium
which looks as though it dated from Lobb's original introduction in
1846.

Such instances of longevity in other than forest trees seem to be
rather exceptional. I suppose the oldest garden still retaining much of
its original planting is Stourhead, in Wiltshire, dating from 1741. It is true
that various flowering shrubs have been added, but the original con-

ception still stands, without much variation having taken place, as it relied almost entirely on water, architecture and forest trees. On the other hand, Sheffield Park in Sussex must now be very different from Capability Brown's original scheme, although the main layout of the central water-garden means that differences are mainly in details. Many of the best trees at Sheffield Park were not in cultivation in Brown's day.

If gardens are treated as living places and constantly renewed, they seem to be able to continue for a very long time, but if they are designed and planted and then left, I would think that they have a life of from fifty to seventy years. Many of the great gardens started at the beginning of this century are now beginning to decline. This may well have been accelerated by the crisis of 1914–18 and 1939–45, when neglect was unavoidable, but I would imagine that every garden would be the better for a good overhaul every half-century.

Some failures will be inevitable. If you have a large tree of, let us say, *Styrax japonica*, you will want to enjoy its marvellous display as long as possible. The tree may start to weaken after fifty years, but it is asking too much of human nature to fell it then and start another. After all, if you have planted it, you are probably in the seventies yourself and having watched the tree develop from a sapling to a noble tree, you cannot be expected to throw away the fruits of fifty years. Doubtless if you were really prudent, you would have planted another Styrax after twenty-five years, so as to have a replacement when your original tree had passed its best. I suppose that is possible, now that we know that fifty years is about the life of a Styrax in this country, but the plant has only been in cultivation a little over a century and, probably, to start with a few people kept their plants so long. With many plants we simply have no good idea of their life-span and unless the garden is being continually watched by members of the family, with the younger generations taking over from their elders, we shall get to a stage of stagnation and death.

I would imagine we might get some idea of a plant's potential vitality from its rate of growth, the time it takes to come to flowering size and its ultimate size. Most rhododendrons, for example, come into flower some five or seven years from seed, but many of the Taliense series seem to take fifteen to twenty years, and it would seem reasonable to suppose that they must be rather longer-lived than the quicker maturing species. Berberis are fairly rapid growing, but do not make extremely large plants, so it might be implied that they do not have a very long life-span. I do not think this line of inquiry is foolproof. *Nothofagus antartica* grows very rapidly in Britain, growths of up to three feet a year being by no means uncommon. In its native Chile it reaches up to 100 feet in height, which suggests that it is probably a long-lived tree. On the other hand it is definitely not long-lived in this country. No plants survive from the original 1830 introduction, nor from a subsequent introduction by Joseph Hooker in 1843 and, according to W. J. Bean, all the plants in Great Britain date from an introduction by H. J. Elwes in 1902.

The same strictures apply to the nearly equally rapid-growing *N. obliqua*, although plants from the 1902 introduction are still in existence. It does not seem to be recorded whether plants in the wild have similarly rapid growth and it may well be that the ease with which the tree can grow in cultivated ground induces it to expand its energy prematurely and that trees that were not given VIP treatment might grow slower, but prove longer-lived. This seems a fairly safe suggestion to make, as it is very doubtful whether anyone will take me up on it and try some comparative tests. Even if they do, I shall not be around to see the result.

Climbers certainly cannot have their longevity equated with their rate of growth, as it is essential for a climber to make its growth rapidly so as to emerge from darkness into light. *Wistaria sinensis* is a rapid grower, but it would seem fairly long-lived; there is a plant over a century old at Kew. Still, where so little is known, any indication should be accepted, even though it will almost certainly not be 100 per cent correct. I feel that there would also probably be some correlation between a plant's life span and its height in feet, but again this would not always work out at all accurately. It is known that Catalpas seldom survive for longer than fifty years, but whether this standard should be applied to all trees that reach about 50 feet seems a little dubious. It might not, however, be a bad working hypothesis, although I suspect it would fall down when we got to the smaller shrubs, and would of course be meaningless with shrubs that are normally prostrate, although it could, I suppose, be correlated with the lateral spread. The idea would certainly fall down with dwarf shrubs; capricious as it is, *Daphne cneorum* can survive for a number of years and *D. collina* will certainly last for longer than three years, although rarely exceeding three feet in height.

In any case it is obvious that not all plants mature and decay at the same rate, but for long-term planning it would be convenient to have some idea as to how long a tree or shrub might be expected to give of its best. Probably in the private garden this may not much matter. You are only going to worry about your own lifetime; but in public gardens the matter may be of greater importance. You do not want to find your shrubs and trees dying before you have supplied replacements and some information here would be helpful.

The cases of herbaceous and alpine plants are rather different as, for various reasons, they are rarely allowed to live out their natural life in the same place. Plants get too large and are broken up or they tend to get bald in the centre and are renewed. With a few exceptions neither herbaceous nor alpine plants are grown with the intention of their remaining *in situ* for many years and I think that if we estimated the average lifetime of most of these as from seven to ten years we would not go far wrong. This does not, of course, mean that you have to re-make either your herbaceous beds or your alpine garden every decade, but simply that the plants will probably have to be renewed in some form during that period. It is usual practice nowadays to break up the clumps of tall bearded irises every three or four years and replant as single rhizomes, which means that in the case of some of the older hybrids the actual life of the iris may be as much as a hundred years, a few of the earlier hybrids having been that long in cultivation. But this survival has been possible only because the original hybrid has been unceasingly propagated, so that a large population has been built up from a single plant and this is constantly being placed in fresh soil. The life of a tall bearded iris which is not shifted at regular intervals may be much less, although I have no evidence as to how long it might be. Indeed, as we shall see later, some sterile clones have been known in cultivation for at least four centuries, so that, given the inability to produce seeds, the life of some herbaceous plants must be very extended.

I have mentioned the inability to set seed as a possible cause of longevity, and it seems plain that there is liable to be a correlation between the life of a plant and its ability to reproduce itself. Plants that produce abundance of seed with good germination are liable to be short-lived. The most obvious examples are plants like the Iceland poppy, *Papaver nudicaule* and the alpine poppy, *P. alpinum*. Although capable of perennating, they must for all practical purposes be treated as biennials, as they will usually die after setting seed, even though not much may be produced. This monocarpic habit is also found in most of the related genus *Meconopsis*. On the other hand, *P. orientalis* is a good perennial, although it will come into flower from seed as soon as the monocarpic *Meconopsis*. *P. orientalis* comes from the mountains of Iran where, in order to survive, plants must either be short-lived annuals or deep rooting perennials. The oriental poppy opted for the latter alternative. In the climatic conditions of the Iranian mountains, seed germination may be delayed for a season, owing to drought conditions, and for this or some such reason *P. orientale* evolved into a long-lived perennial, a rather unusual phenomenon among the poppies and chiefly found in plants living in hot, dry conditions, such as *P. atlanticum* from the Atlas, *P. lateritium* from the Caucasus, and *P. pilosum* from western Asia, although not all these are particularly long-lived.

It would, indeed, seem fairly obvious that if a plant can reproduce itself rapidly, it has no need to survive for a long time and it may well be that a plant that seeds itself abundantly around the garden will not in itself be long-lived. On the other hand, we must beware of generalising from the conditions of cultivation. I have two plants in my garden, which I collected in the lower Pindus mountains, neither of them particularly common in the wild. One, *Geranium asphodeloides*, was confined to a small area near a village, while the other, *Lathyrus laxiflorus* was a rare plant in turf rather high up. In my garden they have both proved extremely prolific and the geranium could be considered a menace in gardens tidier than mine. Yet I still have the original plants that were collected about six years ago and were of flowering size even then. Indeed many geranium species seem to be extremely long-lived.

I have a G. *phaeum* which must be at least sixteen years old, although it has been moved into fresh soil during this period on one or two occasions. On the other hand, *Linum salsoloides*, although not particularly prolific in producing seed, has always proved short-lived with me, although with its woody stems one would have thought that it would prove fairly long-lived. This may, of course, be due to climatic conditions, although I would not have thought there was much difference between the conditions of the lower Pindus and those of the majority of localities I know for *L. salsoloides*. On the other hand, it is evident that the Linum reproduces itself with great profusion in the wild, so that it has no need to be particularly long-lived. So it is to its behaviour in the wild that we must look for an estimate of a plant's length of life, although even here matters are not clearcut. I have already mentioned a long-lived G. *phaeum*, yet this, at subalpine levels, seems to reproduce itself with enormous vigour. It is one of the main components of the alpine hay meadows. Possibly it could not reproduce itself so fast during the period before human cultivation began, but by no means all geraniums are so long-lived.

The handsome if slightly tender G. *palmatum*, from Madeira, is very liable to prove monocarpic, in spite of its woody base, which would seem to presage a long-lived plant. As it is obviously related to such annual plants as Herb Robert and G. *lucidum*, this is not, perhaps, so surprising and it may well perennate more regularly in the wild. Plants that increase by means of stolons, such as, for example, some of the herbaceous artemisias, *Campanula rapunculoides* and *Fragaria indica*, are always colonising new ground, so that they can prove extremely long-lived, as soil exhaustion, which must be one of the factors controlling plant longevity, can be avoided. We know that many primulas are liable to exhaust rather rapidly the soil in which they are growing and that if they are not moved and broken up at regular intervals they will be lost. However other plants do not seem to suffer in this way at all, probably owing to a more extensive root growth. It is well known that many—indeed most—primula species are shallow-rooting, and plants like the polyanthus can be pushed out of the ground as a result of severe frost.

We seem rather to be proving the platitude that not all plants have the same life-span, even though they may inhabit similar localities. I would still like to know why this happens. The fact may be obvious, but the reason is not. The most one can say is that there seems to be a tenuous connection between the amount of seed a plant can produce, its rate of germination and the potential life of the plant.

It is a commonplace of gardening writing to say that some plants are naturally short-lived, but the reason for this is not always apparent. Sometimes, maybe, it can be traced back to the natural habitat of the plants in question. Both the wallflower and the antirrhinum (*Antirrhinum majus*) are chasmophytes in the wild, settling in rock crevices, in which they do not produce a very large root system. In the garden they are treated as biennial at the most, but in the wild they may persist for a few seasons. However, the amount of seed that they will produce in any one flowering is probably in excess of any nourishment that the roots can provide, so that the plant eventually dies from sheer exhaustion. However, by no means all chasmophytes are short-lived, but the long-lived ones, such as the aretian Androsaces, produce a very long root system and, if they are unable to do this, presumably die off as young seedlings. It would seem simple to say that if you grow in rock crevices and do not make a large root system, you are liable, if you are a plant, to be short-lived; a statement that is immediately contradicted by *Corydalis lutea*, which often colonises brick walls and survives for many years, apparently living on air and a little mortar.

Although we can produce some fairly specious reasoning for the short life of some plants, that of others is less apparent. It seems accepted that *Gentiana verna* has a life-span of about five years on an average and there would seem to be no apparent reason for this, and in any case it may only be true of plants in cultivation and not of plants in the wild. With woody plants the rings can be counted to estimate the life span of the plant, but no such aid is available with herbaceous plants. I am continually amazed at our ignorance of matters that should be easy to establish, although I am just as bad as anyone else. I live in a place where it would be easy for me to make observations with regard to a variety of wild plants, but I do not seem to do it. The knowledge so acquired may not be of any immediate practical use, but that is not really important. It seems rather silly that we should know more about the structure of the moon than we do of the life-span of a daisy.

With bulbs and tubers it would seem that, barring destruction from outside causes, a plant can survive nearly indefinitely. Indeed the plant is perpetually renewing itself, so that a bulb in 1972 may not have any trace of the same plant five years earlier, while many corms and tubers renew themselves annually. On the one hand there are crocus and gladiolus, which produce a fresh corm annually and on the other hand is the cyclamen, in which the corn increases in size from year to year, but is never renewed in the same way as such plants as crocus or some terrestrial orchids. Yet another method of achieving a long life is illustrated by some tropical orchids, which produce a fresh pseudobulb each year, but retain the old pseudobulbs as a reserve of food and a possible source for a new pseudobulb, should the current new growth be damaged. The old Dutch yellow crocus, so often the first flower of the year, is a sterile plant that has been known for some four hundred years; all the millions of plants now in existence may be considered to have come from a single corm since the sixteenth century. The same may be said of the double daffodil known as Van Sion, and there are still in existence some tulips first recorded in the seventeenth century ('Zomerschoon', for example). Indeed it would seem that if a plant is perennial and sterile it has an almost indefinite capacity for survival, as we shall see in more detail on page 143.

There are exceptions. As a general rule the madonna lily (*Lilium candidum*) appears to be sterile in cultivation, but the double form of this, although known from the sixteenth to the eighteenth centuries, has now vanished. In the nineteenth century Sweet records double forms of both the purple and the white martagon lily, but here again the plants have been lost (and probably just as well; a double martagon lily sounds revolting). Nor can it be assumed that the madonna lilies now in cultivation are necessarily descended from sixteenth-century plants, as these have been continually reintroduced from eastern Europe and western Asia.

In spite of their potential long life, bulbous plants, using the term in its wider sense, are vulnerable. It only needs a slug to eat off the growing point for two successive years for the plant to perish. Herbaceous plants can produce fresh shoots, but the bulb is restricted to a single shoot per bulb and if this is destroyed the whole plant goes. In gardens many bulbs produce numerous offshoots, but this is not found so commonly in the wild. The bulb-growers tend to select plants that multiply rapidly and often the commercial bulbs differ in this respect from the wild forms. I have a collected wild *Hyacinthus orientalis*, which has been with me for some eight years. It flowers yearly, but I still have only the one bulb. Indeed in the wild, the ability to produce offshoots is often regarded as a substitute for producing seeds.

Another collected plant I possess is *Scilla hyacinthoides*. I think I have had it about nine years and during that time it has produced innumerable offshoots, but never a sign of a flower. I suppose the record for not flowering so far as I am concerned, is *Lycoris radiata*, of which I purchased six bulbs in 1947. If I had kept them I would now have many hundreds, but I have only once seen it flower, which it did fifteen years after I purchased it. One understands only too clearly why it is not a popular plant. Incidentally, in the wild the scilla seemed to be flowering regularly, but *Tulipa saxatilis* seems just as prodigal of offshoots and shy of flowers in the wild as it is in cultivation. There is a curious pendant to my wild hyacinth; at the same time I planted in my Mediterranean house a commercial Roman hyacinth. I have always found that these, when grown in bowls, produce a number of offsets, but planted fairly deeply in soil it has also maintained itself without producing offsets, although I think I now have about three where I originally had one; a very unexpected result.

Among shrubs that seem to be short-lived, even under their natural wild conditions, are brooms and cistuses. Brooms have our criterion of rapidly germinating seed and rapid growth, so we might expect them to be short-lived, but cistuses are less rapid in their growth and there seems no reason why they should not survive for some time. Indeed the taller ones, *CC. ladaniferus*, *laurifolius* and *populifolius* which tend to form a maquis do appear to survive for longer than the small white *CC. monspeliensis* and *salviaefolius*. On the other hand the related helianthemums seem to have a rather longer life in the wild, although direct observations seem to be lacking. One does not often see a dead helianthemum, but dead cistuses are commonplace in Mediterranean

96

regions. We can find exceptions to everything and, in cultivation at least, the sycamore *Acer pseudoplatanus* produces vast quantities of seed that germinate very rapidly and freely, but it is far from being a short-lived tree. It does certainly take many years to attain a flowering size, which provides one reason for its longevity; but it will certainly survive for longer than a Catalpa, for instance, which has a much shorter life-span, although taking nearly as long to reach flowering size. The whole matter might well be investigated by some youthful student; those of middle age or more might never see their research finished.

There are certain herbaceous plants which for preference should not be moved or broken up in any way, as they are very intolerant of root disturbance. Chief among these are the hellebores and the paeonies. They can usually be moved without actually losing the plant, but they will take two or three years to get back to their former state. Both genera, I suspect, are fairly long-lived. The exception among the hellebores is *Helleborus foetidus*, which tends very often to be mono-carpic, and is always short-lived, and the same might apply to *H. vesicarius*, were it hardy and were it in general cultivation. Otherwise they may be expected to remain in the same positions for as long as you wish to keep them there. The same should apply to all the herba-ceous peonies, although the increased incidence of peony mildew may kill off many plants prematurely; it seems, however, to be more lethal to the shrubby species, notably the cultivars of *P. suffruticosa*, the tree peony. Provided that the seed is sown as soon as it is ripe, hellebores can easily be raised from seed, so that renewal is not difficult.

In the case of particularly fine colour forms of the hybrid Lenten roses, there is no guarantee that the seeds will reproduce their parent's colouring, but it is probable that at least some seedlings will be reason-ably close. Incidentally, it is by no means easy to establish when helle-bore seeds are ripe, as the carpels dehisce while still appearing green and you often find that the seed has already been shed when you go to look for it. Towards the end of May it is advisable to open a capsule and see in what stage the seeds are. If they appear ripe, or nearly so, gather the other capsules and hang them upside down in a paper bag, until they are shed, when they should at once be sown. They may not germinate until the following spring, but they will not germinate at all if left too long out of the soil. Peony seeds take two years to germinate, and then another five before they attain flowering size, so that increasing peonies is a slow job. The cultivars of *P. albiflora*, the Chinese peony, can only be increased by dividing the clumps, but they do not enjoy it. However, they are certainly long-lived; the double white 'Whitleyi' has been in cultivation since 1808, while no one knows for certain how long the old double red peony has been around, but it would seem at least since the sixteenth century.

Your estimate of the probable life of your trees and shrubs may be upset if your soil has a high water table. Some plants, such as many poplars, willows and alders, like this, but others once they get their roots down into permanent stagnant water will quickly die. There is nothing much you can do about this, although the provision of land drains would doubtless solve this problem, but at considerable expense, and this operation is probably not possible once the garden has been planted up. If you have a very high water table, the presence of rushes will give you an indication, but it is when the water table is some two or three feet down that you remain unaware of it, until suddenly the trees start dying. Once you know of this you can concentrate on either water-lovers or on shallow-rooting trees and shrubs, of which there are a good number.

There are always liable to be exceptions to any plant, but I suppose that one can take the average life of an herbaceous or alpine as from seven to fifteen years (although most are capable of indefinite prolongation by vegetative propagation); for shrubs from ten to thirty years; for moderate-sized trees from thirty to sixty years; and for forest trees anything from a century onwards. These potential life-spans will be dependent on the ground being kept in good heart and on renewing the nourishment which the plant will take when making its yearly growth; this does mean that some feeding—whether organic or inorganic—is desirable. Of course, many plants will survive for far longer than the times suggested here, but they will probably decrease in attraction and vigour, while on the other hand others may start to deteriorate before these ages are attained. I believe, however, that if you act on these ages and establish replacements some years before they would become due, the garden can be kept in full beauty for as long as you wish.

11

TAILPIECE

The remainder of this book is going to concentrate on plants and the details of gardens rather than the garden considered as an entity. That is to say that it will be aimed mainly at the plantsman, and so it would seem only fair play to let the other side have a word. Here, then, is a salutary warning to people like me, whose main interest is in the contents of the garden rather than in its design. In these days, to call someone a perfect lady is to sound rather patronising and faintly pejorative, but it seems to me that, taken literally, it is a very good description of the late Gertrude Jekyll; it is from her pen that the following extract is taken.

'It is not possible to use to any good effect all the plants that are to be had. In my own case I should wish to grow many more than just those I have, but if I do not find a place where my critical garden conscience approves of having any one plant I would rather be without it. It is better for me to deny myself the pleasure of having it, than to endure the mild sense of guilt of having placed it where it neither does itself justice nor accords with its neighbours, and where it reproaches me every time I pass it . . .

'Often when I have had to do with other people's gardens they have said: "I have brought a quantity of shrubs and plants; show me where to place them"; to which I can only answer: "That is not the way in which I can help you; show me your spaces and I will tell you what plants to get for them" . . . There are many people who almost unthinkingly will say, "But I like a variety." Do they really think and feel that variety is actually desirable as an end in itself, and is of more value than a series of thoughtfully composed garden pictures? There are no doubt many to whom, from want of a certain class of refinement of education or natural gift of teachable aptitude, are unable to understand or appreciate, at anything like its full value, a good garden picture, and to these no doubt a quantity of individual plants give a greater degree of pleasure than such as they could derive from the contemplation of any beautiful arrangement of a lesser number. When I see this in ordinary gardens, I try to put myself into the same mental attitude, and so far succeed, in that I can perceive that it represents one of the earlier stages of love of a garden, and that one must not quarrel with it, because a garden is for its owner's pleasure, and whatever the degree or form of that pleasure, if only it be sincere, it is right and reasonable, and adds to human happiness in one of the purest and best of ways. And often I find I have to put upon myself this kind of drag, because when one has passed through the more elementary stages which deal with isolated details, and has come to a point when one feels some slight power of what perhaps may be called generalship; when the means and material that go to the making of a garden seem to be within one's grasp and awaiting one's command, then comes the danger of being inclined to lay down the law, and of advocating the ultimate effects that one feels oneself to be most desirable in an intolerant spirit of cock-sure pontification. So I try, when I am in a garden of the ordinary kind where the owner likes variety, to see it a little from the same point of view; and in the arboretum, where one each of a hundred different kinds of conifers stand in their fine young growth, to see and admire the individuals only, and to stifle my own longing to see a hundred of one sort at a time, and to keep down the shop-window feeling, and the idea of a worthless library made up of odd single volumes where there should be complete sets, and the comparison of an inconsequent jumble of words with a clearly-written sentence, and all such naughty similitudes, as come crowding through the brain of the garden-artist (if I may give myself a title so honourable), who desires not only to see the beautiful plants and trees, but to see them used in the best and largest and most worthy of ways.'

The ignorant, unrefined and unteachable plantsmen may leave quietly.

PART TWO

PLANTS

G

12

GARDENS AND CONSERVATION

We started the first section with some rather high claims, and we might as well do the same with this part. Were it not for gardeners it may well be that many plants that still exist in cultivation, but are unknown in the wild, would now be extinct. I suppose the largest of these is the maidenhair tree, *Ginkgo biloba*. Apparently there are numbers of Ginkgos to be recognised in fossil deposits, but the only one still extant has been preserved by the Chinese, who planted it near their temples. It has never been found convincingly growing wild, although it is safe to assume that it must have originated in China. Nowadays it is not a rare tree and can be found growing in most temperate climates. It is not very clear why it should have become extinct in the wild, as it sets fruit well in cultivation (though rarely in Great Britain, where the summers are not sufficiently hot). Admittedly it is dioecious, but so are many other trees that show no signs of becoming extinct.

Another Chinese conifer, which is not quite extinct but which is apparently confined to a single stand, is the *Metasequoia glyptostroboides*. This, again, was only known from fossils, until its discovery in 1945. An expedition was mounted to collect the seed, which was distributed in 1947, and the plant is now quite common, as not only does it come readily from seed but also from cuttings. It would seem safe to say that there are more Metasequoias in cultivation than survive in the wild and if anything should happen to the wild plants (and they were not, apparently, in very good shape) the plant will still survive.

It would seem probable that there may be other trees in China that are sliding towards extinction, as the country is so vast that it is still not thoroughly botanised, although the Chinese themselves are now working on the matter. In any case we can still cite a couple more Chinese plants that have not been found growing wild. *Malus spectabilis* is one of the most attractive ornamental crabs, with deep pink buds opening to a paler pink in April. It has been a long time in cultivation; Dr Fothergill was growing it in his garden in 1780, but it has never, apparently, been found as a wild plant at any time. Another plant that lacks a wild ancestor is that popular cool greenhouse plant, *Primula sinensis*. There are a number of wild plants which are allied to this, but the actual plant is known only from cultivation. In this case, as the plant has obviously been selected for flower size and colour over many centuries, it may well have altered considerably from its wild ancestor.

From the banks of the Alatamaha in Georgia grew at one time that relative of the camellia, *Franklinia alatamaha*. It was first found by John Bartram in 1765, when he was accompanied by his young son William, who found it again and collected specimens in 1776. He may well have collected seed for his father's botanic garden at Philadelphia but apparently the plant was introduced into cultivation in Great Britain in 1774. The date seems slightly odd, as no one is known to have visited its only station between the elder Bartram's visit and his son's, but possibly John Bartram sent back seed from the 1765 visit. The last known time the plant was seen in the wild was when John Lyon, who combined plant collecting with running a nursery, saw it in 1804. From what we know of Lyon's voraciousness, he may well have contributed to its extinction, as it has never since been recorded in the wild. It is a spectacularly beautiful tree with large white flowers and extremely brilliant autumn colours, although it is too tender to survive outside in many parts of Britain. However, the plant has so far been preserved and we may reasonably hope that it will not be lost altogether.

It would seem that there is something in the vegetation of Georgia which is possessed of a death wish. In the valley of the Savannah grows a curious member of the Ericaceae, *Elliottia racemosa*. It is a deciduous shrub or small tree, usually only four to ten feet high but, apparently, occasionally making a small tree up to thirty-five feet. It has terminal racemes of four-petalled white flowers, the racemes up to ten inches long, and so quite handsome. It was, it appears, first detected by William Bartram, who describes it in his *Travels*, but it was first brought to the notice of botanists when Stephen Elliott introduced it to cultivation in the United States in 1813. At that time, although restricted in its distribution, it appeared to be a perfectly sound plant, forming seeds and maintaining its population. However, towards the end of the nineteenth century it suddenly ceased to produce any seed, so that, when Bean came to write his famous book he had to state 'fruit and seed unknown'. Rehder, in his *Manual* was able to describe both these parts of the plant, presumably from herbarium specimens. The plant proved extremely difficult to propagate from cuttings or layers and there seemed only too much reason to fear that it would become extinct. Fortunately a few years ago a successful method of propagation was discovered so there is reason to hope that at practically the last moment the plant has been saved from extinction. This action has only been taken because the plant is attractive horticulturally.

There is a rare member of the *Proteaceae*, *Orothamnus zeyheri*, which it seems is likely to be very hard to preserve from extinction. It produces only a single stem and if the terminal bud is damaged in any way the plant dies. It also produces very little seed and most of this is not viable. The plant is very attractive and efforts are being made to preserve it, but with such a marked death wish, it is difficult to be optimistic about its survival.

Provided that the plant is attractive and reasonably easily propagated, cultivation will often ensure survival. The Flamboyant is a widespread tree for parks and avenues in the tropics, yet in the wild it has always been rather rare and is now, apparently, reduced to a single stand in its native Madagascar. The Horse Chestnut was a well-known ornamental of temperate climes long before its native country was known, which appears to be Albania and northern Greece.

Occasionally we are given a second chance. In a lecture to the Royal Horticultural Society on 2 April 1970, Mr R. Melville stated: 'Another species on Hong Kong island, *Camellia crapnelliana* was . . . known only from a single tree when it was discovered in 1903. No one took the trouble to propagate it and it must be presumed extinct. This was another white-flowered species, but it had brick-red bark which I believe was unique in the genus. It is a tragedy that this species is lost.' Fortunately this has proved erroneous. Other plants have been found and the species is now being propagated.

So far as gardeners are concerned, it is only the attractive species that are going to be preserved. Large islands usually manage to produce a number of endemic species, which may appear rather weedy to the average flower-gazer. The introduction of grazing animals, or the clearing of ground for airports or other appurtenances of modern life may threaten the existence of these plants, but if they are to survive it is the botanic gardens that will have to bestir themselves. Doubtless many a private botanist may preserve the odd plant or so, but unless he propagates these plants they will eventually disappear, either through age or through accident. You may ask, people often do, what does it matter in practical terms if some species do become extinct? There are, after all, plenty of others. I think the only answer to this question is that we do not have the slightest idea. Certainly in many cases it may affect the climate. When the Portuguese landed on St Helena in 1502 it was covered with forest; they released goats on the island and when Burchell did a botanical survey of the island in the early nineteenth century, most of the forest had disappeared. During this survey he described thirty-one endemic species, that is to say plants that existed nowhere else in the world. Since that time eleven of these species has disappeared. The disappearance of individual species may be of only trifling import, but the disappearance of forests can have the gravest results. Dust bowls and deserts are often man-made, and induced particularly by deforestation, and the disappearance of a single species may be the first link in a chain that will lead to widespread devastation. Where our ignorance is so widespread it is obviously safer to err on the side of excessive caution and to preserve everything. Mankind seems to have survived quite happily the disappearance of the dodo and of the Phillip Island Glory Pea, but we cannot be sure.

Although gardeners have preserved a number of species that would otherwise have disappeared, they have also contributed to the depletion of many others. The great financial reward from collecting orchids at the end of the last century and beginning of this one has caused some species to be nearly wiped out. Nearer home, *Narcissus cyclamineus*, now a rare plant in Portugal, was formerly very common, but has been gravely depleted by ruthless collecting. *Lilium pomponium* was entirely removed from one valley in the Maritime Alps by a single commercial collecting. The Oncocyclus irises are so attractive that many people try to grow them, but most fail, so that we cannot say that the population is being maintained in cultivation. The lady's slipper orchid, *Cypripedium calceolus*, is becoming rarer every year. Indeed terrestrial orchids present a problem to the gardener. At the moment we do not know how to raise them from seed, although we know that a rhizoctonia fungus must be present in the soil to allow the young plant to develop. Techniques have been worked out for raising tropical orchids from seed, by placing the seeds in special conditions, but either these do not work with terrestrial temperate orchids, or, somewhat improbably it would sound, no one has actually tried. It follows therefore that every orchid in a garden must be presumed to reduce the world population. In some gardens it is possible that the soil contains the right fungus and the plants will seed themselves, but this cannot be guaranteed.

Many orchids, however, have such an immense wild population that moderate collecting will probably do no harm. When one sees acres of marsh in central Spain purple with *Dactylorhiza elata*, it is hard to feel that the species is in any danger, but the related Madeiran endemic, *D. maderense*, certainly is and gardeners would probably be well advised not to encourage its collection by purchasing tubers. Once we can grow their seeds as easily as we can grow the seeds of the tropical orchids the matter will be different, but at the moment the conscientious gardener will abstain from Cypripedium species, from *D. maderense*, and indeed from any species that is not extremely widespread.

Orchids that tend to grow in pasture are particularly vulnerable. At the start of the century *Orchis morio* could be seen in hayfields by the thousand, and was regarded as a very common orchid; but the chemical treatment of pastures to improve the herbage, and the practice of having temporary rather than permanent pasture, has turned the plant into a great rarity in Britain. The two colonies I knew in my immediate vicinity have disappeared, and I have been told of many more that had already disappeared when I came to live in east

Kent. It would seem, therefore, that even the presence of large populations does not necessarily indicate permanence if its habitat is altered.

Provided that we can maintain the plant in cultivation, there is obviously the greatest incentive to have as many plants in our gardens as possible, but where, for some reason, this may prove difficult or impossible, a certain amount of self-restraint is advisable. We should distinguish here, perhaps, between private collecting and commercial collecting. To bring back a few orchids from your holiday may be a little naughty, but will probably make little difference to the population balance; to collect plants by the thousand obviously will. I, myself, have collected a number of orchids in my time, but I have never dug up a Cypripedium on the few occasions when I have come across them. The case of Oncocyclus iris is somewhat different. The populations, so far as my experience goes, tend to be rather small individually, so that collecting on a large scale from any single stand is to be deprecated. On the other hand in suitable districts, such as parts of the United States and around the Mediterranean, they can be grown from seed. The seed tends to be of uncertain germination and may take several years before it germinates, but in theory at least the stock can be increased in cultivation and, bearing in mind their restricted wild distribution, it is obviously desirable that they should be brought into permanent cultivation. Whether we in Britain are doing anything constructive in growing them with some difficulty in bulb frames I am not sure. They are so easily lost. But, on the other hand, if efforts are not made the plants might disappear in the wild. We cannot all live in Arizona, but although we can grow them in this country, it is a risky business.

The trouble arises when it becomes a profitable business. *Iris lortetii* cost five pounds a rhizome some time ago and it is not surprising that it has become extinct in many of its localities. Most of these irises grow in near eastern countries, where poverty is widespread and the temptation to make more money by pulling up wild flowers must be overwhelming. It is useless to tell such people that they may be killing the goose if they pull up too many; after all, probably the number of people who know the status and distribution of these irises is only a few thousand; to the local peasant it will just be another weed. The onus of conservation should rest primarily with governments and only secondarily with nurserymen. I would imagine that in impoverished countries with plants like the Oncocyclus for which there is great demand, encouragement could be given to the establishment of nurseries on the spot to cultivate such plants. Such establishments exist in South Africa and in Australia and they might well be started elsewhere.

13

SOME FAMOUS PLANTSMEN

It is a rather devious step from the Oncocylcus iris to the Rev Henry Ewbank, but Siehe did name *Iris ewbankiana* in his honour and he was, at the end of his life (he died in 1901), very successful in growing these recalcitrant plants. He attributed this to dosing them with bone meal and from this, surely incorrectly, he proclaimed that lime was an essential for their successful cultivation. Since bone meal also contains phosphates, it may well have been this that contributed to his success; in any case most cultivators have used bone meal since that time.

Ewbank was the rector at St John's, Ryde, in the Isle of Wight, and he was inclined to give most of the credit for his success to the genial climate he enjoyed; to which his contemporaries replied that many other inhabitants of the Isle of Wight enjoyed similar advantages without being able to obtain the fantastic results that Ewbank did. In *The Garden* of 29 December 1900 he gave an account of his work and garden. His style is somewhat prolix, and makes one wonder what his sermons may have been like.

'About thirty years ago, from causes which were rather clerical than horticultural, I found myself the possessor of nearly an acre of land on the east side of Ryde. To this was soon after added, for purely horticultural reasons, another bit of land of about the same size. I might possibly have been contented with what pleases my neighbours so much, if it had not seemed to me a sin to waste the glorious climate that we have here, the splendid sunshine and the good soil on anything less than the best of the best, which the case seemed to admit of . . . I trace to the fact that we are where we are, a great part of any success I may have had. A man must be a fool who cannot do anything here.'

Indeed his soil and climate were such that 'if I were to leave them severely alone, such good things as Gladiolus purpureo-auratus, Brodiaea multiflora, Homeria collina, Hesperocordeum lacteum, Milla ixioides, and many others which are indigenous to California or at the Cape of Good Hope would soon take possession of my garden, after the manner of Groundsel or common dock, and entirely cover it.' However, although, 'I believe it to be a sort of ideal place for the cultivation of flowers . . . it is not pretty at all. Brick walls on two sides and a Laurel hedge on the third do very little to set it forth. I have treated it merely as a receptacle for shrubs and flowers which reward me for my trouble. I have never once thought how the garden would look, but times without number I have proposed to myself the enquiry how the plants would grow. If the plants are all right, it seems to me that the garden may be left to take care of itself . . .

'It was a big business to try and find out how many of the most beautiful bulbs and plants of the whole world could be put together and would settle down in the Isle of Wight, and I knew that I must be content with a very faint representation of it . . . It is an immense delight to me in a garden of this sort completely to overcome and conquer an apparently intractable subject. That is, perhaps, not quite a pretty way, as it certainly is not a correct one of speaking of such a matter; but the difficulty of growing some things well at first is so great that it almost looks like a struggle. I love to see a beautiful flower or shrub, which once seemed to me as though it could not be managed at all, at last docile and responsive in my hands. It very likely all turned upon some small or trivial consideration . . . a lucky hit, a bright thought, a slightly better arrangement has made all the difference in the world. Of course in a garden of this sort, where climate helps one so much, it is a great point to fill it with as many exotics as can be found to live here with contentment; but who they are . . . can only be found out by experiment and by trying a large number in different situations and in different ways. The very last thing I should go by is the rules that are laid down in nurserymen's catalogues, for the divisions that are made between stove, greenhouse and hardy plants are often arbitrary in the extreme . . . I believe that a much larger number of things will do better in the open air than is sometimes supposed, and in a place like this it is a most interesting amusement to put it to the test . . . but it would not do to come to a decision about them all at once, one failure or two should never deter, for it is a very good thing to get a good start for a plant or shrub, and if two or three mild winters occur in succession, it very often will not matter at all if the fourth winter is hard, and *vice versa*, if the first winter after exposure should be severe, it should not be concluded that there is no chance of success till another effort is made.'

As a result, 'I have this year blossomed four or five fine things which I have never heard of nor seen recorded as blossoming in the open air in this country before.' And he cites *Hulthemia* (*Rosa*) *berberifolia*, which so bemused the alpine authority Henri Correvon, when he visited Ewbank, that he could only with difficulty be induced to take an interest in any other plant. Ewbank lists among unusual plants for outdoors, *Poinciana gilliesii*, *Mandevilla suaveolens*, *Ipomaea purga*, *Beschorneria cornuta*, *Dasylirion glaucophyllum*, *Crinum yemense*, *Lapageria rosea* and *Gerbera jamesonii* as names that 'occur to me at once and the list is by no means exhausted'. But his greatest triumph was the giant Burmese honeysuckle, *Lonicera hildebrandiana*, which has flowers up to six inches long and four inches across. Ewbank built what he termed a 'sentry box' at its base, which could be stuffed with bracken to protect the base from frost, but the plant only flowers when fairly large and eventually there must have been more outside the sentry box than inside.

Indeed, the last years of the nineteenth and opening years of the twentieth century seem to have had a large number of clergymen who were also great gardeners. The most famous was Canon H. N. Ellacombe, at Bitton in Somerset, whose garden was a storehouse of unusual plants, which were also arranged with unusual taste. One tends to forget, or else one has never learned, that he inherited many marvellous plants from his father, the Rev Henry Thomas Ellacombe. In *The Garden* for 31 July 1880 there is printed a list of the herbaceous and bulbous plants grown at Bitton Rectory in 1830 (when the future canon was only nine years old). The list, which also includes ferns and aquatics runs to over 2,100 names, which—even allowing for various cultivars and possible plants described under more than one name—is still an astonishing total. At Ludgvan in Cornwall, another canon, Boscawen, was growing a number of unusual plants and also hybridising them. The Rev F. D. Horner had a curious range of interests. He was a specialist in florists' flowers at a time when they were falling into desuetude. He had a great interest in growing Orobanches, which one would have thought remarkably difficult, and his main success seems to have been with the annual *Orobanche speciosa*, which parasitises broad beans, while in his early ministry he used a lean-to greenhouse as a source for groceries growing 'tea, coffee, and, of course tobacco; rice, arrowroot, ginger, cotton (of which one villager said he had thought *that* grew on sheeps' backs), black pepper and a few other things, which, like the plants of chocolate and mahogany, had to be kept within bounds. My live groceries, however, did not meet with much appreciation' (*The Garden*, 5 May 1900).

The Rev Harper Crewe is now known chiefly for the double Cheiranthus which still bears his name, but he was a renowned grower in his day, while the Rev Wolley Dod at Edge Hall, Malpas, is mainly remembered today for a semi-double form of *Rosa pomifera*, which still gets listed as Wolley Dod's rose, although there cannot now be many who know who he was. He also used to import *Anemone fulgens* yearly from its wild site in south-west France, which may be one reason why it is no longer there. His son A. H. Wolley Dod, split the British wild roses up into far too many species.

Leaving the clergymen, we come to a rather shadowy figure in Mr T. H. Archer Hind, who specialised in hybridising Helleborus species and to whom we may owe the race of Lenten roses, although, as we shall see, the matter is not clearcut. According to his own account he started work in the 1850s. Writing in 1900 he said:

'The interest attached to the subject is almost inexhaustible. By crossing one species with another and again and again crossing the hybrids thus produced, endless new varieties are obtained; new forms, new combinations of colour result from year to year and the present generation of experimentalists have the benefit of a goodly field to carry on the work. It is worth all their skill, since, whether as they appear in the border or as cut flowers, the unique effect of so much beauty and variety in the earlier months of spring is wonderful, and would have astonished gardeners in my early days or even thirty or forty years ago. It was before that date that I first took them in hand, but with slight success. Not more than five or six were to be had; some had been lost, most never introduced; but by watching my opportunities I ultimately collected nearly thirty reputed species. In the meantime those I had gave me spontaneous hybrids of considerable interest, and by subsequent systematic crossing, both hybrids and varieties have multiplied yearly. Two species I have long wished to obtain, but without success, viz. true H. lividus from Majorca and vesicarius from Syria; the former has long been lost, but I remember it seventy years ago and its exact habitat is still known. The latter has, I believe, never been seen in England . . .

'I have never succeeded in crossing the Christmas Rose (H. niger) outside its own family, neither have I so far raised any cross from our native H. foetidus nor the Helleborus argutifolius, the only representative of the class in Corsica. With regard to the Lenten Roses, I am inclined to think that all of them, whether with persistent or with nonpersistent leaves, may be crossed one with another, and their hybrids still further indefinitely extended into varieties. This is the task I would set before young lovers of their gardens.'

From this it might seem that Hellebore hybridisation was the work of a single man, but this is not the case. Here is an article from the pen of W. G., writing in *Gardening Illustrated* for 13 December 1884. I suspect W. G. to be W. E. Gumbleton of Belgrove near Cork, a famous gardener and gardening botanist, who sometimes signed articles W. E. G.

'Few seem to be aware that other Hellebores besides the common Christmas Rose and its varieties possess beauty. The general impression seems to be that all other kinds of Hellebore are green-flowered, unattractive plants, only fit for botanical collections . . . Besides H. niger there are about a dozen species in cultivation at the present time, though only about half that number can be recommended for general culture, the rest being green, unattractive and often malodorous. These half dozen select species are named: atrorubens and abchasicus, both with deep vinous purple blossoms, bright and showy when well grown; colchicus with deep claret-red flowers; olympicus with pure white cup-shaped blooms; guttatus, like olympicus, but spotted; and antiquorum, with flowers greenish-white but handsomely shaped.

'Within the past few years these half dozen so-called species have been taken in hand by hybridists, the result being that a numerous race of seedling varieties has been obtained by inter-crossing. It is astonishing what strides have been made in this direction in so short a time, having regard to the length of time which it requires for a Hellebore to grow to a flowering stage. [I do not follow this; Hellebores usually flower in the third year from germination, only one year longer than a lupin or delphinium.] This work of hybridising has been carried out chiefly in continental nurseries and gardens, as may be gathered from the German names which have been given to the majority of the produce. Of these named seedlings about a dozen are already in commerce in this country, by far the best being . . . Commerzienrath Benary . . . best described as an improved guttatus. The flowers are cup-shaped, perfectly white and copiously spotted with purple . . . Two other seedlings in the way of C. Benary are "guttatus leichtlinii", a much shallower flower, but quite as profusely spotted and "sub-punctatus" which lacks the copious spotting for which the two just named are remarkable. The seedlings obtained by crossing colchicus with guttatus appear to be F. C. Heinemann, rosy-purple freely spotted with a deeper hue; Gretchen Heinemann, Hofgartner-Inspektor Hartwig, Frau Irene Heinemann and Apotheker Bogren are all similar . . . H. olympicus "Professor Schleicher" and "Willi Schmidt" are both pure white and may be regarded as improved forms of the typical olympicus. They are probably only seedlings from the species.

'These are the principal continental seedlings already in commerce in this country . . . There are several other fine seedling Hellebores belonging to this section that have been raised in this country; for instance Mr B. Hook, who is quite a specialist as regards Hellebores, has several of his own raising quite as handsome as the continental kinds.'

We have, therefore, not only continental raisers working concurrently with Archer Hind but also the mysterious Mr B. Hook. We can find a little more about him from another article by the same writer in *The Garden* for 26 March 1881. Hook used to garden at Bradfield in Berkshire, but he left this garden about 1878 and presented his collection of Hellebores to Kew Gardens. 'Mr Hook not only enriched his collection from every available source both in this country and on the Continent, but worked assiduously among them, annually raising new kinds by hybridising and judiciously selecting the finest forms.' After leaving Berkshire he went to Torquay, where he was near Archer Hind, so perhaps they worked together for a time. With regard to the continental raisers, in the *Gardeners' Chronicle* of 1874 there is a reference to a series of crosses between *H. abchasicus* and *H. guttatus* raised in the Berlin Botanic Garden which were to be offered for sale by Ant Roozen & Son the following year. There were eleven different cvs, offered under number, and No 6 had pure white flowers, which suggests that *H. olympicus* (*kochii*) was also used. It would seem as though parallel work was going on in England and Germany, with the German seedlings getting earlier into commerce. Still, if Archer Hind really started in the 1850s he is probably entitled to the credit for pioneer work.

14

PLANTS TO AVOID

One of the desiderata of all gardening books, so far as I am concerned, is a list of plants that should never on any account be allowed into a garden. What follows is an attempt to fill up this lacuna. I am not here concerned with personal tastes. There are a number of plants that I dislike and would not allow in my garden, but they are perfectly civilised plants and will do no harm in your garden if you should happen to enjoy them. The plants I am thinking of are, quite often, not unattractive, but they take such a hold of the soil that they are ineradicable, or nearly so.

Most of these are plants with a stoloniferous habit of growth. That is to say that they spread by means of underground stems, so that you will suddenly find them coming up quite a distance away from where they were planted. If you decide that they have outstayed their welcome and attempt to remove them your wishes are thwarted. They have got a hold and will resent fiercely any attempt to oust them. Others of this tribe spring from bulbils or tubers. These proliferate, and the smallest vestige remaining in the soil will produce a fresh plant. Another tiresome group are those that produce an abundance of wind-dispersed seed. In the case of ornamental thistles, it is possible to remove the flower heads before the seeds ripen, but if you have the misfortune to have a sycamore either in your own or your neighbour's garden, there is nothing that you can do except to remove seedlings every year. I am still surprised that most of the gardens of England did not turn into sycamore forests during the war, when gardens tended to go to wrack and ruin.

We may as well start off our survey with a plant that I cannot imagine anyone allowing willingly into the garden—only to find that it was recommended by no less a person than Gertrude Jekyll, a lady with whom one may disagree, but who never wrote nonsense. It was as a foliage plant that the Queen of Spades, as Dean Hole nicknamed her, recommended it, and this is what she wrote: 'Their leaves have almost the grandeur of the Gourd tribe, but without their luscious weakness, and the vigour of the Rhubarb without its coarseness. I never cease to admire their grand wave of edge and the strength of line in the "drawing" from root to leaf-point. It is a plant that for leaf effect in the early year should be in every garden; it would hold its place as worthily as Veratrum or Artichoke. Later in the year there are other plants of bold leaf-beauty, but in April and May they are so few, that none should be overlooked.'

Well, she is quite right; the plant does have a very handsome leaf (I cannot say I ever looked at them properly before I read that passage), but I raise my eyebrows at the suggestion that they should be in every garden. The plant is *Arctium lappa* (or perhaps *A. vulgare*) the great burdock. This distributes itself by attaching its fruits to passing animals or to one's clothing, and manages to do it extremely effectively. Once it is in the garden it is not easily got rid of; although only a biennial, it produces a very long tap-root, so that unless caught as a young seedling, it is well-nigh indestructible. If you prevent it flowering at all, you will lose the plant, but if it does flower it will prove very invasive. The flowers are an unattractive purple-magenta.

We have had Miss Jekyll recommending one dubious plant, and here is William Robinson with another. In this case there are two very similar species and about one he was later to change his mind. In what we may, for the moment, call case A, he wrote in 1872 that it 'is the most stately and at the same time the most graceful hardy perennial now in blossom. The stems rise 6 to 9 feet high, and are laden with branchlets strung with small racemes of creamy-white blossoms. The plant is most valuable, and well deserves good treatment and a good position. It is seen to most advantage as an isolated tuft on the grass in the pleasure ground. It loves rich deep soil.'

Of the similar case B, he wrote in *The English Flower Garden*: 'A huge perennial with bright green leaves upwards of a foot in length, the flowers greenish-white in slender drooping racemes. It thrives in moist soil near water, where it is effective, and it makes a fine feature on the turf or in a spot where it can run about freely.' However, by the time that he had published his book Robinson was having second thoughts about case A, although I suspect, judging from the wording, that the afterthought did not come until well after the first edition. 'Of fine graceful habit, its creamy white flowers borne in profusion, it should be grown apart on the turf or in the wild garden. It is easier to plant than to get rid of in the flower garden; a rank weed, right in copse or pond-side.'

These plants are the so-called Japanese bamboo, *Polygonum cuspidatum* and *P. sachalinense*. Either one could probably overrun a medium-sized garden in a couple of years and they appear to be completely unkillable. You can water them with any weed-killer you like to select, but you will never check them for long. Indeed the only way to contain them at all is by pulling up the growths at regular intervals. They are quite impressive plants and one can see that when they were new introductions they must have seemed rather attractive, before their spreading habits and lasting grip on life had been learned. Both plants have long escaped from the confines of the garden and naturalised themselves in parts of the country, but anyone who has let them into their gardens can only be commiserated with.

Another plant that has become so completely naturalised, that most of us have always thought of it as a British native, is the winter heliotrope. This could well be described as an excellent ground-cover, which indeed it is, although less showy than creeping buttercup, another ground-cover plant that most of us would rather be without. The plant produces tufts of sweet-scented mauvy-white flowers in February or earlier in a mild winter and its name is *Petasites fragrans*. All the petasites behave rather like their near relatives the coltsfoot, and spread very rapidly by means of underground stolons. Their invasive habits were soon learned. Here is some anonymous person writing in January 1884:

'Just at the present time there is not a more fragrant plant in the out-door garden, or one that is better able to brave our worst winters. It is chiefly for the delicious vanilla-like perfume of its flowers that it is desirable, a few cut heads of its bloom being sufficient to scent a good-sized room . . . It is a native plant, but, as already remarked, its flowers are so welcome in the depth of winter that an odd corner should be allotted to it where convenient, so that a few of its sweet-scented blossoms may be cut to mix with other flowers. Care must, however, be taken not to allow it to take root in any choice border, for it is a difficult plant to eradicate, its underground stems spreading rapidly and widely. A dry bank where little else would grow might profitably be devoted to the Winter Heliotrope, and if the soil is of a strong loamy character, it will produce luxuriant foliage, by no means unhandsome throughout the year.'

Rather surprisingly, this sparked off a considerable correspondence, chiefly from people who had read Henry Phillips' *Flora Historica* and who made haste to point out that the petasites was not a British native. Henry Phillips was a rather naïve and uninquiring writer but writing, as he did, in 1824, his prose style is not without its charm and I will here reproduce a few of his remarks on what he called the sweet-scented tussilage:

> He trudg'd along, unknowing what he sought
> And whistled as he went for want of thought.

'That even classical ground provides minds of this description, is instanced in the long-neglected plant of which we are about to speak. Although *Tussilago fragrans* is a native plant of Italy, it remained in obscurity until the nineteenth century, when M. Villan, of Grenoble, was attracted by its agreeable fragrance at the foot of Mount Pilat, from whence he brought it to perfume the winter gardens of the continent, and it cast its first odours on British shores in the year 1806.* As its perfumed flowers expand in the months of January, February and March, it cannot fail of being welcomed amongst us by every lover of sweet smells, and it is already become naturalized to our climate, as to discharge its fragrance as freely over our walks in the winter months, as the Egyptian Reseda disperses its odours over those of the summer.

* A Mr C. L., writing in *The Garden* for 12 February 1881, says that when first introduced it cost a guinea a plant.

We may hail it as the Heliotrope of the open garden, and as a vegetable winter friend of no small importance in the parterre.

'The modest flowers of this plant were too insignificant to have attracted the notice of the ignorant, who have not souls to admire humble merit, whether in men or flowers, until it has received the sanction of fashion or the patronage of the great . . .

'The thyrsi of this fragrant plant are of a whitish-lilac tint and the odour greatly resembles that of the Heliotrope. It is easily propagated by parting the roots in the summer, and planting them in a free light and fresh earth, in a warm and sheltered situation. It is also planted in pots for the purpose of perfuming our winter apartments; and thus the plant which so short a time back could not by all its fragrant charms obtain a corner in a cottage garden, now fills a situation in the proud saloon, to the admiration of all the crowd that usually attend the decorated apartments of gay routs.'

We do not, alas, write like that nowadays. One advantage of going round the garden is that we can saunter in byways and I would not leave Phillips without quoting his remarks about *Zantedeschia aethiopica*.

'The more polished part of society admit the Ethiopian Calla, a species of Arum, into their most embellished saloons, where its alabaster calyx expands into so elegant a vase-like shape, that Flora seems to have intended it for the hand of Hebe, when she presents the imperial nectar to Jove . . . it is only within these few years that it has become generally known, and the fashion of ornamenting the houses of London with plants when routs are given, greatly contributed to bring it into celebrity, its time of flowering being January to June, which is the period of our metropolitan festivals. It was soon found to be a conspicuous candlelight plant, and therefore increased by all the rout-furnishing florists. Thus introduced to public notice, its charms could not fail to obtain it a favourable regard among all the admirers of nature, for its appearance in a group of plants reminds us of a beautiful antique lamp for burning incense, which illusion the flame-coloured spadix, arising out of the centre of the white calyx considerably increases. This vegetable cup also pours out an agreeable perfume from its graceful and beautiful horn.'

To return to his remarks about the winter heliotrope, I find them slightly baffling. M. Villan of Grenoble is presumably M. Villars, who wrote a flora of the Dauphiné. But if the plant was a native of Italy, what was it doing at the foot of Mount Pilat? I assume that is the same mountain as Pilatus near Lucerne, but possibly there was some other mountain with that name. In any case it does not sound particularly Italian.

The winter heliotrope at least looks as though it might be a menace, which is more than can be said of some of the *Oxalis*. I would tend to be very cautious of bringing any of the genus into the garden, although *O. adenophylla* and *O. enneaphylla* appear to be perfectly safe. Many of the species come from underground bulbils and these split up into innumberable sections, each one of which is capable of producing a fresh plant very rapidly. It thus follows that even if you dig the plant up, you are liable to leave a fragment in the soil, as well as distributing fragments elsewhere, so that the plant spreads and spreads.

O. rubra (*floribunda*) with its clover-like leaves and heads of crimson flowers, looks attractive and innocuous, but once in the garden it is there for keeps; since the plant comes from Brazil, this seems surprising. I suppose the most successful of the genus is not bulbous at all, but the herbaceous *O. corniculata*. This can spread in a number of ways. It sends down a longish taproot from which radiate procumbent stems, which root as they go. In addition it produces seeds, which explode from their capsules and distribute the plant even further. The plant has been so successful in penetrating not only temperate but also tropical countries, that no one can say for certain where its first natural habitat was. One would have thought that a plant as dangerous as this would have been barred from gardens at once but such was not, it would seem, the case—not, certainly, for the purple-leaved form. Here is a plangent cry from a Mr T. Williams in *The Garden* of 9 November 1872:

'*Oxalis corniculata rubra*. This is an exceedingly beautiful little plant forming patches of deep brownish-red leaves, studded with golden stars. I once had a small round bed of it, edged with a silvery Saxifrage, and dotted over with Echeveria glauca, the effect of which was charming; but such is the astonishing fecundity of the plant, that I bitterly repent ever introducing it into the garden. Every part of my garden is now covered with it, even the gravel road and the walks. Every pot on every shelf in my little greenhouse swarms with it, and I fancy I can see some bits on the top of the house. Much against my inclination, I have destroyed this summer thousands of this beautiful plant. If you have any spite against a person, advise him to plant this Oxalis in his garden and you will have ample revenge. I never look at it, but I think of the plagues of Egypt. Still it may have its proper place. Old quarries and rough, rocky places, especially in a calcareous district, would suit it well, and their bareness might with advantage be hidden by a handsome plant which speedily covers the most unpromising surfaces.'

Terrible as *O. corniculata* is, its menace is as nothing compared with the Bermuda buttercup, *O. pes-caprae*, fortunately not hardy in this country,* which has become one of the worst of all cornfield weeds in the Mediterranean and in some Atlantic islands such as the Canaries, and, I presume, Bermuda. This article, which concerns the Mediterranean, seems to me so interesting that I feel it should be better known. It is from the pen of quite a well-known botanist, George Henslow, and first appeared in *The Garden* for 8 June 1901.

'This plant, a native of South Africa, is occasionally exhibited at the horticultural shows, but if any one wishes to see it in perfection, let him go to Malta, where the Maltese call it the English Weed. It has a remarkable history. Father Hyacintho was a teacher or professor of botany and medicine at the beginning of last century, and received a plant from the Cape on, or before, 1806.

'It is a trimorphic, like our loosestrife (Lythrum salicaria), but only one "form" the short-styled one is present. It appears to require the others for fertilisation, as, although it has thriven for 100 years, it has never been known to set seed in the northern hemisphere. It propagates itself solely by tiny bulbs.

'From this beginning it has spread, not only all over Malta and Gozo —indeed the fields are sometimes as yellow as our own meadow with Buttercups—but through the intercourse between Malta, North Africa, Italy &c., it reached Egypt (with the Mandarine Orange tree) about 1820. It got to Gibraltar in 1829, and, in fact, it is now to be seen at intervals from Egypt to Morocco and from Gibraltar to the Greek Islands.

* Except in the Scillies, where it is a serious pest.

'It has a remarkable rhizome, being thread-like in form, which penetrates to great depths . . . The Maltese simply pull it up as a weed from the fields and lay it to die on the tops of the low stone walls, but *as it withers it develops bulbs*. Even when drying it under pressure for my herbarium, I found the long rhizome had produced several bulbs, while the foliage and the flowers were dead.'

It is undoubtably amazing that a plant that never sets seed should have spread from a single specimen in the Malta Botanic Garden to so many parts of the Mediterranean, but none the less infuriating. Moreover it is increasing all the time. When I first visited Crete in the 1930s it was not a common plant, but by the 1960s it was all over the place. In the Canaries, so far as my observation goes, it is not a particularly dangerous pest (although it is some years since I was there)—and it is the double form which has become naturalised there—but it was spreading there as well.

It is not only in temperate climes that *Oxalis* can be a pest. Here is the superintendent of the Hong Kong Botanic Garden writing of Hong Kong weeds:

'Oxalis martiana [= *corymbosa*] is an exceedingly obnoxious one. It is included in the list of tender exotic plants grown at Kew, and if that establishment should run out of it at any time (which I do not think is likely) I can safely say that Hong Kong is not likely to be without it for many years to come. It is not a native, but an introduction; nevertheless from the persistency with which it forces itself upon one's attention, in spite of continuous rebuffs and harassing treatment it receives, one is almost forced to the conclusion that it is the legitimate owner of the soil. Having a bulbous rhizome it is a most difficult subject to deal with, and the rapidity with which it propagates itself by division is amazing. It is particularly fond of rich soil, but if it cannot get that it will put up with any other and accommodate itself to circumstances. It is a native of the Mascarene Isalnds [possibly; the list of habitats in the Royal Horticultural Society's *Dictionary* gives South America, southern and eastern Asia and the Pacific Islands], but is now naturalised in many tropical countries. It is a pity it did not stay at home as it was certainly not wanted in Hong Kong.'

It would be interesting to learn how these pestilential weeds do behave in their native lands. Our own wood sorrel (*O. acetosella*), which looks as though it could be just as dangerous, is reasonably restrained in the wild, although it can, of course, colonise large areas of woodland. It does not, however, seem to leave its woodlands with any success, although it is to be presumed that if it strayed into pasture the animals would not eat the leaves, which are impregnated with oxalic acid and presumably distasteful to most animals. Possibly if that pest in the garden, *O. rubra*, could have its site grassed over and mown regularly it might eventually disappear.

This is more than can be said for that enchanting plant *Veronica filiformis*, sometimes known as blue devil. I believe that there is some dispute among botanists as to whether our plant is really *V. filiformis* or another plant of the same name but, whatever its correct name may be, it is a plant that cannot be easily got rid of. The Royal Horticultural Society's *Dictionary* says that it is annual or perennial, but since it has apparently never set seed at all consistently in this country, it must be regarded as a true perennial. It forms a pretty little creeping plant, with prostrate stems which root as they elongate and which bear circular bright green leaves about a quarter of an inch in diameter and in June quite large, circular, flat blue and white flowers. It is extremely pretty. This can get into the lawn and dismay the purists by turning the lawn pale blue during June. As far as I am concerned I can observe a blue lawn with equanimity; indeed I wonder that it has not been put forward as a material for lawns that would need no mowing. It is when it gets into the cultivated part of the garden that most of us would get restive, as the slightest bit of rooted stem left in the ground immediately starts to spread; also it covers all the ground very closely and seems to prevent air getting to the roots of the plants it surrounds. It looks an ideal plant for the alpine garden, but here it can do more damage than anywhere else, as it penetrates the more choice subjects and then cannot be removed without lifting the plants. It can, presumably, be used as ground cover beneath shrubs and, as we shall see in the next section, the dividing line between some ground-cover plants and pestilential plants is occasionally extremely hard to establish. I suspect the blue devil may be a bit finnicky about its soil. In my old garden it swarmed everywhere and was a menace. A piece came with a plant I brought from that garden, but in my present one it has not increased particularly rapidly and looks quite mild compared with its activities not many miles away.

Another plant with the unfortunate capacity of rooting all along its annual growths is *Soleirolia* (more usually known as *Helxine*) *soleirolii*. This plant belies its common name of mind-your-own-business, by covering all the ground in its vicinity with a dense mat of slender stems, bearing circular leaves and occasionally producing small green flowers which have to be sought for with a lens. This used to be a common greenhouse subject, being grown in pots to provide backing to some gaudy subject such as a cineraria or calceolaria. It usually managed to colonise beneath the greenhouse staging fairly rapidly and has since come out of the greenhouse and into the garden, where it continues to thrive, growing in every conceivable position, from cracks in the wall to the lawn. The plant is native to Corsica and Sardinia and one would think it would be killed off during severe winters, but it usually manages to survive, although quite a mild frost will blacken the leaves. It is thus not a suitable subject for lawns and would indeed seem to have no good reason to be in the garden at all.

Another Corsican plant with much the same leaves but with minute mauve flowers, and the same habit of rooting as it goes, is the little mint, *Mentha requienii*. I have never heard of this as being a menace, but it does look as though it could be without much encouragement, and I would be very cautious about letting it loose in the alpine garden. As a filler of cracks in crazy paving it probably has some virtues, as it gives out a minty scent when trodden on, but can one rely on it staying in the paving? I have no knowledge of its behaviour in cultivation, but it looks as though it could be deadly.

The rose of Sharon, *Hypericum calycinum*, is a most beautiful plant, with its large rose-like yellow flowers, full of golden stamens, but alas it grows too easily. We can all admire the similar flowers of *Fremontodendron californicum* (formerly *Fremontia*), because this is a tender shrub that has to be grown against a south-facing wall; but the poor old St John's wort, which will colonise the most unpromising situations, including embankments made from clinker, is despised. Fashion plays a larger part in flower appreciation than it should. (Imagine the fuss we would make over laburnum if it had to be grown in a greenhouse and only flowered at irregular intervals.) The big St John's wort is a very handsome plant and it is only its excessive vitality which prevents us recognising the fact more often. Unfortunately once it is in the garden, it is there for keeps and it should only be admitted to places where its spread can be confined by natural obstacles.

Of course, if one applies oneself over a sufficient length of time, even the most recalcitrant plants can, eventually, be defeated. When I was a boy many gardens still displayed the purple and double pink forms of the bellbine, *Calystegia japonica* and *dahurica*, as well as a pink form of *C. sylvestris*. All these plants will grow with the vigour of our own native *C. sepium* and were recommended by Robinson as 'excellent for covering bowers, railings, stumps, cottages, etc. and also for naturalisation in hedgerows and copses'. For *C. sylvestris* he does say that 'the wild garden is the place where it is most at home, and where its vigorous roots may ramble without doing injury to other plants'. Of course, in one sense he was quite right; Calystegias are rather handsome plants with their heart-shaped leaves and big convolvulus flowers, and were they controllable we would be happy to have them in the right place. But since most of us spend a large part of our gardening lives trying to get rid of this terrible weed, one can only be amazed that anyone should ever have considered deliberately planting them. I wonder if perhaps it was a less widespread weed in the past. The various pink ones do seem to have been controlled, as they are rarely met with nowadays, although there are reports that some hybrids have been found in the wild and *C. sylvestris* appears to have naturalised itself and more or less supplanted *C. sepium* in northern England and Scotland. Still neither *C. dahurica* nor *C. japonica* infest many gardens nowadays, so it seems they can be controlled.

Plants that root as they travel above ground can be very alarming, but plants that spread underground by means of creeping rhizomes can be even worse. *H. calycinum* belongs to this group and so does the charming *Campanula rapunculoides*. This has always seemed to me one of the nicer campanulas, with its spikes of nodding purple bells reaching a height of about nine inches (I am always fascinated by the entry in the Royal Horticultural Society's *Dictionary*, which gives the height at two to four feet), but the plant has a very bad reputation and is probably quite unsuitable for the herbaceous bed or border, where it will inter-penetrate its neighbours. However, under spring-flowering shrubs it can surely bring a touch of colour later in the year, and it seems a pity to have to bar so attractive a plant solely on account of its invasive qualities. Most of us have parts of our gardens where plants can invade if they wish, and there the campanula can be allowed to spread at leisure. The trouble will come if we wish to change our garden and then it will prove very tenacious of its territory and continue to appear long after it has outstayed its welcome. There are rather too many plants which seem to have modelled themselves after Lear's Old Lady of Looe ('when they said "Go away", she continued to stay').

I suppose we should really differentiate between plants that are in-vasive and those which are only removable after many years' work, if at all. The silver-leaved herbaceous artemisias from North America, *AA. purshiana ludoviciana*, *palmeri* and *stelleriana*, have a bad reputation, and *A. stelleriana* has become naturalised in at least one locality in Cornwall, but although they may spread widely and be a nuisance in the herbaceous department by tending to smother their neighbours, they are usually little more than a nuisance. The same can be said, in some gardens, for the flame flower, *Tropaeolum speciosum*. This is a very handsome perennial scarlet nasturtium from Chile, which is often very difficult to establish at all in the garden, although it has the reputation of being much easier in the northern half of the country where it is cool and wet, rather than in parts like the south-east, which is warm and dry. It has been suggested that a number of plants should be obtained, and placed in various parts of the garden until a spot is found which they will enjoy and where they can be left. It is when they have established themselves that trouble may begin, as the plant appears to spread rapidly underground, and even the smallest bit will then make growth. I suppose the plant might be a nuisance on young shrubs, which it could conceivably smother if left, but most of us would be only too happy to have the display of scarlet flowers in the late summer and autumn with which the plant delights us.

Tropaeolums, then, do appear to be fairly indestructible once they are established. *T. polyphyllum*, an attractive trailer for the alpine garden, is nearly unobtainable commercially, as it sets no seed in this country and is very difficult to propagate, yet you can see it at Waterer's nursery at Twyford in Berkshire, coming up through the gravel path, which must have been laid some time ago on a place where it was growing. Like quite a few Chilean plants, it is very deep-rooting and so it is not easy to remove all the roots.

Another plant that is troublesome to establish, but once established unremovable, is *Alstromeria aurantiaca*. All the alstromerias have very brittle tuberous roots, which will eventually descend several feet. Until they have done that, or if for some reason they are unable to do so, they make little growth and may, indeed, not survive at all. When they eventually do establish themselves, they show quite a different aspect, growing with great vigour and spreading widely. The so-called *Ligtu* hybrids (in which, apparently, *A. ligtu* plays no part) are more difficult to establish, but equally strong and invasive when they are happily and deeply rooted. Since they are all very attractive flowers (although some forms of *A. aurantiaca* are rather fierce in colour) most people are happy to settle for their permanency and it is only if one wishes to remove the plants that any trouble is liable to arise.

Plants with wind-borne seeds that germinate readily can be a great bore and the giant hogweeds (*Heracleum villosum* and *H. mantegazzianum*), which are rather large for most gardens in any case, do manage to put themselves in the most uncalled-for places, if allowed to seed freely. If the seedling is quickly recognised it can be removed, but it takes only a few days to send down a tough tap-root, after which the job becomes more difficult. Since it is only in fairly large gardens that it is possible to grow these enormous plants at all, it is very easy for seedlings to develop to quite sizable plants before they are detected. The seeds are disc-shaped, and can skim on the breeze for longer distances than one would imagine, so that the plants distribute themselves rather more widely than one would suspect from the size and weight of the seed. They can, of course, have the flower heads removed before the seeds ripen, but many people, apparently, find that they are liable to get serious blisters if they interfere with mature plants, so that all things considered, it is probably best not to allow the plant into the garden at all.

Even more invasive are the various ornamental thistles, although they are much more rewarding garden plants. I once brought back a golden-spined thistle from Greece, which made an exceptionally ornamental rosette of leaves. Like so many thistles it was a biennial, and in the second year it produced a head of extremely weedy-looking and dirty purple flowers, not one of which produced any viable seed. Where, however, they do thrive and set seed, the seed is very widely distributed and will appear all over the garden and probably in your neighbour's garden as well. They anchor themselves with deep tap-roots and these must be dug out to be sure of killing the plant. Taking off the top is liable to encourage the formation of two tops to take the place of the original one. Such is the perversity of plants, that if you inadvertently take off the top of a plant you wish to preserve, it will probably die; it is only those that you wish to kill which turn out to be tenacious of life. Here again you can cut the flower heads off before the seed is ripe, but the stems are extremely solid as well as prickly, and cutting them down requires a brushing-hook and gloves; secateurs are often not powerful enough. There is also the problem that if you want to keep your giant thistles, you will probably want to preserve some seed, as most of them are biennial. Many of them are noble plants, with what gardeners are liable to call architectural value, and they can be very attractive in the garden, but they do pose problems. One's best plan is to be able to recognise the seedlings in the cotyledon stage and look for them at least once weekly during spring and early summer.

Plants that throw out runners which then root are much employed as ground-cover plants, but one of these, yellow archangel (*Galeobdolon luteum*) is really more than a ground cover; it is an invasive pest. It is a fairly common wild plant of the woodland, but there is a variegated form which is often offered by nurserymen. The plant grows as vivaciously as the wild form and will soon cover not only the ground but any low-growing plants in its vicinity. It throws out long stolons, which root at the tips and then proceed to throw out further stolons, so that a single plant does not take long to make ten or twenty more. Whether the variegated nettle-like leaves are ornamental depends on one's taste, but the yellow flowers are not particularly attractive and if you decide that you do not like it, you have probably made your decision too late. Once in the garden it is extremely difficult to eradicate.

An attractive plant for the bog garden or for any badly drained situation is *Houttuynia cordata*, which will also grow in shallow water. This belongs to an obscure family, the *Saururaceae*, which is closely akin to the pepper family, *Piperaceae*. The actual inflorescence lacks any petals, but is surrounded by four white bracts which are ornamental and long-lasting. The plant has a creeping rhizome, and roots as it goes. It will invade any other plant growing near it and, once established, may be regarded as ineradicable unless the whole complexion of the soil can be changed. It does need ample water to thrive, so that if its site could be well drained and made fairly dry it can be presumed that it will eventually die off. In a favourable situation there is nothing that can be done except to enjoy it. If you have it at the edge of a pond, it should be firmly discouraged from getting into it, otherwise bits are liable to float around and colonise other parts where they may not be wanted.

Ponds, indeed, have a number of potentially pestilential plants which are offered for their embellishment, and any aquatic plant is liable to spread with a speed that land-based plants cannot hope to emulate. We all know the damage that the attractive water hyacinth, *Eichornia crassipes*, has caused in tropical rivers around the world. I suppose the two most alarming plants offered to pond-owners in temperate climes are the arrow-head and the water hawthorn.

The arrow-head, *Sagittaria*, is an attractive plant, with large leaves sometimes a foot or more in length in *S. latifolia* and quite sizable in the native *S. sagittifolia*. Since the plants are monoecious, seed is rarely a problem, but the plants spread stoloniferally and can soon invade large patches of water, although they cannot survive if it is deeper than eighteen inches. The plants bear tall spikes of white, three-petalled flowers in whorls and are really very good value, but the plant can soon surround the fringes of the pond if not kept well controlled, and will usually smother any other aquatic that may be in the vicinity. If it is planted right on the edge of the pond, and every vestige that enters the water is pulled up in the autumn, it can be kept under reasonable control.

I do not think that there is any way of keeping the water hawthorn, *Aponogeton distyachum* under control if it is happy. It is a tuberous plant, with floating leaves and sprays of white hawthorn-scented flowers which are borne over a long period, from April until the autumn frosts. It seems to grow happily in almost any depth of water, although probably thirty inches to three feet is about its maximum depth. Once established, the plant seems to seed itself with great abandon, and also spreads in other less easily established ways, so that it can soon infest a large pond. The plant is attractive, so that if you have no objection to your pond eventually being covered with aponogeton, there is no cause for alarm. If, however, you want to see the surface of the water or want to grow other aquatics you have a problem. Or rather you have to make a choice. Once the aponogeton is well established the matter is out of your hands unless you drain your pond or indulge in some rather expensive spraying with an aquatic herbicide, which is probably not very desirable. Like some of the other menaces mentioned in this section, the plant is not very easy to establish, and usually it has to be put into very shallow water to begin with and then moved into deeper water.

The above would represent my personal black list of plants, although I must confess that I have consulted many other gardeners before writing this section. There are numerous other plants that can be irritating from the frequency with which they seed themselves around. Many of the violets are bad offenders in this respect, particularly the charming yellow *V. glabella* and the purple *V. arenaria rosea*. There are also numerous attractive geranium species which tend to fill the garden with their seedlings. Now that the spurges are coming into fashion, one should perhaps issue warnings about *Euphorbia coralloides*, which also seeds with great freedom. However, I would not exclude any plant from my garden just because it seeded itself around with considerable abandon.

So far we have said nothing about bulbous plants, and warnings should perhaps be hoisted for *Allium moly* and for *Nothoscordum inodorum*. This latter plant is not usually introduced deliberately, although—in the equivalent of estate agents' particulars—it can be made to sound quite attractive: rush-like leaves followed by pendent white, pink-flushed bells which are slightly perfumed; resembles an allium, but lacks the pungent garlic scent of that genus. This description is a roseate picture of a dirty white, rather weedy plant which seems to proliferate with almost as much abandon as our wild ramsons, *A. ursinum*, although it is far less handsome. On some nurseries it appears to have become endemic and is liable to arrive as an undesirable extra with plants that you wish to have in the garden.

A. ursinum itself is a well-known menace, but this is very rarely introduced deliberately into the garden. Most bulbous subjects can be killed off fairly rapidly with paraquat, so that their menace is now far less than it used to be. However if you get either the nothoscordum (sometimes, incidentally, masquerading as *A. fragrans*) or moly among some choice bulbs, this remedy is not available. *A. moly* itself is a charming little plant with glaucous leaves and heads of starry yellow flowers in May or early June. It has, however, responded very eagerly to cultivation. I have seen it growing wild in central Spain, where it is much less of a coloniser than is, for example, the early spider orchid, *Ophrys sphegodes*.

In cultivation the ophrys is not a particularly easy plant, which does not spread at all, while the allium will proliferate both by means of offsets and by seed. However, the seed tends to fall quite near its parents, so that the plant need not be a menace at all if placed with sufficient forethought. Don't put it among fritillaries or choice crocuses, but among shrubs it can run without any damage being caused and both its leaves and flowers are ornamental. Most alliums tend to do rather well in cultivation, with the natural exception of some particularly choice ones, which tend to be rather shy and difficult.

There are those who curse at the very handsome *A. siculum*, which in some gardens seeds itself around with as much freedom as a dandelion. This, like some of the other menaces we have been discussing, sometimes takes a year or so to establish itself and the hopeful owner wonders what he is doing wrong as the plant produces a few unhappy leaves and no flowers. Two or three years later he will understand why the plant has its reputation. Or perhaps he will not; in some gardens it will grow quite satisfactorily but the seeds do not germinate. It has a large bulb which produces offshoots rather sparingly, so that unless your soil suits it, the invading seedlings will not be forthcoming. Since the large bulbs are very easily removed if they appear in the wrong place, I cannot see that this plant needs to be placed on the Index Expurgatorius. I imagine that ants must carry the seeds around, as the seedlings often appear a long way from their parents. The plant may be up to thirty inches high and bears an umbel of drooping, bell-shaped flowers, which are greenish-white with a red band on the outside of the petals; if the flower is pure white it may well call itself *A. bulgaricum*. It is a splendid woodland plant but, although suitable for the herbaceous border, should even there be watched a little warily. It is easy enough to remove the seed heads before the seeds have ripened.

The curious thing is that there are almost certainly some gardens where many of the plants I have mentioned will not thrive at all or will barely subsist, though probably this does not apply to the appalling Japanese polygonums, which seem to grow in any situation with more than nine inches of soil. Be that as it may, for most gardens all the above-mentioned plants should be left severely alone.

15

GROUND COVER

The majority of gardens nowadays have, perforce, to be of the do-it-yourself kind. Most of us cannot afford to employ a gardener and for those fortunate ones who can, the supply is not equal to the demand. Gardening tends to be a job of long hours and poor pay and only a few dedicated people are prepared to undergo the arduous training for a meagre reward. As a result, we have come face to face with that creation of fantasy, the trouble-free garden. This is a contradiction in terms. You can have the surround to your house trouble-free by laying it all under concrete or paving stones, or you can have a garden, which must inevitably invite trouble. The trouble-free garden is a chimera, but some forms of gardening are less trouble than others. If you had a wild urge to revive the carpet-bedding of the 1860s and wished to make a bed of alternanthera in which the following legend could be emblazoned in plants of iresine: 'Chelsea for the Cup', you are obviously setting yourself a difficult task. The plants have to be raised in the greenhouse, hardened off in frames and then planted out, while the bed has to be carefully marked out with string and pegs to get the legend correctly spaced and the letters to size. After that you have to manicure the bed at regular intervals, so that the carpet-like effect is preserved. It is obviously less trouble (quite apart from being more ornamental) to plant your garden with shrubs, which will increase in size yearly and which entail comparatively little attention.

For many years after the war we were told to plant shrubs and have a trouble-free garden. Naïve gardeners who fell for this idea were brought sharply back to reality when they discovered that a shrub that might well spread over twelve feet, when fully grown, was received from the nursery as a small plant about a foot in height and as much across. If the shrubs were planted correctly there was an awful lot of bare earth between them. Unfortunately it would not stay bare. Seeds drifted in and the spaces between the shrubs were soon covered with a carpet of greenery, which all too soon revealed itself to be a mélange of tiresome weeds. On the excellent principal of if you can't beat them, join them, nurserymen began propagating plants that would behave with the vigour and virulence of garden weeds, but which would be agreeable to look at. These he termed ground-cover plants.

In fact, with a few exceptions, a ground-cover plant is an attractive weed. Sometimes, indeed, there is some doubt about this attractiveness. I have already mentioned yellow archangel, and in an American book I saw ground elder recommended as a ground cover. Apparently in New England the winters are so severe that the plant is less invasive than it is in our gardens, as much of it gets killed off every winter; but granted that, it still seems to me a curious plant to select for ground cover. We have it as unwanted ground cover in so many English gardens that it is not easy to see the plant impartially, but I would not have thought the leaves were particularly attractive (there is, however, a variegated form, which is apparently in commerce in the United States) while the flowers, although not unattractive, are rather tall for the ideal ground-cover plant. Also one would have thought that the plants were rather too esurient to be altogether satisfactory. Plants that root too deeply are liable to take too much nourishment from the shrubs and trees, which are after all the principal concern.

I imagine that the main points to look for in a ground-cover plant are first its ability to cover the ground and to suppress annual weeds or the seedlings of any perennial ones; secondly its ability to exist without seriously depleting the nutrients in the soil; and thirdly that it should be agreeable to look at. Another desirable quality is that it should be fairly low-growing. We certainly do not want the ground cover to smother the young shrubs, and we may also want bulbous plants to pierce the carpet that has been formed. A certain toleration of shade is also required, although eventually, once the shrubs have made their full growth, these may be expected to take most of the light from the ground cover, which will no longer be necessary and may be expected to die out to a large extent. It is really only a temporary feature of a permanent planting. Of course any ground cover will deplete the soil of nutrients to a certain extent and some extra nourishment must be provided to compensate for this, but it is liable to be less greedy than such plants as stinging nettles, docks or creeping buttercup.

Ground-cover plants themselves are not trouble-free when you start off. Although they may suppress annual weeds or perennial seedlings they will be no good against deep-rooted perennials that are already there, so all these must be removed before you plant your ground cover. Indeed it is best if you get rid of these before you plant anything at all, and ground that is fallow can be treated with herbicides or, if you dislike these, thoroughly and frequently cultivated; if you have already put your shrubs in, you may well harm them while trying to clean up the land. Nor are your troubles over when you have cleaned the land. Your ground-cover plants will be quite small when you receive them and you will have to have had them established for two or three years before you achieve an unbroken carpet. This entails hoeing for the first year and hand-weeding for the next two; only then can you relax, although even so not entirely. Plants such as groundsel seem able to come up through ground cover from time to time, although heavy infestations are rare. However, if they should be left, they would no doubt increase, so that even with your unbroken carpet, you still have to remove weeds from time to time.

Ground-cover plants can be just as temperamental as any other plants, and some that will do excellently in one garden may be a total failure in another. A friend of mine living quite near me uses *Vancouveria hexandra* (a North American relative of the epimediums) as a ground cover with great success. The plant has a fairly rapid running rhizome, which throws up attractive foliage, not unlike a giant maidenhair fern, and also has spikes of rather small white flowers; an ideal ground-cover plant one would have thought. I have lost count of how often I have been given pieces of it, but I have never been able to establish it. If it comes to that, the epimediums too, which also give excellent ground cover in many gardens, are slow to establish with me. *Epimedium perralderianum* is said to be able to smother even weeds like creeping elder, but if you do not have a rather light, peaty or leaf-mouldy soil, it may well prove hard to establish. However, where they can be grown epimedium and vancouveria do make a good thick canopy that will obliterate most unwelcome visitors. They have fairly attractive leaves (very attractive in the case of the vancouverias) and many of the epimediums have enchanting flowers. Once the vancouveria is established it spreads fairly rapidly; the epimediums are rather slower, and probably an increase in width of six inches each year is what should be expected.

Plants that spread by means of runners are usually fairly effective as ground cover. A plant that some people find far too invasive, but which suits my particular kind of gardening, is the Indian wild strawberry, *Fragaria indica*. The leaves of this look rather like our own wild strawberry, but the flowers are borne singly and are bright yellow in colour, while the resultant strawberry, which is larger than the normal wild one, although it looks delicious, is so entirely devoid of any flavour that birds tend to ignore it, so that you can have a mat of strawberry leaves with yellow flowers and red strawberries from mid-May onwards. The plant throws out its runners with all the enthusiasm of our own wild strawberry, and covers the ground quicker than most plants, I suspect it might be damaged in a very severe winter, but even so it seems to re-establish itself very rapidly. The plant is to be seen in quite a number of gardens, but I do not remember ever having seen it catalogued, although I suppose it must be somewhere. People who have it are only too pleased to give runners away, so I suppose that is the method that has circulated it. It seems to grow in most situations, wet or dry, shaded or sunny, but I know at least one garden where it was never established. Most of the runner-producing Potentillas are too coarse and deep-rooting for our purpose, but there is a comic little Japanese one which came into my possession and which has the charm of rarity, even though it has very little else to offer. This is *Potentilla centigrana* which is a fairly minute plant with grey strawberry-like leaves, which spreads rapidly by runners and also, as its name implies, by seed. The yellow flowers are so tiny that you can scarcely see them and the plant is remarkably unexciting, but the leaves have a mild attraction.

Speaking of Potentillas, whatever happened to *P. ambigua*? This was almost a sub-shrub with a running underground rhizome, attractive, slightly silvery leaves, and quite large yellow flowers. As a plant in the alpine garden it could be a menace, as it would dive underground and come up in the middle of some cosseted gem, but I would have thought it would have had a future as ground cover in the early stages of shrub plantings. It looked very much a sun-lover and would probably vanish as the shrubs shaded the ground, but it made large clumps quickly and, since it was deciduous, it would obviously not interfere with bulbs, as would most of the other plants we have mentioned.

To return to our runnering plants, the common bugle of our woods, *Ajuga reptans*, has several cultivars with coloured leaves; both a purple bronze and a white variegation are available. I am not, by and large, a great one for coloured leaves, and I cannot say I like these bugles very much, but to those who do they are easy to grow and spread with great rapidity. I brought back once from Corfu a bugle with larger flowers than our own wild plant and also of a far more brilliant blue. This was named for me as *A. orientalis* and was certainly a better plant, from the floral point of view, than either *A. reptans* or that other good blue, *A. genevensis*, which does not spread particularly rapidly but which is an attractive plant. *A. orientalis* did spread with great vigour and might have proved a valuable plant for the ground-coverer. At Wakehurst, that branch of Kew Gardens in Sussex, they have an attractive runnering geranium, which has quite ornamental leaves and handsome purple flowers from August onwards; it suggests a Himalayan plant, as the Himalayan geraniums tend to flower later than those from Europe or from China. It is labelled *Geranium collinum*, but it does not seem to agree with the *G. collinum* of *Flora Europaea*, which is a relative of *G. palustre*, confined to Rumania and the adjacent parts of the Soviet Union, nor does it agree with the *G. collinum* in the Royal Horticultural Society's *Dictionary*, which says that it flowers in May. Whatever it may be, it is an attractive plant which one would like to find available.

Although Galeobdolon may be a menace, the creeping lamiums are fairly harmless plants, although not wildly exciting. *Lamium garganicum* is low-growing and has a somewhat variegated leaf and long, purple-pink, dead-nettle flowers which appear sporadically over quite a long period. *L. maculatum* is rather taller, with a more pronounced variegation and, in the case of the cultivar called 'Chequers', with good deep-pink flowers. Although it looks like an attractive weed, it cannot put up with much competition and I rather doubt whether any of the lamiums really deserve their reputation as reliable ground-cover plants. They look as though they ought to be, but most of the plants I have seen have not really been very effective. Of course the wild dead nettle, *L. album*, can be an all-conquering weed, although in the eastern Mediterranean there is a form with blotched leaves and a black blotch in the flowers which is really very handsome.

The garden is so liable to abound in ground-cover plants which one would rather not have that it is always risky to cultivate their respectable relatives. Thus *Convolvulus arvensis*, looked at dispassionately, is a very attractive plant in its place—which is definitely not the garden. Its Mediterranean relative, with silver leaves and deep-pink flowers, *C. elegantissimus* (if that is still its name), should be an admirable ground-cover plant, and owing to its provenance it tends to get weakened every winter so that it does not become the *menace* of the field convolvulus. On the other hand it does want as much sun as it can receive, so that it is excellent as ground cover in the early days, but is liable to be suppressed as the shrubs increase in their shade-bearing potentialities. This makes it sound the ideal ground-cover plant, and I cannot help wondering why it is so difficult to obtain. Gardeners tend to put it on the alpine garden, where it is rather too exuberant, although its combination of deep-pink flowers and silvery dissected leaves makes it a joy to behold in any situation. Like most of these spreading convolvulus, the roots tend to descend very deeply, so that once established, which may take a year or so, it is not easily shifted. It is thus, potentially, rather a dangerous plant, but I do not know any garden where it has proved unmanageable. I should think that it would be rather hard to establish in heavy clay soils.

The spurge family often figures high in lists of ground-cover plants, but most of them are rather dreary. The best spurges tend to be rather too tall for this purpose. *Pachysandra terminalis* and its variegated form have only one virtue so far as I am concerned and that is their ability to survive in very dense shade. The flowers are nearly invisible and little would be lost were they completely so, while the leaves are unattractive. A much better plant, but one that takes quite a time to become established, is *Euphorbia robbiae*. This is a dwarf relative of our native wood spurge, *E. amygdaloides*, with glossy green leaves and spikes of large greeny-yellow 'flowers' in April. Once established, it will spread quite rapidly by means of stolons and eventually colonise large areas. It is evergreen and the leaves often assume quite attractive bronzy shades during the winter. It is easily the best of the spurges for this particular purpose. The deciduous *E. cyparissias*, the Cypress spurge, is an attractive plant which increases with the greatest vigour, but which seems quite incapable of suppressing any weeds at all. It is a difficult plant to find a home for in the garden. It is graceful and mildly attractive, but barely sufficiently so for a situation in the herbaceous department, while it is not an effective ground cover. Its real home is the Wild Garden, but this is now rarely met with. Every feature is mildly attractive, from its stems which do look like miniature cypresses, to its yellowish inflorescence and in autumn often quite vivid tints, but it spreads far too freely to be near other herbaceous plants and besides being ineffective as a weed-smotherer, is also rather tall for a ground-cover plant.

I suppose the ideal ground-cover plants, where the soil is suitably acid and open, are the various hardy ericas and callunas. They can only be introduced as comparatively small plants, as large ones do not move readily, and they are far from trouble-free, even when well established; if not pruned hard back after flowering they tend to become tall and leggy. Since they come in as small plants, they have to be kept clean for some two or three years until the plants have expanded sufficiently to coalesce. I suppose the showiest are those cultivars of *Calluna vulgaris*, the Scotch heather, which have ornamental foliage as well as their purple flowers in early autumn. Some of these are rather slow growing; plants such as *Foxii nana* never make a very large bun and it is necessary to select the right type of cultivar. Here again, once the shrubs have grown, the ericas and callunas will tend to die out, as most of them are sun-lovers.

The early flowering *E. carnea*, which will tolerate some lime, is also often found in shady situations in the wild, and may be expected to persist for longer. One can usually manage to grow spring bulbs through the ericas, so there is some advantage in having the species that flower at a different period, such as *EE. cinerea, vagans* and *ciliaris. E. tetralix* likes a rather moist situation and is less suitable as a ground-cover plant. All these plants are dwarf shrubs, and if left to themselves get leggy and lanky, so as we have already said they want yearly trimming, if the cover is not to be too dense and untidy. I suspect that heathers require some mycorrhizal association, and in some soils may fail to progress at all, so it is obviously worth your while to try a pilot plant before you lay out too much money. The fungus, if it is a fungus, is usually present in moss peat, so a top-dressing with this will probably help to establish the ericas or callunas more rapidly. They are also rather intolerant of drought, until well established, so that they are far from being the trouble-free plants that exponents of heather gardens would have us believe. They do not seem to be particularly greedy, not taking too much out of the soil, and they are easily removed once their usefulness is over. Most people find them easy to propagate through tip cuttings, so it is not difficult to work up a stock fairly rapidly. Since I have red fingers (if that is the opposite of green fingers) where ericas are concerned, I wouldn't know if propagation is really so easy. I have never had any success in that line, but that should probably be ascribed to my incompetence. I would never put myself forward as a good propagator in any line.

Plants which even I can propagate easily, and which spread with great rapidity, are many of the dwarf sedums. These soon make a mat, although not one which will suppress every weed. On the other hand, they are so shallow-rooting that they take practically nothing from the soil, so that the shrubs themselves will remain unaffected by their presence. My favourite in this line sometimes masquerades under the name *Sedum hispanica*, to which it has no right, as *S. hispanica* is an annual. Its correct name is *S. bithynica* and it has greyish, almost needle-like, fleshy leaves and heads of pale pink starry flowers in late June or early July. It can be a slight menace, as any portion that is removed and then dropped on to the soil is liable to root and start growing at once. There are a number of other dwarf stonecrops which are equally rapid in growth, the only one to avoid being *S. amplexicaule*, which looks splendid during the winter but, being a Spanish plant, drops all its leaves to get through the summer, which it thinks, poor fool, is going to be hot and rainless. It may well prove rather tedious keeping the interstices clean until such time as the stonecrops have made a solid foundation. The same may be said about both thyme and *Dianthus deltoides*, although both will eventually make good carpets. The dianthus has the advantage of dying back to a central head of rosettes in the winter, so that the ground between them can be easily cleaned of any weeds that may have insinuated themselves. The dianthus will also continue to persist when the shrubberies have become quite shady; it tends to seed itself around, which may or may not be an advantage.

An excellent ground cover for a more shady situation is lily of the valley (*Convallaria majalis*). Although the fragrant flowers are amongst the most delightful for arranging in vases, when growing they tend to be hidden beneath the leaves so that neither the flowers nor the red berries which may succeed them are particularly ornamental in the garden, and it is usually more convenient, if space allows, to have a small patch reserved for this plant a little out of the way, where the flowers can be picked but where the eye is not offended by too much of its characteristic foliage, although this is not really unpleasant in moderation.

I have already mentioned the runnering geranium, and there are two other species which may be considered in this connection. One has the rather alarming name of *G. pylzowianum*, a name doubtless highly gratifying to Mr Pylzow's feelings, but hard for Anglo-Saxons to pronounce. This is one of Farrer's introductions and he thought very highly of it. One can well imagine it looking very charming in the high mountains of Szechuan, but in the alpine garden it tends to be rather invasive. It produces a thread-like rhizome, on which at intervals very small tubers form. In the spring these throw up finely dissected leaves, which are ornamental in themselves, followed by few-flowered umbels of one-and-a-half inch wide pink-purple flowers of a slightly distressing colour. They are really a rather muddy pink, I suppose. The plant spreads very rapidly and will soon make a sizable carpet, but not one that is impervious to annual weeds. On the other hand, bulbous plants can pierce this carpet with ease and the plant is certainly meritorious. I suspect, however, that it would prove difficult to dispose of, should its welcome be outstayed. The other geranium I call G. *sibiricum*, but without much confidence that I have named it correctly. This is a superb foliage plant in the spring, when it makes neat little rosettes of rather buttercup-like leaves, each ornamented with a crimson blotch and really looking very ornamental. Unfortunately, about mid-May it starts to throw out its flowering stems and the crimson fades from the leaves. The plant is covered with flowers in July and August, but these are both minute and fugacious, so that the floral display is not worth considering. The plant will then ripen tons of seed which will germinate all over the place with the greatest readiness, so that it will rapidly colonise considerable spaces.

And so one could go on, listing plants which will form a low carpet that, once established, will suppress most weeds. I rather wonder if it is really worth it. Until the carpet has joined its seams you have as much or more work in weeding, and most of the available plants are not really ones that you require too much of in the garden. Moreover, there are a number of very desirable plants which are at their best growing between shrubs and which are preferable to most of the carpeters. The large autumnal colchicums are very welcome from August until October, but the following spring they will produce extremely bulky and (with the exception of the tender and rare *Colchicum latifolium*) rather unattractive foliage, which is far too large for the alpine garden and unattractive in the herbaceous department. Planted in the front of the shrubbery this unsightly foliage tends to pass nearly unnoticed. The various hellebores are, I would imagine, the most valuable of plants flowering in late winter. They like semi-shaded conditions and they resent any root disturbance. They too produce a lot of leaves during the summer and though these leaves are not unattractive they are copious and bulky. Here again the spaces between shrubs seem to be designed to give suitable living space for hellebores. In the wild the various paeony species tend to grow in semi-shade, and here again they will look and grow well among the taller shrubs. Admittedly you will have to weed around these plants, but once either peonies or hellebores are established they manage to cast a lot of shade, so that the weeding will not be very onerous.

Of course, if you have suitable soil the spaces between lowish shrubs are ideal for most lilies, which I imagine many of us would prefer to grow over most other garden plants. They will not, of course, grow anywhere, as they require a light, well drained soil (as far as I can make out, both these desiderata must be filled). A heavy, well drained soil will tolerate one or two of the less attractive species, such as *Lilium martagon*, while *L. pardalinum* seems to put up with much damper conditions than most other lilies, but for the majority I doubt if one will have much success unless both these essential conditions are present. Although by no means all lilies are woodland plants, they do seem to occur where there is ample spongy humus and this is obviously a big help to the lily-grower. With the appalling spread of lily virus, it would seem as though one's best chance of establishing a healthy stock is to show great patience and grow your lilies from seed, as the virus is not transmitted in the seed. This does mean that you may have to wait some years for some of your lilies, but *L. regale* will usually flower in the second year and *L. phillipinense* may flower eighteen months after sowing. Growing from seed means that you must eschew named clones and hybrids, but that is a small price to pay for having healthy stock.

However, owing to their strict requirements very few of us can grow lilies with much hope of success. We can probably all grow *Lithospermum purpureo-caeruleum*, a beautiful plant which is not easily accommodated. In the spring this throws up quite short stems, which bear umbels of the most brilliant blue flowers. It then throws up sterile stems which elongate considerably and then arch down and root at the tips, so that during the later summer the plant looks fairly untidy. It is not evergreen and the sterile shoots eventually dry off, leaving their offspring scattered around the original plant.

There is another method of suppressing weeds, which we in this country seem loath to try, although I believe it is frequently resorted to in the United States. This is covering the ground between your plants, be they woody or herbaceous, with a weed-suppressing mulch. Usually when we mulch we do it to enrich the soil and to prevent excessive desiccation, and use such materials as compost, farm-yard manure, or even peat. Occasionally sawdust is used to suppress weeds, which it does very effectively, and this is probably the only material readily available. Unfortunately, sawdust seems lethal to the nitrifying bacteria in the soil, and it is necessary to supply extra nitrogen in some chemical form when much sawdust is used. It is also rather slow to break down, so that its continued use could do considerable damage to the soil.

I suspect there are a lot of waste products which could be effectively used for this purpose and which might also prove beneficial. Think of the tons of peas that are annually frozen or tinned. What becomes of all the pods? Surely it would be simple to dry and pulverise them. Possibly it would then be found, as it has been in the case of the residue from coffee powder, that a useful animal feeding stuff could be manufactured, but if that were not the case I can well imagine that a useful mulching medium might result, which would not only suppress weeds but would also have some slight manurial value. This is only one example, but I suspect that there are many waste products of industry which might be employed in this way.

The main essentials are that these materials should be fairly light and inexpensive, inoffensive to handle, and should not be too persistent. Also, of course, they should not be brightly coloured. If the earth between your plants was coloured scarlet or bright yellow, it would not please most people. In the United States, where buckwheat flour is used in many recipes, buckwheat hulls are frequently employed as a mulch. I would imagine that there might be some risk of them blowing about, as they are so light, but otherwise I am sure they are admirable. They are not, however, liable to be available to us, though no doubt similar materials are. It is surely preferable that these waste products should be used, rather than be dumped and left to fester in waste tips. I recommend the scheme to some entrepreneur.

When such materials are available, all one need do is to spread them over the surface of the unplanted soil every spring and trust that any weeds will be suffocated before they can pierce the mulch. This mulch must, of course, be sterile. Many of us tend to use grass mowings as a mulch around such plants as roses, but they bring more weeds than they suppress and are not very satisfactory. The whole business of mulches would seem to be a new idea in gardening, and it would be as well if some research station did some tests on the effectiveness of the various mulches, both as weed-suppressors and also as to their effect on the cultivated plants. It would not be much use suppressing the weeds if the plants were weakened as a result, but if we could find a mulch that had some mild manurial value as well, we would obviously have found something worth using. Although it seems that there is never anything new in gardening, from time to time some new idea does arise.

16

THE HERBACEOUS DEPARTMENT

SOME GARDEN MYSTERIES

There are a certain number of plants in the garden, mainly ones that have been in existence for centuries, whose origins remain doubtful and whose continued existence seems to have depended chiefly on propagation by means other than by seed. Heading the list is the old flag iris, which has a number of names, such as *Iris germanica*, *I. albicans* and *I. fiorentina*. The cytologists have proved that none of these is a genuine wild plant, but hybrids, and sterile hybrids at that. There are a large number of wild bearded irises known, and the number of chromosomes in each cell is always some multiple of 8. Thus, there are some with 16 chromosomes, while others have 24, 40 or 48. The *germanica* group have 44. It seems fairly certain that they have resulted from hybridisation between the dwarf *I. chamaeiris* with 40 chromosomes and one of the tall bearded species (or probably, as we shall see, more than one of these) with 48 chromosomes. When plants hybridise, half the chromosomes come from one parent and the other half from the other, so that in the hybrid we are considering, *I. chamaeiris* would produce 20 chromosomes, while 24 would come from the tall bearded species, giving the total of 44. It would seem certain that *I. chamaeiris* must be the parent providing the 20 chromosomes, because no other 40-chromosome iris is known, except for the Portuguese *I. subbiflora*.

So far, everyone is agreed as to the origin of these irises. What no one seems to have asked hitherto is where did they meet? In the wild, *I. chamaeiris* ranges from Sicily westwards to Provence, while the range

Page 149 *Hellebore* hybrids. The product mainly of amateur gardeners

Burnards Formosa.

Page 150   A florist's polyanthus

of the tall bearded 48-chromsome plants seems to be mainly confined to western Asia, with one outlier in Cyprus and a more interesting one, *I. kashmiriana* in Kashmir. This latter plant is interesting for many reasons, but the one that most concerns us is that not only is it a white iris, while the other species are all various forms of violet, but that this white is dominant when the plant is crossed with other colours. It would seem, therefore, probable that it played a part in the creation of such plants as *I. albicans* and *I. fiorentina*, both of which have white flowers. If that should be the case, and I do not know if it is provable or no, it would seem more probable that the original crossings took place in the near east. *I. albicans* is much planted in Moslem burial grounds, which again suggests an Asian origin. But in that case we must assume that early in the Christian era some Asian gardener imported *I. chamaeiris* from Europe. The old herbals give no particular medical virtues to this plant, so that it seems we must imagine an expedition to gather ornamental plants from the Mediterranean. We know that in the sixteenth century there was a thriving trade in ornamentals based on Istanbul, including such favourites as tulips, hyacinths and forms of *Ranunculus asiaticus*, which suggests a fairly long established gardening tradition in Turkey (or possibly in Persia), and the plants in which they specialised seem to have come originally from their immediate vicinity. We do not know whence came the ancestors of the florists' tulip, but both *Hyacinthus orientalis* and *R. asiaticus* abound near the Asian Mediterranean shores. Hence we can also postulate, without too much extravagance, the possibility that they were cultivating the tall violet flags of the vicinity.

To go off at a tangent for a second, these tall bearded irises never seem to have been very thoroughly investigated. They were mainly brought to Europe by missionary friends of the great iris expert Sir Michael Foster, who named them after the place of collection; thus we have *I. trojana* from Troy, *I. cypriana* from Cyprus, *I. mesopotamica* from Iraq and *I. amas* (also known as *I. macrantha* and *I. germanica* var. *amas*) from Amasia in Turkey. No one seems to have decided whether we really have four species here or just a single species from four different localities, and the plants are not generally obtainable, although they have formed the main parent of all the modern tall bearded irises.

It should, perhaps, be mentioned that there is a European iris with 48 chromosomes, although it is unlikely that it played any part in the creation of *I. germanica*. This is *I. aphylla*, whose range starts in Hungary and extends east as far as the Caucasus. It is distinct from the other bearded irises in that it shows no leaves whatsoever during the winter while all the others show at least the tips of the new leaves, in the few cases where they are not evergreen. *I. aphylla* does not meet *I. chamaeiris* in the wild, so there would seem little chance of it being a natural hybrid.

There is one factor which might suggest a western origin for *I. germanica*. In the famous *Nativity* by Hugo van der Goes in the Uffizi, there is depicted a purple iris growing in a pot. This does look like one of the tall 48-chromosome plants, so it is possible that some of these might have been brought back in the fourteenth century and planted near *I. chamaeiris*. One always conveniently ascribes these early plant introductions from the near east to the crusades, and if the German iris were only a plant of ornament one might agree that it could have arisen in a western garden. Against this are several factors. First, so far as we know, ornamental gardening was not usual in medieval times; secondly, *I. fiorentina* was being extensively grown for orris root, which is the dry and powdered rhizome of this plant. This was traditionally brought from the east. Thirdly, both *I. fiorentina* and *I. albicans* (assuming that they can be distinguished) have white flowers. The only white 48-chromosome iris known as *I. kashmiriana* and, as we have seen, its progeny in hybrids tend to be white also. Presumably albino forms of *I. chamaeiris* and the tall bearded Levantine irises must occur from time to time, but they are not common and the most probable parentage of *I. fiorentina* and *I. albicans* would be *I. kashmiriana* × *I. chamaeiris*. On the other hand, the probable parentage of *I. germanica* would be *I. chamaeiris* ×, a purple 48-chromosome plant.

My reason for assuming different seed parents is based on the rather shaky ground of the time of flowering and the fact that, despite all probability the seed parent does seem to have more effect on hybrid progeny than the pollen parent. *I. chamaeiris* tends to flower in April in this country and so does *I. germanica*, while the white irises tend to come into flower a month later, nearer the time of the tall bearded irises. Another reason for assuming a near eastern origin for these hybrids is the occurrence, in India, of yet another of these sterile hybrids, Wallich's *I. nepalensis* (not to be confused with D. Don's plant of the same name, which is, correctly, *I. decora*. Wallich) which is found in various parts of India and Nepal. As we must postulate a two-way traffic to account for the use of *I. kashmiriana* in the near east, we might assume that some of the newly bred irises would also be brought back on the return. Almost all these irises are found most abundantly in Moslem countries, so that religion does seem here to be the link in distribution. The main exception is *I. germanica* itself; although plants with the same sterility and chromosome count are not uncommon in the near east, it does seem to have become more established in the west, where it has become naturalised in the most unlikely places.

If healthy plants are sterile, they conserve energy by not setting seed and make more vegetative growth with this unused energy. As a result all the irises in the *germanica* group grow with considerable vigour. They are also practically indestructible and their rhizomes can grow in places where no other plant can venture. I remember once in the Pyrenées Orientales seeing them dripping a hundred feet over a cliff, presumably obtaining all their nourishment from the plants at the top, but the rhizomes had continued elongating down sheer granite, in which not a crack appeared to allow any roots to enter.

What is written here is only a reasoned guess as to the origin of this widely distributed group of irises, and that is probably all we can manage. Judging from the length of time they have been in cultivation, it would seem improbable that the cross were made deliberately. However, we are still left with one problem. In the wild, *I. chamaeiris* flowers in April in the south of France, probably earlier further south, while the Levantine irises flower a month later. Even assuming that some gardener in the near east imported *I. chamaeiris*, the chances of them flowering at the same time would have seemed remote. However it is not impossible (obviously so), as such parts can have sudden hot springs which will bring out the flowers of March, April and May simultaneously and presumably this is what happened. The rest was the result of an intelligent and enterprising bee.

I may seem to have gone on rather about the German iris, but, so far as I know no one has raised this question before. The cytologists were so pleased to have found the origin of *I. germanica* that they left the matter there. Anyway there is no reason why a cytologist should be a botanist and have plant distribution at his finger-tips.

We know how the German iris came into existence, even though we may not be certain where it originated. The case of the old double red paeony is different. Everyone seems to agree that it is a double form of *Paeonia officinalis*, and so far as I know I am the only person to have questioned this attribution. It seems to me that, for the reasons I shall be giving, the garden plant seems to bear little resemblance to any form of *P. officinalis* found in the wild. On the other hand, it shows very little affinity with any other wild species, with the possible exception of *P. peregrina*.

The nomenclature of paeonies, particularly the European ones, is so wildly confused that one is never quite certain to what plant any of the writers before about 1900 are really referring. *Paeonia officinalis*, as now understood, refers to a plant that has a fairly wide distribution from near Avignon through the Basses Alpes and Alpes Maritimes, in northern Italy and the Tirol and in Istria. There is also a record from southern Albania, which sounds very improbable. The plant is usually rather short, about fifteen inches high, although plants up to two feet have been recorded. The leaves tend to be smooth on the upper surface, but slightly hairy below, while the flower is crimson with a very strong perfume. The petioles are usually slightly hairy. Our old double paeony has no hairs on the stems or leaf-stalks, while the veins of the leaves stand out very prominently on the underside of the leaves, a feature not found in the wild form. The leaves are also larger than those found in wild plants, although this may not be significant. The flowers are more purple in colour than any wild form that I have seen, which are usually a dark glowing crimson, and the delicious perfume is barely perceptible in the cultivated plant. In fact, to put the matter in a nutshell, the double paeony does not look remotely like any form of *P. officinalis*.

As I have said, the plant does somewhat resemble *P. peregrina*, a plant that is found in eastern Europe from Albania and Rumania eastwards to Asia Minor. This was early known in western Europe under the name of *P. byzantina* and had more in common with the garden plant than *P. officinalis*. However, the colours of many forms of *P. peregrina* tend more towards scarlet than any other paeony and it flowers a month later than the old double paeony. Both the species have been found in both diploid and tetraploid forms and there is evidently close kinship between them; their distribution is practically contiguous. It would seem most likely that the record for *P. officinalis* from Albania would refer to *P. peregrina*, which has been recorded elsewhere in that country.

The matter is further slightly complicated by the fact that *officinalis* is an adjective referring to plants with medical properties, the paeony used by the early herbalists being *P. mascula*, while the present-day *officinalis* was known as *P. foeminea*. Although the double paeony lacks any stamens, it has perfectly good carpels and could, presumably, be pollinated both by *P. officinalis* and by *P. peregrina*; it might be possible to arrive at some idea of its true identity from the resultant plants. In spite of the fact that the original *officinalis* paeony was *P. mascula*, I think we can exclude that from our consideration, as it has leaves dissected into far fewer segments than either *officinalis*, *peregrina* or the garden paeony. Lobel, in his writings which appeared towards the end of the sixteenth century, refers to the double paeony as *P. promiscua neutra*. I have wondered if the adjective *promiscua* could refer to a possible hybrid origin. What, I wonder, would result from hybridising *officinalis* and *peregrina*? Presumably the plant has survived entirely through vegetative propagation for at least four centuries.

It might be as well here to consider what Philip Miller had to say in his *Gardener's Dictionary*. Of *P. officinalis* (which he still calls *P. foeminea*) he says that the leaves are hairy on the underside and also that the flowers are a deeper purple than those of *P. mascula*. 'There are several varieties of this sort with double flowers, which are cultivated in the English gardens; these differ in the size and colour of their flowers, but are supposed to have been accidentally obtained from seeds.' Of *P. peregrina* he says: 'The large double purple peony, I suspect, is a variety of this sort.'

I think there may be a possible clue here. It is not clear what colour was envisaged as purple by Miller, but if he thought that the flowers of

P. officinalis were of a darker purple than those of *P. mascula* he must mean a more or less purple-crimson. In that case the 'large double purple peony' may well be the old plant still with us, while the double forms of *P. officinalis*, with flowers of different sizes and colours, may now be lost. Double paeonies are normally rather larger than single ones, but our old plant certainly has very large flowers, larger than one would normally expect from *P. officinalis*. Miller also notes that *P. peregrina* flowers after the other species. In gardens the double paeony does flower later than *mascula* or *officinalis*, although it does open earlier than the forms of *peregrina* now in cultivation.

It should also be noted that Miller specifies that the underside of the leaves of *P. officinalis* were hairy. Let us assume that he was correct and we get a number of different double forms of *P. officinalis* and a large double-flowered *P. peregrina*. In my time I have collected seedlings of quite a few wild paeonies, and the one that I have found most difficult to establish has been *P. officinalis*, which may be due to my inefficiency or may point to the fact that this particular species does not take readily to cultivation. Should this be the case, we might assume that the 'large double purple paeony' of Miller has survived, while the double form of *P. officinalis* has been lost to cultivation. We have different colours in our double paeonies—a white, a very pale pink and a deep pink, as well as the old crimson—but we do not have plants with varying sizes of flowers, and this again suggests that Miller's plants are no longer with us. If we can assume that Miller was right, then the matter is explicable. There formerly existed a number of double paeonies, most forms of *P. officinalis*, but one a form of *P. peregrina*. In the course of time the double forms of *officinalis* were lost, while the vigorous form of *P. peregrina* persisted. Since there were originally more double forms of *officinalis*, it was assumed that the surviving plant was also a form of *officinalis*, no one having noticed that the leaves did not agree well with any wild form of this plant. As a result this double-flowered form of *P. peregrina* is now universally known as *P. officinalis*. The wild forms of *P. officinalis* are not, so far as I know, in cultivation. There should be an opportunity here for some research.

As a footnote to this I would mention a short note from that great hybridist Victor Lemoine, which appeared in *The Garden* for 1 January

1881, about the new paeonies being produced by himself, Crousse and Victor Verdier. He said that they were formed from *P. edulis, P. officinalis* and *P. sinensis*. The first and last of these are both the Chinese paeony, now known as *P. albiflora*. This is the first comment I have seen suggesting that *P. officinalis* has ever been used in the modern production of hybrid paeonies, and since most forms of *P. officinalis* have 20 chromosomes, while *P. albiflora* has only 10, it would seem unlikely that the hybrids were successful. In fact I doubt if any of these so-called *officinalis* crosses ever took. The resultant plants, in so far as they have survived, all look like cultivars of *P. albiflora* and only differ in degree from such old forms as 'Whitleyi' and 'Humei', which were imported from China at the end of the eighteenth century.

Most of our mystery plants appear to be sterile and to have been propagated only by division. In this class comes *Hemerocallis fulva*, the orange day lily. This has been known in cultivation since 1576, but has probably been around for longer than that. The plant is a triploid, which accounts for its inability to set seed, although there is some suggestion that it may on occasion have produced usable pollen. Presumably there is a diploid form of this plant, but its ancestor has never been convincingly found in the wild. Most of the species come either from China or Japan and a species was known to Pliny and Dioscorides at the beginning of the Christian era. The plant was regarded as having considerable medical value, the flowers in particular being regarded as very efficacious in relieving pain, particularly during childbirth. The dried flower buds of *H. flava* are also used as a vegetable in China. It is assumed that it was brought to Persia along the silk trail in the earliest times and thence, later, to western Europe. The plant is easily cultivated and tends to naturalise itself if flung carelessly around. A double form was raised, or preserved, in Japan and this reached cultivation in 1860. The plant is not, one would have thought, outstandingly attractive and its survival might have been thought problematic. However here it still is, although recently the hemerocallis have been transformed by hybridisation. The plant would also seem to be remarkably stable. Two double forms have been recorded, one with variegated leaves, and occasional slight colour variants turn up, but by and large we may assume that we are seeing exactly the same plant as the Elizabethans. Probably it came from China, but its origin is wrapped in mystery.

So too is the Dutch yellow crocus, which is one of the first flowers to brighten our garden in mid-winter. This is obviously fairly close to *Crocus aureus*, a plant with a wide distribution in eastern Europe, but from which it differs in being completely sterile. Apparently the first reference to it is in a publication by John Rea of 1665. Here again one would suspect a triploid form, but no one seems to have established this. Bowles, in his classic work *Crocus and Colchicum*, suggests that it may have occurred in more than one place and form, 'because there are at least three distinct stocks of it in cultivation, varying in the colour of the outer segments, both in a lighter and duller shade of yellow in some, and also in the length and depth of colour of the grey stripes, invariably present, but most marked in the richer-coloured forms'.

The simultaneous occurrence of unusual forms in cultivation is quite a common phenomenon. It occurred with the giant forms of *Cyclamen persicum* and with the 'Spencer' sweet peas, so it may well have happened with *Crocus aureus*. During the course of time some variants appeared, which were described by Joseph Sabine in the journal, *Transactions of the Horticultural Society* in 1829. All these are characterised, among other things, by the virtual disappearance of the anthers, which would make it probable that the main deficiency of the Dutch yellow crocus lies in its pollen. There are other sterile crocuses known in cultivation, notably the saffron crocus, while the commerical form of the autumn-flowering *C. medius* also appears to be sterile. In many ways it is an advantage for bulb merchants to have sterile plants, as the inability to create seed is compensated for by a superabundance of offshoots.

This applies to our last mystery, the dwarf double daffodil known as Van Sion. The only mystery here is of what particular species this is a double form, as it does not appear to agree very well with any extant species. The most probable candidate would seem to be the Tenby daffodil, *Narcissus obvallaris*, which is itself a rather mysterious plant. Its occurrence at Tenby, in Wales, has been thought to be an escape from cultivation but no convincing population of wild plants has been found to agree with it, although I have collected plants of *N. pseudo-*

narcissus from the Alpes Maritimes which seemed fairly close at a superficial glance. But in any case Van Sion does not agree very well with what one might imagine a double Tenby daffodil would look like. Wilmer's great double daffodil, mentioned by Parkinson, has been equated with this and also called *Telamonius plenus*, but Parkinson's description that 'the stalk riseth to bee two foote high' and his description of the flower 'diversely intermixed with a rowe of paler, and a row of deeper yellow leaves, wholly dispersed throughout the flower, the pale colour as well as the deeper yellow', cannot be our dwarf, deep yellow, trumpeted double flower but must be some other plant.

Peter Barr in his *Descriptive Catalogue* made after the Daffodil Conference of 1884 says of *Telamonius plenus*: 'This Daffodil is common at Florence, from whence it may be supposed it was introduced into this country about the year 1620. The single form is to be found growing with it, but not abundantly.' However the only pseudo-narcissus mentioned in the Italian flora is *N. pseudonarcissus*, and it would not seem that this were liable to produce a two foot stem, so one has to think Mr Barr must be incorrect. He, like everyone else, confesses himself baffled by Haworth's *Lobularius plenus*, which seems to be our Van Sion. Since *N. pseudonarcissus* is a very variable plant, perhaps too much should not be made on this point.

PLANTS THAT MIGHT BE REINTRODUCED

In the hills of the Lebanon and elsewhere in Asia Minor grows *Eremostachys laciniata*. According to the Royal Horticultural Society's *Dictionary* it is an 'easily grown, hardy perennial', and it has certainly been in cultivation. Although herbaceous plants are a bit under a cloud at the moment, this particular plant surely should be reintroduced. It bears long pinnatisect leaves, which I have always thought must have provided the inspiration for the Corinthian capital, rather than the acanthus, which is always credited with this. Certainly the leaf looks exactly like the leaf on one of these capitals, which is more than can be said for any eastern Mediterranean acanthus. The commonest of these is *Acanthus spinosus*, which would be the one most likely to be seen by a Greek sculptor. This is barely distinguishable from the leaf of a thistle and is not particularly like the Corinthian leaf.

I am not sure from what time the legend of the acanthus leaf arose, but probably in classical times acanthus would refer to any plant with a pinnatisect leaf and may well have been our eremostachys. The plant makes a handsome rosette of these leaves and then throws up a stout, rather woolly spike, which can reach three feet, although eighteen to twenty-four inches is seen more frequently. This bears whorls of yellow labiate flowers, which from a distance suggest a lupin, although closer inspection will soon reveal its labiate character. The plant is really extremely attractive, and since its habitat is easily attainable I cannot think why some enterprising traveller has not brought back seeds. In the wild the plant is found at low levels, but also in situations where snow lies in winter and it would be from these that the hardiest forms would, no doubt, be found.

From the same part of the world come two very striking annual plants, one of which was formerly in cultivation but has dropped out, while the other has apparently never been in cultivation, although it seems incredible that it has never been tried. Possibly there are some cultural difficulties about which we know nothing. This latter plant is *Linum pubescens*, growing about six inches high and with large, rose-pink flowers, usually two inches or more across. To see this plant massed in olive groves is a remarkable sight and there seems no reason why it should not be as easy to cultivate as the North African *L. grandiflorum*, which has maintained its popularity as a hardy annual for a long time. The only thing to do is for someone to collect some seed and try it out. If it should prove as easy as it looks, it would be a notable addition to our stock of ornamental annuals.

That common arable weed of the near east, *Veronica syriaca*, was popular in the middle of the last century and certainly looks very attractive in the wild. It is a small, prostrate plant with extremely vivid blue speedwell flowers about half an inch across, in four-inch spikes. In the wild it is extremely floriferous. It is possible that it might prove less so in more temperate climes, but in view of its long period of popularity I would have thought that it must have been a success in our gardens. Of course, as we have already mentioned the number of annual plants that were available from fifty to one hundred years ago was very much larger than today and probably many attractive plants require reintroduction. The Royal Horticultural Society's *Dictionary* lists *V. syriaca* as a half-hardy annual, but it does turn up fairly high in the mountains where frost is not unknown. I imagine both this and the *Linum* would prove satisfactory if sown outside towards the end of April.

One of the most agreeable entries in that famous list of Kew in 1812, the *Hortus Kewensis*, is that for Lord Anson's pea, *Lathyrus magellanicus*. It reads: 'Introduced 1744 by the Cook of H.M.S. Centurion.' Miller tells us why. He says it 'hath a biennial root, which continues two years. This was brought from Cape Horn by Lord Anson's cook, when he passed that Cape, where these Pease were a great relief to the sailors. It is kept here as a curiosity, but the Pease are not so good for eating as the worst sort now cultivated in England; it is a low trailing plant; the leaves have two lobes on each foot-stalk; those below are spear-shaped, and sharply indented on their edges, but the upper leaves are small and arrow-pointed. The flowers are blue, each foot-stalk sustaining four or five flowers; the pods are taper, near three inches long, and the seeds are round, about the size of tares.'

Incidentally Miller calls the plant *Pisum americanum*, which surely gives our taxonomists a chance to rename *L. magellanicus L. americanus*. To judge from gardening books, one would assume that this plant has been almost continuously in cultivation since its introduction, but apparently this is not true. It is not to be found either in Loddiges's catalogue nor in the list of plants grown by the elder Ellacombe in 1831. In addition to this, we have an article by J. C. L. (whoever he was) in *The Garden* for 1 April 1899, which treats this plant as follows in an article on the hardy *Leguminosae*:

'I remember reading a few years ago in some gardening paper or pamphlet an article on these sort of things, in which Lord Anson's Blue Pea (L. magellanicus) was treated with the knowledge of complete familiarity. The venerable writer (he must have been close on ninety and may have been a half-brother or first cousin once removed of Mrs Loudon) had evidently seen the vegetable sea-serpent in the flesh, dealt with it, cultivated it and knew all about it: but unfortunately (as is often the case with the memories of very old people) he probably confused the present with the past and, at any rate, he forgot to tell us when or where he had last seen it, so the veil of obscurity cannot even now be said to be lifted.'

Evidently the plant had been lost to cultivation by the end of the eighteenth century. Incidentally no one so far as I know, except Miller, has ever suggested that the plant was not perennial. The colour of the flowers would seem to be rather dubious. Miller, as we have seen, says they are blue and this tradition seems to have survived, but Sweet says that the flowers are purple, while Loudon says they were purple, with some blue, while the Royal Horticultural Society's *Dictionary* says purplish-blue. In any case it sounds a desirable plant.

Some years ago I wrote a book about climbing plants, in which I mentioned this as sounding as though it merited reintroduction and received a query from a reader, asking where it could be obtained. The only suggestion I could make was that the writer should try and find some correspondent in Patagonia who would send him seeds. Then two years later I received another letter, telling me that he had done just that and received some seeds, some of which he most generously offered to me. They germinated well, but none survived the mild winter of 1971–2, though my correspondent managed to flower his. He has since sent me some more seed, indeed so much that I was able to pass some on to Wisley, Surrey, so that we may see it reappearing in cultivation. We may also see whether it was worth all our trouble. A blue everlasting pea sounds marvellous, and even a purple-blue one sounds attractive. There is another good really blue pea in *L. sativus*, but that is only an annual. It is equally out of cultivation, but since it is a European native it should be easy enough to obtain.

Thermopsis montana is an attractive plant from the time that the blue-green shoots come through the ground in early spring until the rich yellow lupin-like spikes open in May and June. Once established, it spreads very rapidly and might well be something of a menace in some situations. It is not uncommon in gardens, although it seldom appears in nursery catalogues. In the early 1850s, that amusing writer Lt-Col Edward Madden (you will have to take my word that he was an amusing writer, as his writings are all buried in the *Asiatic Journal* of

Bengal of the 1840s; I have hopes, one day, of reprinting them) introduced *T. barbata*, a Himalayan plant with purple spikes springing from a woody rootstock. The spikes are not so densely flowered as those of *T. montana*, but the individual flowers are at least an inch long, and judging from the illustration in the *Botanical Magazine* (t 4868) the plant should be very attractive. What happened to it I have no idea. The Royal Horticultural Society's *Dictionary* says that it is hardy, although one doubts that the writer was speaking from personal experience. I certainly have never heard of anyone growing it in my time. Most of the *Thermopsis* come readily from seed, so it should not be difficult to reintroduce the plant.

I think the best herbaceous plant I have is *Erodium carvifolium*. This is found in central Spain. It tends to be a local plant, but where it does occur it is plentiful. The plant has long feathery leaves, more like those of a carrot than of the carroway (*Carvi*) after which it is named, and throws up umbels of inch-wide magenta, black-blotched flowers from mid-May until the frosts come in the autumn. In the garden it seems very shy of setting any seed, and possibly it requires cross-fertilisation to get a satisfactory set, this inability to set seed is amply compensated for by its incredible production of flowers.

There is another Spanish species to which it is evidently closely allied. This is *E. daucoides*, which has coarser leaves and which is more alpine in character, sending out its umbels sideways rather than erect, and starting to flower a fortnight later. I suspect that in my gardens these two plants have hybridised and that my best plants are a combination of the two species. Although seed is produced so sparingly, the plant is easy enough to propagate both by detaching rosettes and by root cuttings and I am unable to account for the fact that so floriferous a plant should have dropped out of cultivation. It seems to be as hardy as any other plant in the garden and to grow in most soils. There are, after all, very few plants that flower for at least six months non-stop. Some people have strong feelings about magenta, but this particular magenta is set off by the blotches on the upper petals and it is far less glaring than, for example, *Geranium psilostemon* or *E. manescavi*.

I am doing my best to distribute the plant to various friends, so I hope eventually it will be well re-established in cultivation, but why did it ever drop out? Robinson mentions the plant as an afterthought in *The English Flower Garden*, but does not sound very well acquainted with it. It is not mentioned in Sweet's *Hortus Britannicus* of 1830. Indeed the plant was only diagnosed by Boissier and Reuter in 1842, a surprisingly late date for what is a not uncommon plant. Since the plant now exists in my garden, in some of my friends' and, presumably, some from seed supplied to the Alpine Garden Society, I suppose I can say rather pompously that I have reintroduced it to cultivation; but that will not do much good until some nurseryman propagates it on a commercial scale.

Among the introductions that the great plant collector William Lobb made was *Dicentra chrysantha*, which sounds a magnificent plant, growing from three to five feet high according to the Royal Horticultural Society's *Dictionary*, with very finely cut glaucous leaves and golden-yellow flowers in erect racemes in the autumn. The plant is native to California, and since there are now many people in that state collecting seeds (although mainly of alpine and bulbous plants) there seems no good reason why so splendid a plant should not be reintroduced. Another dicentra that sounds attractive is the climbing *D. scandens*, with large yellow or purple flowers in eight to twelve flowered racemes. This comes from the Himalayas and should not prove too difficult to obtain again.

The above are only a few of the plants that used to be in cultivation and which sound as though they merit reintroduction. Doubtless there are many more of which I have not heard, as well as some of which I have heard but have now forgotten.

PLANT-COLLECTING

The erodium mentioned above was collected by me in Spain, and there are many plants which can be collected in the wild with advantage. Moreover, no purchased plant can have the associations of a plant you have yourself seen growing wild; plant-collecting, under certain safeguards, is interesting and potentially valuable. There are, however, certain basic points which should be borne in mind.

First, in many countries wild flowers are protected and it is against the law to dig them up. One should always remember, when on holiday, that one is a guest of the country one is visiting and take care not to give offence. Do as you would be done by is always excellent advice and should be borne in mind by any tourist, whether he is collecting plants or not. Most countries that prohibit the lifting of plants have no objection to the collection of seeds or of cuttings. The exception is South Africa, where most people are not even allowed to pick wild flowers, the right of propagating the wild plants of the country having been given to certain nurseries. Apparently, alas, this stringent effort at conservation does not have any effect when it comes to industrial or building sites, and many local South African plants are said to be at risk, owing to their habitats being in land scheduled for other purposes.

In countries where there are no laws of conservation, you should make your own. If you know that a plant is rare, withhold your hand. The flower may be blushing unseen, but it is present and if there are very few of them, do not make the number less. If you can collect seeds, or if you can take a few cuttings, that will do no harm, but if neither of these openings are available, show self-restraint. Take a photograph and lament over the one that got away, but rejoice that you have not further diminished a rare species. There can be exceptions to this rule, which normally should be stringently applied. If the plant's habitat is obviously about to be destroyed, either through road construction or through agricultural processes, it is better that the plant should survive in your garden than not survive at all. But this is really the only valid excuse for collecting rare plants.

I can give an example, not fortunately of a rare plant, from my own experience. In northern Greece I once came upon a field that was white with a particularly good form of *Leucoium aestivum*. At the time I got there the field was being ploughed up and there could be little doubt that the plants would all be destroyed. *L. aestivum* is not usually a rare plant, although I have never seen it elsewhere in Greece, but even if it had been rare there would obviously have been no objection to collecting a few bulbs, which is what I and those who were with me did. (The sequel is instructive though depressing. The plants did not do well in this country and did not appear to be any better in form than the usual commercial bulbs. It was obviously the combination of soil and climate that had made them so outstanding.)

Apart from not collecting rare plants, one should take care that one's collecting does not cause offence to other passers-by. One should not root up some attractive plant that is growing beside the path when one can get an equally good one by leaving the path for a few yards. Other people want to enjoy the wild flowers and do not want to see a gaping hole. Do not be greedy. It is only very exceptionally that one needs to take more than two plants of the same species. Provided one can establish them one can then propagate from them and increase the stock. It is easy enough to think that when one sees, for example, a meadow white with *Anemone narcissiflora* that no harm would accrue if one took as many as a dozen and, indeed, if one were the only person collecting plants one would be quite right, but if seven other people also arrive and collect a dozen that is already a hundred gone from the native population.

In point of fact it is rare that the amateur collector will do much damage with a normal population; it was commercial collectors who nearly caused the extinction of *Narcissus cyclamineus* in Portugal, who stripped the Vésubie Valley of *Lilium pomponium* and who caused the extinction of *N. alpestris* in the Pyrenees. Fortunately, a couple of new colonies have since been discovered but that was luck. It might well have become extinct in the wild, owing to the demands of gardeners and the short-sighted greed of bulb firms. All these bulbs come perfectly readily, although slowly, from seed and there was never any need to make such massive collections. The red form of *L. pyrenaicum* has never, so far as we know, been found in the wild, which rather suggests that there was only a single population, which was completely destroyed by the first collector. Fortunately it has persisted in cultivation, but had it not it might have been completely lost.

If it is possible to collect a plant without removing it entirely, this is obviously desirable. At the present time there is considerable collecting going on of the marvellous Oncocyclus group of irises. These all exist in local populations, which may be quite numerous. There is no need to collect a whole plant; a portion of the rhizome with two fans

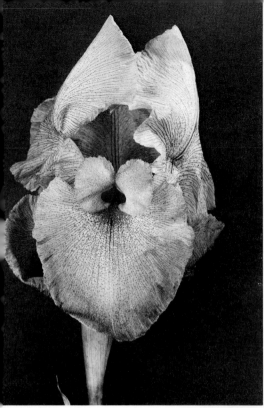

Page 167 *(left) Iris lortetii* tottering on the brink of extinction;
(below) Digitalis obscura. A shrubby foxglove from Spain, with mahogany flowers, that should be reintroduced

Page 168 Show pansies. Pansies still exist, but not like these

is more than enough and the rest of the plant can be left to increase again.

Small plants move and establish much better than do large ones. It may be tempting to take up a great clump of *Gentiana verna* in full bloom, but it is really a waste of time. It is very unlikely that it will survive the move, and equally unlikely that it will ever make a satisfactory plant again, whereas a seedling plant will usually re-establish quickly and grow with success. Ideally, plants should not be moved when in flower, but this is not always possible. If you are sufficiently learned and sufficiently sharp-eyed, you may be able to find the plants when they are not in flower, but this is not easy even for experienced collectors and may be very difficult indeed for amateurs. There is also the point that when you collect plants out of flower you have no idea, if it is a variable plant, whether you have got a good form or an indifferent one. When you collect your plant in flower you at least know what you are getting. So when you are collecting plants in flower, be selective and only collect the best.

Once you have established a collected plant it takes considerable will-power to throw out any inferior plant. I have been looking for more years than I care to remember at a plant of *Geranium phaeum* var. *lividum*, a livery-purple version of the nice black *G. phaeum*, not particularly attractive but which was the first plant I ever collected. Had I had the benefit of reading my own advice I would never have collected it in the first place and my garden would not be burdened with an inferior plant to which I have a sentimental attraction.

Particularly good forms, even of plants commercially available, are always worth collecting. Its genes are probably well distributed among the rest of the wild population, so there is a good chance it will appear again, but it may not be in our gardens. The same applies to any colour variants, be they albinos or other deviants. In the wild these are liable eventually to be hybridised out, generally representing the emergence of a normally recessive gene, so it is only in cultivation that they can be preserved. But here again, if you can leave part of the plant, do so. The probability is that once the genes of this particular form are in circulation, they will surface again to give other good forms. There is always a slight risk too that the good form may not be preserved in cultivation. There is the case of the golden lewisia 'Carol Watson'. Only a single plant was ever found of this, and attempts at propagation were unsuccessful, so the plant is now lost. You may argue, I would say justifiably, that nothing would have been gained by leaving it in the wild (indeed it may well have been flourishing in the wild for some time before it was found). Unless it was self-fertilised, the probability of this unusual colour variant reappearing would be very remote and there was at least a possibility that it would survive in cultivation. I would agree with this. One's efforts cannot always be crowned with success.

This leads me to another precept that I would like borne in mind. If you do get a good plant, propagate it and distribute it among your friends. It can be fatal to keep a good plant in one garden, as a particular set of circumstances can so easily result in its disappearance. The wider the plant is distributed the greater is its chance of survival in gardens; and there is the practical point that if you have given a plant to a friend you can always ask for a piece back if you have lost yours. So far as I know the psychology of the miser, or the collector who gloats over his possessions, is not very frequent among gardeners, who tend to be rather friendly and social creatures, generous with their possessions.

The worse time to lift plants, usually, is when they are in flower, but this is generally what the plant-collector has to do. Of course, if you are abroad for some time, as opposed to most of us on our fortnight's holiday, you can mark the desirable plants when they are in flower and collect them subsequently at a more favourable time. Also if you are a trained botanist, or have visited the region before at a different period, you can probably recognise some plants when they are either yet to flower or after they have done so. However, even the trained man sometimes lacks certainty. It is perfectly easy to recognise an ophrys both before it flowers and after the flowers have faded, but it is well-nigh impossible to determine which particular species of ophrys you are seeing. The same would apply to a number of narcissus species and you will probably have to collect most plants in flower. As we have already said, young plants are easier both to lift and to establish later in the garden, so it may be possible, by searching around the flowering plant, to find seedlings that have not yet flowered. Of course with very variable plants there is always a risk that you may be getting an un-desirable form in this way, but the majority of plants that you will collect are fairly stable and seedlings can be expected to reproduce their parents' characters fairly closely. Plants with bulbs or corms are best collected after flowering if possible, but even if collected in flower, they will usually survive, although somewhat weakened and probably requiring a year or two to get back to their flowering size.

The actual technique and paraphernalia involved in collecting are neither very cumbrous nor at all difficult. You start off by writing to the Ministry of Agriculture, Fisheries and Food asking for a licence to import wild plants. You state what countries you intend to visit, and your date of return, and you then receive a licence without any trouble. With the licence comes a certain amount of literature, which includes a list of plants that you are not allowed to import. The most intriguing item of this is roses from Italy. It is apparently quite all right to bring in roses from anywhere else and I have always wondered about this prohibition. However, none of the plants listed is liable to make the amateur feel frustrated.

For equipment you need a sizable trowel or fork. If you are travel-ling by car you could carry a large garden fork, but usually you must make do with a small one. You also want a small haversack (the ones employed by fishermen I find most convenient), a selection of poly-thene bags of varying sizes, but mainly rather small, some seed en-velopes, some rubber rings and a number of labels. You set off with your trowel and two or three large polythene bags, and your seed envelopes in your haversack, and lift your plants carefully, trying to minimise any root damage. Most plants will probably root deeper than you suspect, so it is as well to excavate fairly thoroughly and to take your time over this operation. As you lift your plants you put them in one of your large polythene bags. If you find any desirable seeds, put them straight into a seed envelope and seal and label immediately. If you are shortly to return home you can also collect cuttings, which may well be more satisfactory, but which cannot be kept in good condition for too many days. Once back in your tent or hotel, you sort the plants out and bag each one up individually.

There are various schools of thought as to how you should do this.

Some people strip all the soil from the roots, others leave the soil on; some enclose the entire plant in the polythene bag, others allow some of the leaves to emerge. My own feeling is that one has to be empirical over this. If you have got the plant up with a good soil ball around the roots, it may well pass the intervening period before it is replaced in your garden with less desiccation. On the other hand, if you are in a district where ample moss is available, it may be better to dispense with the local soil and enclose the roots in moss that has been moistened and then squeezed as dry as possible. It should only be moist, not wet. If you have to travel at some stage by air, then you will obviously reduce your overall weight if you are not transporting soil. (Incidentally, if you are travelling by air, take your plants in the plane with you; they may get frozen in the luggage hold.) If the plant is very succulent, it may be advantageous to let half the plant protrude from the bag, otherwise there is a risk of the plant rotting before you get home, but most plants seem to endure complete enclosure without any damage, provided that they receive ample light; this is the essential point once you have bagged your plants. There is a tendency to feel out of sight out of mind, but the plants require to be stored carefully, so that they get ample light, but are yet shaded from any hot sun, which could cook the plants. Before you bag them, write out a label, giving the plant's name if you know it, or if not some brief description, a note as to where you found it, and remove any flowers or buds that the plant may be carrying. These will now only weaken the plant, so be resolute. In theory, seed capsules should also be removed, but if they are nearly ripe it may pay you to keep a few.

Re-establishment is the most important facet of plant-collecting, and if you are wise you will have taken steps before you leave. Make a nice mixture of half peat and half grit in a well-lit situation but shaded from the direct sun. If you have a frame that may be better than an open bed, but it is not essential. If you have not removed the soil from the roots before, now is the time to do so and plant your plants in this recovery bed, which should be kept always moist. Most of the plants will soon show signs of growth and once this is sufficiently vigorous the plants can be put into their permanent positions. Obviously the shorter the time that the plants have to spend in the bags, the better, so if you are staying at one place it is sound policy to mark whatever plants you wish to collect that are near your hotel and collect these during your last two days. If you are travelling about, this, of course, will not be possible, nor is it usually feasible to revisit sites that are a long way away, but it is possible to strike a happy mean. Do not be in any hurry to collect plants that are easily accessible. Plants that die down in the summer, such as most bulbous or tuberous plants, are probably better placed in pots, rather than in the recovery bed, and kept on the dry side until the leaves have died down, after which you can either put them in their permanent positions, if the bulbs or tubers look good and plump, or should they look rather small, you may wish to give them VIP treatment for a year, in which case they may well be best grown on in pots in a suitable compost.

The number of desirable garden plants that exist in Europe, yet which are not usually available commercially, is surprisingly large. Generally I do not bother to collect plants that can easily be purchased from nurseries, unless there appear to be very good forms. A few years ago in the Soria district of central Spain I found a paeony, which has yet to be identified. There are three paeonies commonly found in Spain, *PP. humilis*, *broteroi* and *coriacea*, which are confined to the extreme south of the country. My plant was none of these, and looked most like the Corsican *P. russii*, which is not recorded from Spain. When found it was no longer in flower. I brought back and established a seedling, which is now quite a sizable plant, but which has yet to flower, so its identity is yet to be established. A curious thing is that though it flowers early in the wild (a few days previously we had seen *P. humilis* in full flower), it is the last paeony to come through the ground in cultivation.

The mountains of central Spain appear to teem with good things; here are just a few that I have noted. *Centaurea macrorhiza* spreads by an underground rhizome and produces rosettes of silver, pinnatifid leaves with a large yellow flower in the centre. I did not keep it very long. *Vicia onobrychoides* has very fine pinnate leaves, a widely spreading habit and very vivid, almost gentian-blue flowers. It seems to be uncollectable. What you think are seedlings, reveal themselves as outliers from a huge central stem; if you trace the slender underground stems down through the soil, you find that it eventually joins a great woody horizontal stem, but still shows no signs of roots. Yet if you take a bit of this woody stem, or even the fine filament that gives rise to the leaves, you will find that the plant will re-establish itself, although you will have to wait a few years before it reaches flowering size.

Lathyrus filifolius is a semi-prostrate plant with rather grassy leaves and racemes of flowers with bluish standards and a purple keel, which is easy to establish. *Thalictrum tuberosum* with a rosette of maidenhair-like leaves and a thin stem, bearing an umbel of large white flowers, is quite unlike most other thalictrums. I have had plants for seven years, but I do not find that they increase at all. Around Tragacete there is a large-flowered, deep-pink Centaurium, which has all the appearance of being a good perennial and which I have not been able to identify, possibly *Centaurium barrelieri*, possibly not yet described. My plant only survived about eighteen months and the plant needs re-collecting.

Artemisia assoana is a very dwarf, mat-forming silver-leafed plant, which is, in my opinion, the most attractive of these dwarf artemisias and much easier to cultivate than such plants as *A. glacialis* or *A. genipi*. Its appearance, and it may well be found practically by the acre, is a sign that the soil is well-nigh exhausted and this should give us some clue as to its treatment in cultivation. If the soil is too good, the plant seems to become soft and rot away in the winter. If given very poor conditions it will probably survive quite happily. In the wild it grows in really horrid places, both where water may lie and in exposed places where everything that our winter can produce is liable to occur. Cuttings root easily, so it can be preserved through the winter under cover, if it is not well established. I think this is slowly coming into commerce. I had no luck bringing it back alive, but my companion, Mr A. Venison, was successful and probably all the plants in the country come from his collecting.

Linum viscosum is a plant not unlike the popular *L. narbonense*, but with slightly wider and greener leaves and rosy-purple flowers. Large plants are very unwilling to move and seedlings seem unobtainable, so the only thing to do is to collect ripe seed, a thing I have never been able to do, having never been at the right place at the right time. Near the town of Guadalajara is the district called the Alcarria and here grows another linum, *L. ortegae*. This makes a tiny shrub, with very narrow, imbricated, needle-like leaves and heads of sizeable white flowers. The plant is quite singularly intolerant of root disturbance, and here again seed is probably the only good method to introduce the plant. Also, although plentiful enough in the Alcarria, it is found nowhere else, so it would be a pity to diminish the wild population. On the other hand it is a very attractive alpine garden plant and should be introduced. I have tried with cuttings with no success, but I am not a good propagator and others might succeed.

Carduncellus mitissimus is a very dwarf blue thistle, much more delicate than the North African species which are around at the moment and equally hardy, although very wet winters can damage it. *Dactylorhiza elata*, the great Spanish marsh orchid, can grow up to thirty inches high; at the moment it is extremely abundant in central Spain and establishes itself very readily in our gardens. Although it likes ample water, it will grow quite satisfactorily under comparatively dry conditions. *Fritillaria hispanica* is often very abundant locally and is one of the easier fritillaries to establish. *Dianthus laricifolius* makes a small, shrub-like plant covered with carmine flowers. It is not particularly long-lived and did not, in my experience, set seed in my garden, so must be propagated by cuttings. The same goes for the mat-forming *D. subacaulis*, which is very local in my experience, although once one hit on a locality, there is liable to be huge quantities of it. This has glaucous leaves and more or less stemless pink flowers.

A plant I have seen only once is the dwarf blue *Veronica boissieri*, which seems to grow perfectly well in cultivation, but is remarkably coy about producing flowers. Here again I suspect that poor soil is required. One of the glories of the Spanish flora from the south to quite far north is the shrubby, orange-brown *Digitalis obscura*. Seed is usually available; it seems to hang on the plants for a long time and seedlings are also usually to be found. The plant varies considerably, and if you can get a seedling or seeds from a good form you will be pleased, while those from inferior forms can look rather wishy-washy. In our climate the plant seems to be very short-lived and must be continually propagated either by seed or by cuttings. We never seem to be able to grow the large bushes that are found in the wild.

Lavandula pendunculata, like a much improved *L. stoechas*, can be found quite high up in the mountains, where it must get plenty of frost and rain, but it seems to be a little dubious about our climate. Here again it can easily be preserved by cuttings, but since it has to make a fairly sizable plant before it is worth seeing, this is not really the answer. Presumably, like so many montane plants it requires a very sharp drainage and might be expected to do well where plants such as cistus do. Once it becomes a sizable plant it is very effective with its long floral bracts at the ends of the flower-spikes, two or three times longer than those of *L. stoechas*.

This list is getting rather tedious, but I would like to mention two more plants out of the many which await collection. The first is the well-known *Erica australis*, which gets further north than I had realised. Between Soria and Logrono it gets really high in the mountains and if seed of these plants could be collected, we would surely have a much more frost-resistant strain than we have at the moment. It is difficult to collect seedlings as it grows with *E. arborea alpina* and you never know which seedling is which until it flowers two or three years later.

The other plant is fairly widespread in the Cuenca area. This is *Euphorbia serrata*, with grey-green leaves, which—unusually for a spurge—are serrated at the edge, and a large greeny-yellow umbel. It seems to spread by means of an underground rhizome and whenever I thought I was lifting a seedling, I found it was attached to a large un-liftable plant. Here again, seed would seem to be the best method of introduction, as even small spurge plants dislike moving, while fresh seed usually germinates immediately. This is a very attractive plant, which the latest Supplement to the Royal Horticultural Society's *Dictionary* says is hardy. Doubtless this is so, although it never seems to get very high up. However it certainly grows among such hardy plants as *Dictamnus albus* and *Allium moly*, so it probably is. I have only seen it in early June, when it was just coming into flower. I could prolong this list quite considerably, but already you have a number of desirable plants, none of them rare, which may be in cultivation but are not in commerce, all of which could easily be found during a fortnight's holiday, provided a car is available. You do not have to go to China or the Andes to get desirable plants; they are on your doorstep.

HYBRIDISING

So far as we know, the first deliberately made garden hybrid was Fairchild's Mule Pink of 1719. This was a cross between the border carnation and Sweet William and seems to have been an isolated example. The real mania for hybridising started in the early nineteenth century, was helped forward by Dean Herbert, and has never since really ceased. By hybridising, a number of plants have been created whose relation to their wild parents are by no means easy to establish, particularly among some of the early creations where the hybridist was liable to guard his secret, so as to prevent others stealing his thunder.

The objects of hybridising were well set out by an anonymous writer in the *Floricultural Cabinet* for April 1857. 'The points to be gained by hybridizing are first, to obtain the properties or qualities of a tender plant upon a hardy one, or secondly, the colours of an ill-habited plant upon one of good habit. Generally speaking, these two points comprise all that can be gained; but there may be another object, which is only comprised in those mentioned by implication— the mixture of colour between plants of equal, or nearly equal claims.'

But in spite of this, in the early nineteenth century they hybridised for the sheer love of creating new plants. The mechanics of heredity were not only not understood, they were barely suspected, although the idea of selection of the best forms had been adopted for some time. A number of rules, based on rather casual observation, had been formulated, more particularly in the breeding of florist's flowers. But for most people the technique was new, it was fascinating, and anyone could do it.

Up to about 1850 the majority of hybrids were created by private gardeners and there was a sort of one-upmanship in the friendly rivalry which resulted. The desirable hybrid might eventually be sold to a nurseryman, but it was comparatively rarely that the nurseryman was himself responsible. There were, of course, exceptions. *Gladiolus* × *colvillei* is the survivor of a number of gladiolus hybrids raised by the nurseryman Colvill, although the ostensible parentage (*cardinalis* × *tristis*) sounds incredible. *Rhododendron* × *nobleanum* was raised originally by the firm of Standish and Noble, but most of the early hybrids were privately raised. It was only in the latter half of the nineteenth century that firms such as Veitch employed hybridists of the calibre of Seden and Dominy. John Dominy (1816–91) achieved fame as the first to make and successfully flower a hybrid between two orchid species. He was also one of the few men to make a successful fuchsia hybrid, without employing as parents either *Fuchsia magellanica* or *F. fulgens*. John Seden was known for his work in many fields from orchids to gloxinias but is probably best known for his work in creating the first race of tuberous begonia hybrids which began in 1867. He also worked among various fruits, unlike the majority of plant hybridists. To John Heal we owe the large-flowered hybrids of tuberous begonias with *Begonia socotrana* as well as all the hippeastrum hybrids with *Hippeastrum leopoldii* as one of the parents. He also continued the work of George Taylor in hybridising the few 'javanicum' rhododendrons that were available in those days and to him must fall the dubious honour of having created the first double javanicums.

In the early days, however, as we have seen, the creation of hybrids tended to be the interest of private gardeners, either amateur or professional. Thus, for example, the hybridisation of the various narcissus species was, to start with, almost entirely in the hands of amateurs, of whom Leeds, Backhouse, Horsfall, Nelson and Engleheart are the best known, while the only nurseryman among the pioneers is Peter Barr. The firm of De Graaf entered the field comparatively late. Pelargoniums, being comparatively easy both to cultivate and to hybridise, seem to have been left, to start with, almost entirely to the amateur, although it is not easy to track down many of the originators. Presumably Rollisson's 'Unique' was created by the firm of Rollisson, who specialised in many South African plants, most notably heathers, and certainly hybridised these rather specialised subjects. In our days the species most frequently hybridised are hemerocallis and rhododendron, the former being almost entirely professional, while the latter is mainly amateur; so even in these days of commercial stringency, the breeders of new hybrids of plants whose commercial value may be dubious is left to the amateur, while the professional tries to improve on known paying lines.

It is arguable that no plant has ever been improved by hybridisation, although other advantages may have accrued from this technique. This is an attitude for which I have great sympathy, but I doubt if it is entirely correct. Loath as I am to admit it, I cannot feel that the various species of hemerocallis have quite the range of interest of the new hybrids, and there is really nothing in the range of species of tall bearded iris of quite the interest of the best hybrids, gawky and graceless though they may be. The main trouble with this sort of plant-breeding is that the raiser is liable to be seduced by size to the exclusion of other considerations. It was the discovery of the immense flowered *Hippeastrum leopoldii* which more or less wrecked the hybrid strain of hippeastrums. They all became very large-flowered and consequently restricted in colour, with the rather harsh brick-red of *H. leopoldii* persisting for most forms. The earlier hybrids appear much more attractive, so far as one can judge from contemporary illustrations; most of them have long vanished. The reintroduction of the large-flowered, tender *Rhododendron griffithianum* in the 1870s eventually resulted in the creation of numerous hybrids with huge flowers, which may be attractive individually but which often look disproportionately large compared to the foliage and size of the tree on which they are borne. In most plants one can see a sort of advance and retreat on this subject. The flower gets larger and larger until they probably end up being too large for the stem to bear it, there is then a *rappel à l'ordre* and the flower size tends to revert to a more convenient size.

This can probably best be remembered by people of my generation in such plants as chrysanthemums and dahlias. I have forgotten its name, but I well recall a dahlia with a flower ten inches in diameter; I doubt if it is available today, although these things do linger on. Few rhododendron-breeders are using *R. griffithianum* today. Instead they are using the scarlet *R. griersonianum* and the dwarf *R. yakusimanum*; this latter plant seems to be a terrible parent from the floral point of view, although the dwarf, compact habit is preserved in the hybrids, most of which look like the old nineteenth-century hardy hybrids suffering from an attack of nanism. The flowers of *R. yakusimanum* itself are rather large for the size of the bush, but the hybrids are far worse. Still, although one may have one's reservations about R. *yakusimanum* as a flowering plant, it is certainly attractive in its foliage, particularly in the winter. This attractive foliage does not seem to have been conveyed to any of its hybrids.

With so many marvellous species among the rhododendrons, the only real excuse for hybridising them can be in the creation of hardy forms of the more attractive tender species. This, indeed, is how the practice began. Before the 1820s, the only broad-leafed rhododendrons known were *ponticum* and *caucasicum* from Europe and *catawbiense* and *maximum* from North America. The introduction of the tender, deep-red R. *arboreum* from the Himalayas brought a completely new colour into the species and one that was obviously very desirable. It was accordingly hybridised with R. *ponticum* to obtain the 'Smithii' variety and with *catawbiense* to give 'Carnarvonianum', both of these appearing in 1826. These were followed a year later by 'Altaclerense' which was *arboreum* crossed with a hybrid of *ponticum* and *catawbiense* and 'Russel-lianum' which had the same parentage as 'Carnarvonianum'. In 1832 appeared the well-known cross between *arboreum* and *caucasicum*, known as 'Nobleanum', while a similar cross was named 'Pulcherri-mum'. Two other early *arboreum* hybrids, according to Loudon's *Hortus Britannicus,* were 'undulatum', with rich purple flowers and 'venustum', which was pink and spotted. Both of these appeared in 1829; I imagine this 'venustum' was not the plant now known as 'Nobleanum venustum', although I suppose it could have been. Loudon definitely lists it as an *arboreum* hybrid, while he classes 'Nobleanum' as a caucasicum hybrid.

In our own day similar crosses have been made to incorporate the late-flowering scarlet Burmese rhododendrons of the Parishii sub-series into hardy plants, as they are all more or less tender, and this has resulted in a number of late-flowering plants, of which 'Firetail' seems to come closest to the parent R. *eriogynum* and which has the same late-flowering recommendation. The introductions of a large number of Himalayan rhododendrons in the early 1850s, from the collection of Joseph Hooker and Thomas Booth, gave a further impetus to the hybridists and so did Fortune's introduction of R. *fortunei* from China in 1855; it is from the introduction of these various species that the main creation of the so-called hardy hybrids dates, in spite of the pioneer work of the late 1820s and early 1830s.

It seems odd that *R. campanulatum* had arrived in 1824 and *R. barbatum* in 1829, but so far as we know neither of these had been used. *R. griffithianum* had been among Hooker's 1849 sendings, but it does not seem to have been much used until a later importation in 1867, when the plant came into the hand of Mr Mangles, who used it on everything he could lay his hands on, or so it would appear. One of his most famous crosses was 'George Hardy', a cross between *griffithianum* and *catawbiense*, and when this was crossed with an early *arboreum* cross known as 'Broughtonii', it gave us the famous 'Pink Pearl', still one of the favourite hybrids after nearly eighty years.

At least in the case of the rhododendrons we can still see the species if we prefer them to the hybrids, but in the case of many herbaceous plants this is no longer possible. It may well be that we might find the various verbena species preferable to the hybrid verbena, which is all that we can now find, as the parents have long since dropped out of cultivation. The same may be said of the various species that went to make up the modern gladiolus, and here, I think there can be no doubt, a very real loss has been sustained, as the modern gladiolus hybrid is not at all attractive as a plant, although undoubtedly useful for cut flowers. Perhaps the most significant hybrids, so far as the history of gardening is concerned, were the various tender, perpetual-flowering plants that gave rise to the nineteenth-century bedding craze. These were first and foremost the zonal pelargonium, and also the verbena, the petunia and the calceolaria. They, perhaps, merit a section on their own.

BEDDING PLANTS

Up to the present day the garden seems to have alternated between the formal and geometrical and the informal and romantic. The intricate knot gardens of the Tudors gave place to what were presumably less formal gardens, but although we know what plants Parkinson and the Tradescants grew, we do not know how they were arranged. In the eighteenth century, according to Henry Phillips, 'the flower parterre was divided into hearts and diamonds, and the garden was made to display octagons, hexagons, circles and semi-circles without number'. This seems to have given way in the early nineteenth century to the romantic garden with shrubberies and flower borders, while towards the middle of the century the geometric garden returned. This was replaced by the informal gardens of Jekyll and Robinson and we are obviously now due for a revival of the geometric garden. Probably, however, the harsh facts of economics will make this impossible and we may, instead, turn to the oriental garden with very few plants, but with sand and rocks arranged with the greatest art.

The earlier geometric gardens were attempts to give interest with comparatively few plants to employ, but in the nineteenth century bedding was used to display the results of what in these days we term advanced technology. Never before had it been possible to plant up an area with a plant already in flower in June and have it still showing flowers at the end of September. Some form of zonal pelargonium seems to have been bred as early as the mid-eighteenth century, but it was the introduction of the compact and floriferous 'Tom Thumb' which established the scarlet geranium as the bedding plant *par excellence*. At the same time the verbena and the calceolaria were being developed and proved equally long-flowering, while the various annual blue lobelias were also entering into cultivation. The petunia was grown rather more as a specimen plant than as a bedding subject and only entered into this field comparatively late. The mainstay of the bedding craze was undoubtedly the zonal pelargonium and this was soon obtainable in whites and pinks as well as in its scarlet form.

In 1867 the *Floral World* was recommending geraniums in scarlet, red, pink, salmon and white, besides various variegated-leaved types to which we will come shortly. The other main bedding subjects were calceolarias, dahlias, petunias, verbenas, dwarf tropaeolums, heliotropes, lantanas and *Gazania splendens*. Some unexpected bedding subjects included in this list were *Convolvulus mauritanicus*, *Nierembergia gracilis* and *Oenothera prostrata*, whatever plant that name covers. Other flowering subjects included pentstemons and, of course, lobelias. The bedding system found its main exponents in the public gardens of the time, including the Royal Horticultural Society's grounds at South

Kensington in London. However, after a time the gardeners began to tire of unalloyed brilliance and a new style of bedding, dependent on attractive foliage, was developed. Although the introduction of the coleus gave the main emphasis to this new style of bedding, it was already being developed when the coleus became available. The brilliant-leaved *Amaranthus tricolor* had been known for centuries, but other brilliant-leaved dwarf plants, such as the alternantheras and iresines, were introduced from South America (it was fortunate that the bedding craze and many plant-collecting expeditions to South America coincided), and this trend was augmented by a number of variegated-leaved plants that Robert Fortune sent back from Japan in 1860.

Other plants, which had remained obscure for some time before the bedders turned to foliage plants, were the nearly black-leaved *Perilla nankingense*, and the silver-leaved centaureas, *ragusina* and *rutifolia* (usually referred to as *candidissima* in contemporary writings). Exceptionally dark-leaved beetroots were also used, while variegated kales were employed to embellish the beds during the winter and early spring. Variegated ornamental grasses also made their appearance. A whole new race of zonal pelargoniums was bred, principally by a Mr Kinghorn to start with, and these were the variegated-leaved zonals of which 'Mrs Pollock' was the first great success. This was a golden-leaved plant, but there were others with white edges or creamy edges and, later, very dark-leaved cvs were produced.

In 1867 Hendersons offered the golden-leaved fuchsia 'Golden Fleece', which was highly recommended for planting *en masse*, but which does not seem to have been maintained for long. The ivy-leaved geraniums also made an appearance at this stage with the variegated 'L'elegante' which remains in cultivation to this day. By the mid-1860s the tricolor geraniums were being bred with great enthusiasm; I rather regret that the golden zonal raised by Messrs F. & A. Smith, which they called 'Pet of the Parterre', was not one of their more successful, as it is a name one would like to have seen preserved.

The interest in ornamental foliage was of more significance than seems to have been realised, and our present cult of ornamental-leaved house plants must derive from this reaction against the excessive brilliance of the flower bed, as well as encouraging at the time the collection and propagation of plants with variegated leaves. The main supplier of these plants was J. Salter of the Versailles nursery at Hammersmith in London; a man who was always prepared to back his own judgement, which eventually he found justified both in his enthusiasm for variegated leaves and in his growing of the large Japanese decorative chrysanthemums, which, on their first introduction, were regarded as far too irregular for a show flower. It was not only variegated plants that were used in bedding; silver-leaved plants such as *Antennaria dioica, Artemisia nutans* (or, perhaps *A. arborescens*, it is not quite clear to what *A. argentea*, as it was contemporarily called, refers), and later *Cerastium tomentosum* and the santolinas were brought in.

In all these cases it was the colour of the leaves which provided the attraction, but in the next development of bedding, the sub-tropical bedding, it was the size of the leaves that seem to have been of the greatest importance. According to Karl Prosper, writing in the *Floral World* for 1867, the main credit for this form of gardening should go to the French. In England its greatest manifestation was in Battersea Park, which was under the direction of that rather important figure, John Gibson. It was he whom Paxton and the Duke of Devonshire had sent to India in 1837 with the main object of bringing back *Amherstia nobilis* for the great conservatory at Chatsworth, but who was also responsible for introducing a large number of greenhouse plants ranging from *Rhododendron formosum* to various orchids, mainly collected in the Khasia hills. He was thus highly skilled in the management of sub-tropical subjects, and this form of gardening again brought into general cultivation a number of obscure subjects. Thus in the articles by Karl Prosper (who was this gentleman?) there are suggested six species of solanum, *SS. giganteum, auriculatum, marginatum, pyracanthum* and *robustum*, as well as a *S. amazonicum*, of which I can find no record, but which he says is 'a fine species of rather small growth, the leaves bronzed on the upper side and silvery on the underside. The flowers are large and handsome, and are abundantly produced in the open air.' The plant from his list which one would most like to see is *S. pyracanthum*, with its 'very elegant pinnate leaves with orange-coloured midrib and fiery red spines. The flowers are bright blue. It grows well when planted out, and is one of the most striking of sub-tropical plants in cultivation.' But, the plant for which he had the greatest enthusiasm was *Wigandia caracasana*, a plant which, I suspect, few of us nowadays have ever seen. Since the plants are covered with stinging hairs, the reluctance of growers to produce it is not, perhaps, surprising, although I see seeds of the equally stinging loasas are still available. The wigandia has large heads of rather small lilac and white flowers, but it was grown entirely on account of its leaves, which according to Karl Prosper, were of a 'sombre green, boldly veined and undulated, and measure two to three feet in length and breadth'. The Royal Horticultural Society's *Dictionary* gives more moderate dimensions of eighteen inches long and fifteen wide.

It was the sub-tropical garden which started the canna on its road to popularity and the hybrids of Anné, who was the first to interbreed these plants, were all directed towards producing large plants with huge leaves. It was only later that breeders turned their attention to the flowers and it was as foliage plants that they were chiefly grown, although they used to grow *Canna limbata* permanently, covering the beds with two feet of straw during the winter, so that the plants produced flowers after growing six or more feet high.

An unexpected plant to find in this list is daubentonia, now known as sesbania. Of these Prosper writes: 'The plants do not flower freely till they acquire some age; therefore much must not be expected the first season when raised from seeds. They are usually classed in catalogues as stove shrubs, but it is one more proof of the small reliance we can place upon these would-be authoritative documents, that all the species grow freely in the open ground if planted out at the end of May, and all may be wintered in ordinary greenhouse temperature with perfect safety; then, of course, they must be kept rather dry.' Sesbanias are leguminous shrubs with pinnate leaves and scarlet or orange flowers.

Prosper's main recommendations, apart from the foregoing, were giant nicotiana and the various forms of *Ricinus communis*, which all received specific names in those days. The nicotiana which he most recommended was *Nicotiana wigandioides*, growing six to ten feet high, 'with leaves over two feet long and one foot wide. The young leaves are beautifully silvered.'

M   185

In 1868 the *Floral World* examined the lists of various seedsmen to see who offered the best selection of plants for sub-tropical bedding and awarded the palm to Rollisson's of Tooting, whose list they reproduced. This included the following plants: *Cannabis gigantea* (which they couldn't get away with nowadays), five species of datura, a number of unrecognisable nicotiana species, named mainly from their native habitats (as, for example, *N. ohio* and *N. porto rico*), thirteen species of solanum, and a plant called *Ferdinanda eminens*, which is apparently now known as *Podachaenium eminens*. Judging from the Royal Horticultural Society's *Dictionary* they must in reality have had *P. andinum*, which, they say, is recommended for sub-tropical bedding. Both the plants are shrubby composites with very large leaves and heads of rather small white flowers; again the main interest was in the foliage. The sub-tropical bedding would also include caladiums.

It was about this time that J. G. Veitch returned from his collecting trip to the Melanesian Islands, which brought back a number of variants of *Codiaeum pictum* and various coloured forms of *Cordyline terminalis*. There was thus an interesting synchronicity in the attraction of ornamental foliage with a big influx of variegated plants from Japan, the coloured leaves of Veitch's introductions, and the sudden interest in sub-tropical bedding. This interest in handsome foliage has been revived, after lapsing somewhat, in the present-day fascination with ornamental foliage, principally for growing in the home, and this interest is now spreading to include plants in the garden. It is by no means unusual now for people to plant trees and shrubs for their attractive foliage and this need not necessarily be coloured. There has always been an interest in purple-leaved trees and in such brilliant plants as *Pieris forrestii* or *Acer pseudo-platanus* 'Brilliantissimum', but nowadays people will also readily plant such things as gleditsichas and *Gymnocladus dioicus*, for the sake of the graceful foliage of the first and the huge impressive leaves of the second. This must be recognised as a modern revival of the spirit of 1866; although some aspects have altered, the basic interest remains the same.

Of the plants grown then, very few are available today. I have looked at our most extensive seed catalogue and I find only *N. sylvestris*, perilla, ricinus. The only wigandia is *W. urens*, which Prosper thought was inferior to *W. caracasana*; but *Sesbania punicea* is still available. Incidentally, on looking again at Rollisson's list I see two plants of the genus paratropia; this turns out to be schefflera and it is surprising that they were in general cultivation so early. One of these was the Indian *S. venulosa*, while the other, which Rollisson called *tomentosa farina*, could have been the Javanese *S. polybotrys*, which was introduced in 1860. If it was not that, I cannot think what it was. They were both described as 'very handsome foliage plants'. One does see from time to time some of the large-leafed solanums, so seed must still be available, even if not commercially. The only canna species left in cultivation, so far as I know, is *C. iridiflora*, the hybrids having driven out all the other species.

It can be convincingly argued that the bedding craze, whatever lunacess it may have led to, had an extremely beneficent result in the promotion of a wide range of plants, in encouraging the breeding of plants that would be suitable for this scheme, and in directing the interest of the eye away from flowers and towards foliage. Incidentally, one of its defenders, when it was under sustained attack, pointed out that it could not have been only for its garish colours that bedding was admired, as the bedding craze coincided with the fern craze; so that part of the garden was very brilliant, while other parts were devoid of flowers but filled with attractive foliage. Since the fern enthusiasts were chiefly interested in atypical forms of their various plants, I have never been able to register much enthusiasm for many of their collectings. Who, I ask myself rather stupidly, can want a pinnate Hart's Tongue, or a depauperate Male Fern; the answer must be that a large number of people did. I am all for growing ferns, but do not see why so much importance was paid to the freaks.

The most convincing argument against bedding was its expense. Behind the fine shows lay a battery of hot-houses and frames and it was obvious that if any substitute for the bedding plants could be supplied which did not need this background of hot-houses, the hardy bedder was almost sure to take its place. There were two main arguments levelled against bedding. First, that the beds were completely bare until the end of May, and secondly the expense. The first objection was quickly overcome by the introduction of spring bedding, in which the beds would be filled with dwarf plants, such as polyanthus or forget-me-not, through which bulbs such as daffodils or tulips would emerge. Suitable daffodils were not available before the 1870s and the tulips, though available, were little regarded as bedding plants, as they were florists' flowers and uniformity was not encouraged. It was not until 1899 that the Darwin tulips were offered as a good plant. Before that there were numerous tulips called breeders, but these were usually kept until the virus that causes flaking made its appearance and no one would have thought of planting out the self-coloured ones. The one bedding bulb that is the same today as it was then is the hyacinth and this was the bulb most frequently used for spring bedding.

Spring plus summer bedding would give a display for nearly nine months, but it was very expensive and, as so often, it was economic factors that were the bedding plants' chief enemy. Nowadays it is mainly the public authorities who maintain bedding in the old way; in private gardens the bedding plants tend to have yielded to the hybrid tea rose. Indeed, once a dwarf ever-flowering hardy plant had been bred, the bedding principle could be applied with plants that could be left *in situ* for year after year, and the hybrid tea rose fitted this category admirably, although in recent years it has tended to be supplanted by the even more floriferous floribundas. This secured bedding from the complaint of expense, although it still left the beds looking flowerless from December until June.

In the early days people used to fill the interstices with bulbs and spring bedding, but this was found to interfere with the proper management of the roses and is now rarely seen. This does mean that the beds are pretty dreary for six months out of the twelve. Fortunately, there is a wide range of colours available, so that the monotony, which at one time threatened to be a serious argument against too extensive use of the rose, no longer supervenes. For this we must thank M. Pernet, who bred *Rose foetida*, with its yellow and flame colours, into the tea rose and greatly extended its colour range, although he also made it more disease-prone. The hybrid tea rose balanced rather uneasily between being a bedding plant and a florist's flower, but the introduction of the polyantha rose into the strain has given us the floribunda, which is a bedding plant pure and simple for the most part, although a few, such as the 'Queen Elizabeth', have proved too vigorous for this work. So where the Victorians had an enormous selection of bedding plants, we only have one. It is a plant of enormous popularity.

I do not think any Victorian nurseryman could have survived by only growing one flower, no matter how many varieties had been bred, but it seems to be quite easy for a nurseryman nowadays to be a rose-grower and nothing else. I suppose the craze will wear itself out in time, as other gardening crazes have done, but it has persisted for longer than most. What does seem to be trickling through the consciousness of the breeders is the fact that the old hybrid tea, while looking very attractive when half-opened, tends to turn into an amorphous mass of petals when fully expanded. The old roses bred before the introduction of the tea rose, R. gigantea, would open out into a handsome shape, and I note that some modern breeders are using these older roses to bring shape into the open flowers of the hybrid teas and floribundas. There has also been a great revival of the pre-China roses, in spite of the fact that they make sizable shrubs and only flower the one time in the year. I suppose if we wait long enough, the single rose will come back into favour and the plant will once more look like a real flower and not like the great cabbagey blob that so many modern roses present to our view. Like so many other plants the rose fell into the error of becoming far too large, so that the flowers were out of all proportion to the size of the plant and people of refined taste (amongst whom, to my great surprise, I found myself for nearly the first time in my life) turned against it.

FLORISTS' FLOWERS

In one of his 'Masters' Lectures' to the Royal Horticultural Society, Dr W. T. Stearn noted that most florists' flowers were designed to imitate either a plate or a mop. I think he should also have included the cup, which dictated the shape of the ideal tulip, but the fact is basically correct and, of the two household implements, the plate was the most popular. I can think of another characteristic of the florist's flower and that is that it is extremely difficult to mix it in with any other flower. Even that oldest of all florist's flowers, the Tree paeony, which has been in cultivation for over a thousand years, is by no means easy to place in the garden, unless it is given a compartment of its own. No one could imagine a show auricula out of a pot, the carnations are such graceless plants that they could only be grown for their flowers, the few florists' tulips that have survived could scarcely show to much advantage in a collection of mixed bulbs; the laced pink, although attractive enough, fails to give of its best except in isolation. Even flowers which will mingle happily enough with other plants, such as ranunculus and polyanthus, would look rather strange in their floristic manifestations.

In fact the real interest of the florist's flower was entirely in the flower, which had to conform to a set of extremely artificial rules. Most of the florists' flowers have now vanished, although there still survive a number of auricula enthusiasts and the Scottish Show Pansy Society certainly existed quite recently. If we look at old paintings of these flowers we must feel that, in spite of their extreme artificiality, we have lost something by their disappearance, and the loss seems the more extreme when we realise that their cultivation was extremely widespread, with, however, a distinct working-class preponderance. The most famous of the florists' societies was that started in Paisley in 1782, but they flourished in most industrial towns. They were more or less all crushed by the Industrial Revolution.

In his attractive *The Victorian Flower Garden* Geoffrey Taylor quotes from the *Horticultural Magazine* for September 1846: 'Those who look upon the thousand of houses which now cover the space that used to boast of the gaudy tulip beds of hundreds of working men, would scarcely think it possible to have made so great a change. There are many small gardens, even now, in the Mile End Road, with their canvas houses looking, in the season, like an encampment, which are doomed at no short distance of time to give place to brick and mortar dwellings . . . unless something be done to provide the mechanic with means of indulging the practice of Floriculture, he will have recourse to the public-house and the skittle ground for less healthy amusements.' Prophetic words, we may well feel. In *The Garden* for 27 May 1882 a Mr W. Brockbank wrote an affectionate obituary for one of the last of these mechanics.

'On Friday afternoon, the 5th inst., a procession of about fifty persons, mostly florists, and wearing flowers in their button-holes, and a few women relatives, who carried two wreaths of white flowers interspersed with fine trusses of Auriculas and Polyanthuses, followed the remains of Tom Mellor to the graveyard at Christ's Church, Ashton-under-Lyne. After the coffin was lowered into its resting place, flowers were strewn upon it by loving hands, quite covering it over. Such was a florist's funeral. Tom Mellor was respected by everyone and beloved by many; he may be said to have died among his flowers. He had long been ailing and the physicians wished him to go into the infirmary a fortnight before he died, as they hoped his life might be prolonged by an operation; but Tom declined to follow their advice. He felt sure that he would never leave the infirmary alive, if once he entered it. The Auricula Show was at hand. He had a lot of pot plants in preparation for it; and amongst these a fine "John Simonite", which he hoped might win the premier prize, and he said: "If I die, I shall die amongst my flowers; if I live I mean to be at the show."

Thomas Mellor was born in Ashton-under-Lyne in 1826. His taste for flowers was acquired in early life, through an acquaintance with S. Fish, a noted auricula-grower, and he was encouraged to begin on his own account by the late W. Chadwick of Dukinfield, who started him off with a number of auriculas, amongst which were six or seven good sorts. His garden was on the Moor, about a mile distant from his home, and here he gradually extended his operations, by preparing home-made frames and simple erections for wintering his plants. These florists' gardens are quaint places, some of which would form capital subjects for a painter, and Mellor's was of this class.

Mr Prescott of Leigh advised him never to buy any plants but what he could win with. 'Have none of their second-rate stuff, Tom,' he used to say. 'Have summat that'll win or it will be o' no use to thee.' This advice Mellor followed, and to obtain a good plant he would travel far and wait patiently. One of his favourite auriculas was Walker's 'John Simonite', and for this plant he went to the raiser's house at Sheffield many times. Mr Walker had promised him a plant a long while before he got it, as this famous auricula passed through many vicissitudes and was for a time nearly lost by its raiser. At last, however,

Tom got his plant and was so successful in its culture that he was able to raise and sell a good many from it. It was this very auricula that he was so anxious to show at Manchester, and if he had been in good health it would in all probability have carried off to its owner the premier prize for the second time. He won the premier prize in 1880 with a grand plant of 'Alexander Meiklejohn'. He was so proud of this that he had a beautiful water-coloured drawing of it made by a pattern designer and it formed the chief ornament of his parlour. He was very successful in raising new varieties. His seedling 'Lord Salisbury', a very fine maroon self, received a first-class certificate in London in 1880; his white-edged 'Reliance' received a first-class certificate at Manchester the same year and is one of the very best of its class. He has left behind him a large number of very fine seedlings, which have not yet been shown, but which are of the highest quality, and it was for these he was so anxious to attend the Manchester show.

As a tulip-grower, Mellor was quite as famous. He acquired his early knowledge of tulips from S. Cock, who started him with a few bulbs and taught him how to manage them. The late Benjamin Haigh, another leading tulip-grower, lent him friendly help, and he was thus trained in a good school and soon made his mark. He won his maiden prize in 1856, and thenceforward became a regular and very successful exhibitor.

In pinks and carnations also he was a noted grower. His maiden prize for pinks was won in 1852 at the great South Lancashire Pink Show, and from that time he became an ardent supporter and exhibitor at all our local shows, frequently acting as steward. He was a successful raiser of seedling pinks, his 'Reliance' (purple-laced) and 'Bertha' (red-laced) being especially good. In July 1855 he was first at Macclesfield with 'Black-eyed Susan' (purple-laced). He had a special liking for this simple flower, and told many good anecdotes about it. One of his axioms was that if his pinks were good, others would be good also; and if his were poor, it might be the same with those of his competitors; and he used to illustrate this by practical instances. One year when the shows were coming on he could only find thirteen decent flowers upon the whole of his stock of pinks. He took them home to dress them and had no sooner begun than he thought the whole lot not worth taking to the show, and so he threw them in the window bottom and left them there lying in full sunlight for about three hours. Happening again to cast his eyes upon them whilst busy at shoe-making, he thought, 'Well, if I dunnut tak 'em to th' show, I'se miss an out.' So he took them up again and was surprised to find them improved by their rough treatment. He dressed them and took them to the Rochdale show, where they won three prizes. Next day he took the same despised flowers to the Oldham show, where they won six prizes out of the thirteen.

In polyanthuses also Mellor was a capital judge and grower. He had some excellent seedlings, amongst which his red ground 'Prince Rupert' received a first prize in 1880 at Manchester, and a black ground seedling won in its class at the show this year. Several other seedlings left behind are of sterling quality. The secret of that lost polyanthus 'Kingfisher', has gone with Mellor, as he alone knew where this famous old flower was to be found, and this knowledge he does not seem to have imparted to any of his friends.

Some curious old hardy plants were amongst his treasures. He had the old double white rocket, the white variety of the American cowslip (dodecatheon), a lovely grey-blue fritillary, a grand lot of *Narcissus horsfieldi* obtained from old John Horsfield himself, a huge variety of the common dandelion, which grew nearly two feet high and which was indeed a glorious flower, and lots of old-fashioned plants of every sort. His garden was a meeting ground for florists in the blooming season, and in it his happiest hours were spent.

I don't know about the reader, but this leaves me profoundly depressed; not for Tom Mellor, who seems to have lived a happy and productive life, but in contemplating the comparison between what was available for the intelligent florist then and what is available today. The debit side of the industrial revolution seems to grow even greater the more one examines it. It is, however, true that the spirit that encouraged the old florists is not entirely dead. Many a man tills his allotment with as much success as his forbears did, but he has only the satisfaction of doing it well. Local flower shows, which are mainly rural, may encourage the vegetable-grower, but the grower of flowers will get few rewards of a substantial nature. Tom Mellor, when he grew his auriculas, could sell plants of the prize-winners for quite considerable sums, and augment his income as well as obtaining prizes, but that source of pocket money has dried up. I suppose the nearest approach to a florist's flower that we have nowadays is the incurved chrysanthemum, but success here is entirely a matter of culture and presentation; no one is raising his own chrysanthemums.

Quite apart from the strict requirements laid down as to form and colour, which we shall examine shortly, the florists' flower had to be hardy (or nearly so, the ranunculus must have needed some protection), easily raised from seed, and flower reasonably soon after sowing; the plants also had to be reasonably cheap. The exception to most of these conditions was the tulip, which could not be grown quickly from seed, while good tulips were expensive. On the other hand, the self-coloured tulips, the so-called breeders, were reasonably cheap and it was with these that the impecunious tulip-grower would start.

There was a certain amount of old wives' lore attached to these breeder tulips and a number of expedients were suggested to encourage them to 'break'. 'Breaking' meant that the plain ground colour became variegated with streaks and stripes, and we now know that this variegation is caused by the action of a virus. The virus does not appear to be particularly malign in its effects as a few such tulips, of which probably 'Zomerschoon' is the best known, are still in cultivation after several centuries. Since this 'feathering', as it was termed, had to conform to a set of rigid rules, the production of a really good tulip was far less liable to occur than practically any other florist's flower, and prices were correspondingly high. Florists' flowers could only be propagated by offsets or cuttings, so that in effect they were all clones.

So far as the tulip went, the conditions required were that 'the stem should be strong, elastic and erect and about thirty inches above the surface of the bed. The flower should be large, and composed of six petals: these should proceed a little horizontally at first, and then turn upwards, forming almost a perfect cup, with a round bottom, rather wider at the top. The three exterior petals should be rather larger than the three interior ones, and broader at their base: all the petals should have perfectly entire edges, free from notch or serrature; the top of each should be broad and well rounded, the ground colour of the flower at the bottom of the cup should be clear white or yellow, and the various rich-coloured stripes, which are the principal ornaments of a fine tulip, should be regular, bold and distinct on the margin, and terminate in fine broken points, elegantly feathered or pencilled. The centre of each petal should contain one or more bold blotches or stripes, intermixed with small portions of the original breeder colour, abruptly broken into many irregular obtuse points. Some florists are of the opinion that the central stripes or blotches do not contribute to the beauty and elegance of the tulip, unless confined to a narrow stripe exactly down the centre, and that it should be perfectly free from any remains of the original, or breeder, colour: it is certain that such appear very beautiful and delicate, especially when they have a regular narrow feathering at the edge; but the greatest connoisseurs of this flower unanimously agree that it denotes superior merit when the tulip abounds with rich colouring, distributed in a distinct and regular manner throughout the flower, excepting in the bottom of the cup, which, it cannot be disputed, should be a clear bright white or yellow, free from stain or tinge, in order to constitute a perfect flower.'

This is quoted by Phillips in his *Flora Historica*, I suspect from Maddock. Only a few years later the requirements were more stringent. 'I consider,' wrote Mr Groom, an authority on this flower, 'a fine rich sharp feather, as it is termed, commencing on the edge of the lower part of the petals, a short distance from the stamina, and continuing round the top, where it should be deepest, to the other side, with each petal alike, and leaving the remainder of the flower of the clear ground colour, without any spots or specks, as the most perfect and beautiful character.' This comes from an article published in 1842. From this too we learn that plants with a yellow bottom were termed bizarres, with a white bottom and a pink ground colour they were roses, with a white bottom and some other ground colour they were byblomens. This comes from the introduction to 'A Descriptive Catalogue of Tulips' in the *Floricultural Cabinet* for that year. The best plant of those years was apparently 'Polyphemus', 'a flamed Bizarre, raised from seed by the late Mr Clark, and broke by the late Mr Lawrecce of Hampton, who sold four bulbs for £50 after it had been broken three years, although it was well known that Mr Clark and his friends had roots in their possession.' The writer, a Mr John Slater, gives some fascinating information about prices. There appear to have been two plants both called 'Pompe Funebre' which was a 'flamed bizarre, cup rather long, bottom pure, and the outside colour a bright lemon colour, and its broad, almost black feathering causes it to rank higher than any other of the same class.' There was a new form introduced in 1780, which sold at five guineas, while the original sold at eight. In 1772 the original cost £20, as we saw in 1780 the price had fallen to eight guineas, but in 1783 it had gone up again to £15, while the new one had fallen to £6. Apparently 'Pompe funebre' was very sparing in its production of offshoots and so maintained a high price.

Most of the other florists' flowers could be raised at less expense. The one whose disappearance I most regret was the ranunculus. Of this, the tolerant Phillips writes: 'The Ranunculus varies in its colours even more than the Tulip, running from a black down to white through all the shades of reds, yellows, browns, and, indeed, all colours excepting blue may be found in these gaily-painted flowers, the criterion of whose perfection is, that they should produce a strong stem, not less in height than from eight inches to a foot, and that they should bear a flower, at least two inches in diameter, well filled with concave petals, that diminish in size as they approach the centre. The corolla should be of hemispherical form; its component petals should be imbricated in such a manner as neither to be too close and compact, nor too widely separated, but have rather more of a perpendicular than horizontal direction to display their colours with better effect. The petals should be broad, and quite free from fringe or indentures at the edges: the beauty of their colouring consists in their being dark, clear, rich, or brilliant; either of one regular colour throughout, or otherwise variously diversified, on white, ash, pale yellow, gold, or fire-coloured ground, either in regular stripes or spots or marble-mottled.'

The mottled ranunculus sounds rather as though we were back with a virus, although, since none of them have survived, this must remain a matter of theory. The spotted and edged varieties were, to judge from contemporary illustrations, of the greatest beauty; the edged ones were like the picotee carnations, while the dots were applied very sparingly over the ground colour and arranged with great symmetry, so that the total effect was extremely artificial. One wonders how the plants could be propagated, once a good form was found. Phillips says that they were propagated by 'dividing the tubers, or by offsets from the tubers' and that 'by this means they will retain all their original character for more than twenty years'. It was customary to grow them in an exceedingly rich compost, so doubtless offshoots were produced, although this seems to happen rarely with the normal forms of *Ranunculus asiaticus* now in cultivation.

The florist's ranunculus was completely double, both stamens and carpels having become petaloid and these were obtained by taking seed from semi-double flowers and then hoping for a perfect bloom eventually to appear among the seedlings. Ranunculus were grown as dahlias are now, lifting the tubers and storing them through the winter. They were usually planted out at the end of February. There were certainly a large variety of colours available. I have in front of me a bulb list of Henry Groom for 1837, which lists something like four hundred named ranunculus, arranged according to colour or combinations of colour. Among the colours listed which we cannot parallel nowadays are black, dark purple, light purple, grey and olive. Compared with the best tulips they were not very expensive. The tulip 'Nourri Effendi' cost £100, but this was exceptional; there were, however, quite a few at prices ranging from £5 to £15 per bulb. Among the ranunculus there were a very few at a guinea per plant, but there were a lot costing only a shilling, which does suggest that they must have been quite easy to propagate clonally. One plant, presumably a pure white, called 'Talisman' cost £2 a plant, but this was easily the most expensive, while if you wished to raise your own plants, you could buy 'semi-doubles for seed' at five shillings the hundred. Well they have all gone now, but nothing has replaced them. We are just that much worse off.

On the other hand, we still have the polyanthus, and even some of the old florists' kinds have survived. One of the odd requirements of florists' primulas, both polyanthus and auricula, was that only thrum-eyed flowers were considered admissible; pin-eyes were immediately rejected for show purposes. The qualities of the polyanthus were, according to Phillips: 'The stem of a perfect flower must be strong, erect and elastic, and of sufficient height to support the umbel . . . of flowers above the puckered foliage of the plant. The footstalks of each separate flower should also be strong and elastic, and of a length proportioned to the size and quantity of the pips; which should not be less than seven in number, that the bunch may be round, close and compact.

Maddox says: 'The tube of the corolla above the calyx should be short, well filled with the anthers, or summits of the stamens, and terminate fluted, rather above the eye. The eye should be round, of a bright clear yellow, and distinct from the ground colour; the proportions of a fine flower are, that the diameter of the tube be one part, the eye three, and the whole pip six or nearly so. The ground colour is most admired when shaded with a light and dark rich crimson, resembling velvet, with one mark or stripe in the centre of each division of the limb, bold and distinct from the edging down to the eye, where it should terminate in a fine point. The pips should be large, quite flat, and as round as may be consistent with their peculiar beautiful figure, which is circular, excepting those small indentures between each division of the limb, which divide it into five heart-like segments. The edging should resemble a bright gold hue, bold, clear and distinct, and so nearly of the same colour as the eye and stripes as scarcely to be distinguished; in short the polyanthus should possess a graceful elegance of form, a richness of colouring and symmetry of parts not to be found united in any other flower.'

Presumably the rules must have been relaxed or Mellor could never have won a prize with his black ground polyanthus, but although the ground colour could vary and the central stripe was no longer *de rigeur*, the rules remained fairly strict. What, I wonder, was that legendary 'Kingfisher'? Could it have been an early blue polyanthus? So far as we know the blue primroses and polyanthus did not arrive until early in this century, but it is conceivable that an odd one or two appeared earlier and were not preserved.

Let us end this section with another mystery plant, the balsam, *Impatiens balsamina*. According to H. L. Li in his *The Garden Flowers of China*, the plant is a native of India. It was introduced into China a very long time ago and was there developed as a garden plant 'with much variation of the colour, size and doubling of the flowers'. It would seem probable that the plant arrived around the seventh century AD. It was certainly in cultivation in Europe in 1564 when Turner figured and described it and Parkinson, a century later, says that 'we have always had the seed of this plant sent us out of Italie, not knowing his original place'. It is tempting, given its early introduction from the far east, and its apparent centre of cultivation in Italy, to ascribe its introduction to Marco Polo, although this would presume a longer period of cultivation in the west than can be substantiated. Still it is curious that this, of all the eastern exotics, should have come so early into cultivation and there remained.

The plant is only half-hardy in Britain and northern Europe generally and is not outstandingly ornamental; although it would seem that we do not grow it nowadays as was done in the early nineteenth century, when a Mr Fairweather described plants 'four feet in height and fifteen feet in circumference, furnished with side branches from bottom to top, and these covered with large double flowers'. Moreover, the invaluable Phillips says: 'We have frequently observed the balsam in the gardens of Paris having more the appearance of a brilliant flowering shrub than an annual plant, ornamenting the quarters of the royal gardens of the Tuileries and the Luxemburg by its petals of scarlet, crimson, brick-red, purple, white, variegated, parti-coloured or delicate blush, this last variety frequently being as double and nearly as large as a moderate Rose, and the whole plant covered with flowers, resembling by their transparent nature a shrub formed of the most delicate porcelain.' How it got to Europe so early must remain a mystery. It is certainly the longest cultivated exotic annual plant.

17

THE ALPINE DEPARTMENT

According to that enthusiastic alpinist Henri Correvon, the first alpine garden was established by the great botanist Pierre Boissier in Geneva. Boissier lived from 1810 to 1885, but we do not know when he established his alpine garden. In any case it could not have been the first. In 1775 two doctors, John Fothergill and a Dr Pitcairn, jointly sponsored an expedition to send Thomas Blaikie to the Alps to collect plants. We have Blaikie's diary of this expedition and we know that he brought back 440 items (not all different species of course), including some difficult plants such as *Artemisia genipi, Viola cenisia, Gentiana ciliata, Phyteuma pauciflora, Saxifraga biflora, androsacea* and *caespitosa, Moneses uniflora* and *Traunsteinera globosa,* as well as some more easily cultivated plants. We do not know how these plants were treated after they were received, but 1776 must surely stand as the year of the first alpine garden.

It is a commonplace nowadays that high alpines are not easy to cultivate at lower levels, and a number of theories were propounded to account for this, mostly based on observations in the mountains. At the same time the rock garden was being developed. A rock garden was by no means the same as an alpine garden. It was often termed a rockery, in the same way that other parts of the garden were termed a fernery or a mossery (a form of gardening that has never caught on; presumably it is too difficult to establish the mosses). In a rockery the interest was in the rocks themselves; it was a sort of Victorian japonaiserie, although there seems no reason to suppose that there could have been any conscious imitation; few Europeans could have visited Japan before 1860. Since, however, most mountains are rocky it soon became natural to associate the rocks with mountain plants, with some very curious results, as we shall shortly see. Indeed, for some time it was regarded as impossible to grow alpines without rocks and the alpine garden and the rock garden became synonymous, although originally they had been quite distinct.

In 1868 Hibberd had recommended raised beds for the cultivation of alpines and in recent years this has become the more usual way of growing these plants. The main reason for this is economic: large rocks were never particularly cheap, even in the 1870s when the rock-alpine garden started on its most popular reign. This cult probably stemmed from the famous rock garden constructed by Messrs Backhouse & Son at York, where such intractable subjects as *Eritrichium nanum* and the Aretian androsaces were cultivated with success even out of doors, and a special cave was constructed for plants such as filmy ferns.

Still, as we have mentioned, rocks were expensive, not so much in their actual purchase, as in the freight and the subsequent labour. Nowadays few people can afford many tons of rocks, so their presence in gardens far from any rocky outcrops is out of the question for most gardeners. Moreover, it has been found that rocks are not essential for the majority of alpine plants; there are some saxatile species, which will not grow very easily away from rock crevices, and some plants such as the ramondas which grow best if placed in a vertical plane; these latter can easily be accommodated in the walls of the raised bed. Saxatile plants can be accommodated in lumps of tufa, provided that this rock is obtainable. Tufa is extremely soft, so that there is no trouble in drilling a small hole and inserting a young plant. It is also soft and spongy, so that it absorbs water, while the roots can penetrate it and eventually emerge into a fairly rich compost. The raised bed also has the advantage that it is easier to keep weeded; one does not have to stoop so low, which makes it admirable for gardeners of advancing age.

The only real objection to the raised bed is that it does not look very attractive. Still, if we are honest (which most of us will find difficult, we have been conditioned for so long to think the contrary), even the best constructed rock garden really looks rather silly. If one lives on a mountain side, one can perhaps get away with it, but otherwise the sudden appearance of rocky outcrops in a rockless landscape and the appearance of gorges or hillocks in an otherwise flat landscape is really pretty ludicrous. The interest of the alpine garden lies entirely in the plants grown therein, rather than in any intrinsic features of its own.

It is not by accident that I am discussing the alpine garden directly after the florists' flowers, as the attitudes are not so dissimilar. It is true that the florist's flower was highly artificial, while hybrids would be looked at rather dubiously by the alpine purist; but the aim of the florist was the perfect flower, while the aim of the alpinist is the perfect plant. Each item in a good alpine garden is considered on its own. The plant should be well grown, what the grower calls 'in character' (which means that it should look like a good wild plant, not a larger and cultivated-looking plant), and well flowered. Where to plant your alpine will depend on the particular microclimate at any point in the alpine garden, and if this means that a blue plant and a magenta one have to appear side by side, this will have to be done regardless of any aesthetic considerations. This may have been one of the reasons that made almost every writer say that the rock garden should be sited away from the house and, preferably, in a secluded situation; although the main reason was the informality of the alpine garden, which was thought to be inappropriate too near the formality of the house. The alpine garden is really the plantsman's property entirely. No one nowadays would put in raised beds or even a rock garden unless they wanted to grow alpines, and once you start on this slippery slope you are not liable to be satisfied for long with aubrieta, mossy saxifrages and *Campanula portenschlagiana*.

Alpine plants tend to induce a certain feverishness amongst authors, when they treat the subject. Here is a passage from the introduction to William Robinson's early book, *Alpine Plants for Gardens*. Robinson was normally a sober and pedestrian writer but show him a mountain valley and we get: 'If the conditions of plant life in our islands are so varied, how are those of the Alps? In no part of the earth are they so wondrously varied, severe, and even terrible. Valleys that would tempt young goddesses to gather flowers, and valleys flanked with cliffs fit to guard the River of Death; beautiful forest shade for woodland flowers, and vast prairies without a tree, yet paved with Gentians; sunburnt slopes and chilly gorges; mountain copses with shade and shelter for the taller plants and uplands with large areas of plants withered up, owing to the snow lying more than a year . . . Lakes and pools at every elevation, torrents, streams splashing from snowy peaks; pools, bogs and spring-fed rills at every altitude; long melting snow-fields, giving the plants imprisoned below them their freedom at different times, and so leading to a succession of alpine flower life.'

Reginald Farrer seems to have got the reputation for being excessively ornate in his descriptions of alpines, but I don't think people who make this claim can have read him very carefully; his descriptions are usually accurate, expressed without hyperbole, but with an amount of witty similes and metaphores. Here, for example, he is on *Androsace glacialis*: 'As for *A. glacialis*, the first sight of it is an epoch in one's life. You have got high, high up towards the glacier, far above the stretches of *Arnica* and *Gentiana acaulis* and *Viola calcarata*. You have trampled lawns of *Aster alpinus* and grey-flannelette Edelweiss and now the last vestiges of grass are disappearing . . . As you wander on in expectation, suddenly, under your very boot, lies a mass of pink. No leaves are visible, nothing but a mat of pure soft rose-pink—a yard across perhaps. It is *A. glacialis*. Nothing so beautiful could the unaided mind imagine. Its colour is so pure, its profuseness of blossom so amazingly generous, not to say prodigal. Unlike the other high alpines of its kindred, too, it is growing loosely, rooting compactly in mere wet *débris*—the easiest thing in the world to dig up adequately, all in a lump. So, think you, here is a glory for my garden,—this wonderful cheerful little person that is evidently as good-tempered as a daisy. You get it home. You plant it, you cosset it, you ultimately weep salt tears over it. Does it flower as it did, does it ramp as it should, as it promised to do? No such thing. It dwindles pines and languishes; if your culture is very fortunate you may have half a dozen pale sickly blossoms. No more. *A. glacialis* soon sulks itself into a better world.'

This quotation comes from *My Rock Garden*, which contains the famous similitudes of the rock gardens then in most vogue, as the Almond Pudding, the Dog's Grave and the Devil's Lapful. This tendency of writers on alpine gardens to destroy their forbears was commented on in 1871 by Hibberd in *The Amateur's Flower Garden*: opening his fourteenth chapter on 'The Rockery and Alpine Garden' (note that in those days they were still distinct), possibly with a thought of Robinson's book which had come out the previous year, he wrote:

'The course of procedure sanctioned by custom in the literary treatment of this subject consists in first destroying all existing rockeries everywhere by unqualified abuse, and then reconstructing them on the author's model, on the hypothesis that they do not exist to please their owners, but to illustrate the writer's theory of what a rockery should be.' Farrer, having followed to a certain extent in the prevailing custom, went on to say that there was only one rule that governs 'the ideal rockery'. 'Have an idea and stick to it. Let your rock garden set out to be something definite, not a mere agglomeration of stones . . . It is, in effect, an imitation of Nature, and, to be successful, must aim at reproducing with fidelity some particular feature of Nature.'

Some of the early rock gardens sound rather entertaining. Here is a description dating from 1837: 'The finest specimen of this kind of work which was ever, perhaps, executed, was laid out . . . for his Grace the Duke of Northumberland at Sion House. The imitation is, indeed, so complete, that when the back of the visitor is turned to the superb conservatory, he might almost fancy himself at the entrance of a Highland glen. The turf on the edge of this rock-work is in part studded with moss, while little knolls, which nobody would doubt being real ant-hills, are covered with wild thyme and harebells. The expense of this, however, must be enormous, as there are blocks of granite of several tons weight; and few amateurs, we think, would attempt to rival this. But when tastefully planned and well executed, rock-work may be made a very interesting feature of a flower garden. The following remarks on the subject from Chambers' *Edinburgh Journal* will give the reader some good hints, which he may adapt to circumstances and situation, should he be inclined to construct rock-work for flowers.

' "The rocky ravine, the mountain's brow, and the sea-beach are the most fertile sources of materials for a rockery; and it is necessary, in selecting them, to pay minute attention to the manner in which the various rocks are deposited in their several beds, and also to the mosses, heaths and ferns which are congenial to them; for, in proportion as the selector shall succeed in imitating nature, will he please his own eye, and gratify his friends. Having fixed on a quarter whence materials are to be procured, the next object is to find an intelligent workman, who may execute the charge entrusted to him with care. On this a good deal depends; and some pains should be taken to make him understand thoroughly what is wanted. The size of the stones should always be varied, but proportioned upon the whole to the intended size of the rock-work. A number of detached erections never look well; they are stiff and artificial. The whole should show an evident and well-defined connection; and, with regard to the stones, the greatest possible variety in form and size should be studied. The foundation should consist of mounds of earth, which answer the purpose as well as any more solid erection, and will make the stones go further. Rocks of the same kind and colour should be placed together; if intermix'd they seldom wear a natural appearance. A dark cave, penetrating into the thickest part of the erection, is not very difficult to construct, and, when encircled with ivy, and inhabited with a pair of horned owls, which may be easily procured, it will form a most interesting object. Rock plants of every description should be profusely stuck around, and, in one short twelve-month, the whole scene will exhibit an impress of antiquity far beyond anticipation ... Water in all cases adds greatly to the general effect ... By a simple expedient, streams of water may be made to issue from the rocks, or spout into the air and fall in beautiful cascades ... A pond, also, would permit the cultivation of native and foreign succulent [aquatic?] plants; and gold fish and perch might be introduced with a water-hen or two, and a few of the ducker species of sea-fowl." '

I think I should repeat that this was written in 1837. The article is followed by a list of recommended plants, which includes such things as *Campanula thyrsoidea, C. alpina, C. pulla, C. collina* and *C. saxatilis*, as well as better known species, *Achillea clavennae, Alyssum alpestre, Anemone (Pulsatilla) alpina, A. baldensis, Aquilegia alpina, A. pyrenaica, Arabis bellidifolia, Diapensia lapponica, Dianthus alpinus, D. petraeus, Hedysarum obscurum, Petrocallis pyrenaica* and numerous other plants as

well as some which cannot now be easily identified. I don't know if
this list surprises you; it certainly amazes me.

In 1866 the youthful William Robinson, then aged twenty-eight and
not yet much of an author, wrote an article in Hibberd's *Floral World*
on 'Rockwork and Rockwork Plants'. This includes a description of
the famous Backhouse garden at York, which lacks some precision but
is nevertheless informative: 'Nearly 500 tons of millstone grit were
employed in its formation, and the whole looks the facsimile of a
choicely selected bit of Wales or Cumberland. By making the huge
slabs and banks surround a little bit of water, every sort of aspect or nook
that could be desired for a plant is at hand, and thus plants the most
diverse in character are accommodated happily within a few feet of
each other: under the shade of the great stones by the water New
Zealand filmy ferns; a few feet higher up, natives of Arctic Europe;
and on the top, in the full sun and free air, the choicest gems of temperate parts of Europe and America.' Robinson observes that the firm
grew 'hundreds of the choicest alpines in the world; but it has been the
result of an expenditure which no other nurseryman would risk, and
of a knowledge of the natural habits of alpine vegetation on the part of
one of the firm, which few other botanists possess'.

This was obviously very impressive, but a hundred years after the
event one would rather have seen another garden described by Robinson: 'By far the most distinct and extraordinary rockwork I have ever
seen is one in a private garden near Chester . . . It is on a large scale,
though there are no colossal stones employed, as at Chatsworth and
York. In the first place large banks of earth were thrown up around a
pleasant garden, oblong in outline, and on the face of this great mound
were built imitations of the various alpine mountains known to the
noble lady, who had it made at great expense. Bays and evergreens are
clipped into conical shape here and there in spots to counterfeit conifers,
and low down where the rocky pathway winds in and out about "the
foot of the mountain" herbaceous vegetation predominates. A little
higher up in a valley are little Swiss cottages (acting also as beehives),
and then another turn round a corner covered with alpine shrubs and
bushes, to look up a deeply worn valley "snow-capped" (with spar)
and so on for several hundred feet. Altogether a very striking and re-

markable scene, which I had better say no more about, as it is very unlikely another of the same pattern may be made.'

Unlikely certainly, but the rock gardens at Sir Frank Crisp's garden at Friar Park, Henley, obviously had something in common with the noble lady's. This garden was described by Henry Correvon as probably the finest rock garden in England, if not in the world, while it, on the other hand, upset Reginald Farrer to such an extent, that in writing the introduction to E. A. Bowles's *My Garden in Spring* he spent most of his space fulminating against this rock garden and barely mentioned poor Mr Bowles. I extract the following information from the enchanting article by C. J. M. Adie in the *Alpine Garden Society Bulletin* for June 1949. There were, indeed, two rock gardens, an upper and a lower. 'The upper was a perfectly well constructed rock garden, built largely of cyclopean blocks and covered with a vast and varied collection of well grown alpines. To those not interested in the plants, its most striking feature was the white-washed concrete replica of the peak of the Matterhorn in miniature which dominated the whole; but, being made reasonably well to scale, it was not . . . intolerably obtrusive, though the idea may seem horrifying enough, especially to those who never saw it. A similar love of make-believe inspired the placing on a projecting rock, near the top, of half a dozen small animal figures, which, viewed through a telescope in the chalet at the bottom, turned out to be a Scurry (or whatever may be the correct noun of multitude) of chamois . . .

'To those who preferred the open air, the Shamrock garden could be reached by merely walking down the hill; but there was another way. The owner, with his love of the bizarre, would make you squeeze between two vertical monoliths near the top into a passage which descended steeply by a stairway into the bowels of the earth. It was lighted by electric light and was painted a greenish white: it had various grottoes, and other delights for the young leading off it and was a highly realistic reproduction of some elaborate igloo or ice cave. On arrival at ground level you found yourself in a large vault with a stream running through it. Here waited boats which brought you by an underground canal into the Shamrock garden.

'This lower garden, as its name implies, was wholly built of artificial rocks, so skilfully contrived that they might almost have taken in any but the trained geologist. They had begun as amorphous blocks of half-dried concrete. These had been shaped, given stratification marks, by scoring them with a piece of broken wood, brushed over with a stable brush to give them a striated and slightly roughened surface, dusted with sand and finished off with a spray of oxide of iron or some such pigment. When set they were ready for use and had the advantage of being made of a shape and size to meet the needs of the plan of construction, rather than, as too often happens, making that depend upon the materials to hand. The finished product looked remarkably like a rock garden.'

It may be felt that Sir Frank lacked the high seriousness of the true gardener, but I can personally sympathise with his feeling that the rock garden was a slightly ludicrous conception. Growing alpines is fascinating and apparently they were grown very well indeed at Friar Park, but they do not blend easily with other parts of the garden and, if you have the necessary income and a rather boyish sense of humour, there is obviously more to be said for whitewashed Matterhorns and model chamois than Farrer could ever have admitted. I am consumed with regret that I never saw Friar Park. I believe it survived in some state as late as 1939, so it was only ignorance that kept me away.

The only reason for an alpine garden is to grow alpine plants, and these will be neither helped nor hindered by model chamois or concrete Matterhorns, but if one wishes to indulge in the sort of follies described here, it is a perfectly allowable eccentricity, on a line with various other 'follies' but less expensive than the more grandiose ones. I hope I am not drummed out of the Alpine Garden Society for saying it, but the emotions of a grower taking his prized androsace or dionysia to the AGS show is much the same as that of Tom Mellor going to his show with laced pinks or his 'John Simonite' auricula. There is nothing ignoble in this and, indeed, the grower of alpines is in the same classless society as the old florists. Very little money is needed to subscribe to the Alpine Garden Society and from its marvellous seed list one can grow at little expense a wide variety of plants that would otherwise be unobtainable. But let us realise that each alpine plant is to be regarded as an object in itself and not try to make the alpine garden an integral part of the whole garden. No one looking at an alpine garden is liable to take the whole thing in a single view; he will be peering at individual plants. This does not mean that the alpine garden need be an eyesore, but only that the interest lies in the details rather than the *ensemble*. Few natural phenomena are more desolate, and indeed repellent, than screes, yet the scree in the alpine garden may well contain the most interesting plants. If we stuck too closely to Farrer's imitation of nature, the scree would be a desolation.

I suppose, if we want to be really deflating, those old rock gardens with numerous rock-girt compartments, each compartment containing one or two species, so that a huge mass of flowers would be present at the appropriate season, were nothing more than a development of the bedding system; not that it would have been any the worse for that, but its practitioners would have been quite convinced that it was very much better. Well, I suppose they were right. A mass of *Gentiana verna* does look better than a mass of *Lobelia erinus*, although the difference in the actual colour may not be great, but the attraction is in the mass of colour in each occasion.

Nowadays the great rock garden has been proved not only very expensive to erect, but very difficult to keep in good condition, and the movement is towards the raised bed, possibly with a stone wall or alternatively with a wall made of peat blocks. These rectangular erections can never be made particularly attractive to look at, but they will grow alpine plants extremely well. Apart from the odd lump of tufa, rocks are rarely employed nowadays to any great extent, while the more recalcitrant plants are not planted out at all, but grown in the Alpine House.

So far as I can make out, we have to thank Shirley Hibberd for this adjunct to the growing of alpine plants. In the *Floral World* for 1870 he suggested 'a low span roofed house, with sliding lights and glass sides, resting on low brick walls: in these walls ventilating shutters; the inside furniture to consist of a simple stage on each side; and *that is all*. The question of heating is intentionally avoided, for this house is not to be heated'. This is evidently an alpine house *in posse* and in the list of plants suitable for growing in such a structure Hibberd lists a number of alpine plants, but there are also a number of rather tender herbaceous plants and low shrubs. However, the following year, at the Royal Horticultural Society's Congress at Birmingham, Hibberd read a paper on alpine plants the last paragraphs of which ran as follows:

'It may appear paradoxical to propose to grow these plants under glass: and yet, when this method is properly conducted, the most happy results may be insured. We need low-roofed unheated structures, with substantial brick foundations and large beds of soil supported by brick walls in place of ordinary stages. By means of free ventilation, the plants may always be kept as cool as the climate will allow, and they can be protected against those destructive alternations of temperature, which characterise the early months of the year, when, lacking their proper covering of snow, they are apt to be forced into growth prematurely, only to be suddenly shrunk up again by biting eastwinds, or washed away by a deluge of rain at the moment of attaining to the full display of their beauties, as though blessed by the brief spring time of their native heights . . . For the structure which we shall designate the "Alpine House" selection should be made of Alpine plants that are especially adapted for pot culture. Their name is not legion, perhaps, but enough may be found to afford in the spring season a display at once attractive and unique . . .

'Should the taste for Alpine flowers continue to extend as it has done during the past few years, the Alpine House will become a necessary and acceptable institution, and probably will acquire an importance equal to that of any other of the many contrivances adopted in connection with decorative horticulture.'

This certainly would seem to give the invention not only of the house but also of the name to Hibberd, but the idea may well have come from the preface to Backhouse's catalogue of 1869, which said, *inter alia*: 'Some species—such, for instance, as *Eritrichium nanum, Androsace lanuginosa, Cerastium alpinum*—and those plants generally which have silky or cottony foliage, evidently dislike having their leaves wet by artificial means, especially in winter; as in a wild state they are buried during that season in dry snow or subjected to frosts which destroy every particle of moisture. These must either be planted where an overhanging ledge protects from snow and rain, or be grown in pots which can be placed under a glass frame admitting full ventilation in winter. Not that these plants are tender. They are nearly as hardy as the rocks themselves, but their winter alpine atmosphere is dry till the spring thaw sets in.' Commenting on this, Hibberd observed that the atmosphere in the frame tended to be rather 'lifeless', presumably with the corollary that damping off was liable to occur.

I don't know if anyone pursued the idea of the Alpine House, for we find in *The Garden* for 18 September 1880 a Mr Thomas Williams suggesting an Alpine House. This turned out to be a rock-garden built under glass and nothing more was heard of this suggestion.

(Mr Williams seems to have been anticipated in any case. I cite the following from the *Gardeners' Chronicle* of 5 October 1878: 'One of the most interesting houses we have seen lately is one in the garden of Mr Joad at Wimbledon; it is simply a rockery under glass, no heating apparatus being employed. The "rockery" . . . consists of tufa and artificial stone so placed as to leave deep pockets, wherein the plants are placed. In the present instance the plants are many of them of the description known as botanist's pets, comprising many rare and interesting species. A perforated pipe at the top of the house allows of irrigation being practised at will.')

Hibberd can not only be credited with the Alpine House, he also suggested the raised bed. In the *Floral World* for May 1869, in commenting on Backhouse's advice he wrote: 'But there is another way of growing Alpines which we have proved to be as good as any, and that is by giving them the soil and moisture they require in a slightly raised bed . . . Suppose, for instance, you receive fifty choice Alpines and have no suitable rockwork, the next best thing to do is to excavate a bed in some fully exposed spot, secure thorough draining and then fill up with fine sandy peat and a little good sandy loam through it . . . place a few rough stakes or slabs around this bed, cropping naturally from the earth, so as to raise your bed a little, say from six to sixteen inches . . . Such things as *Gentiana verna*, *Dianthus alpinus* and *Mysosotis alpestris* will flourish freely in such a situation.' Since Hibberd lived in Stoke Newington, he must have been a reasonably skilled cultivator, if these alpines really thrived as he said.

It might, I hope, be of interest to reproduce some more of Messrs Backhouse's directions: 'It maybe well here to state, that after long experience, and far too much of that kind of "misfortune" which usually attends "experimenting" upon new plants, we find that, as a rule, it is an error to place in the shade in summer, for the sake of coolness, those species which inhabit very high mountain regions. These plants, as a class, hate the soft humid, "lifeless" atmosphere, which shady situations in low districts afford. Living naturally on lofty ridges, they are constantly exposed to high winds, and an atmosphere of crystalline clearness, through which the sun's rays dart down with a vehemence which often heats the rocks till you can scarcely bear to touch them. This brilliant sunshine in the daytime, alternating with excessively heavy dews or sharp frosts at night, are the summer conditions of a large number of the rarest and most beautiful species in their native abodes. And these, born near vast fields of perpetual snow, receive a rapid and permanent supply of moisture at the roots, which is checked only when wintry winds bind everything in a mass of ice. Very rapid and perfect drainage combined with an equally rapid and continuous supply of water are therefore essential to thoroughly healthy development . . .

'Besides the question of moisture and atmosphere, that of soil is generally important. Hundreds of rare Alpines have been sacrificed to the idea that earth is essential to their vitality. We find that, with many species, the less of this they have, the better their chance, especially at first when not established. Grit (coarse sandstone crushed into every imaginable shape and size from sand upwards) is the "life and soul" of a large range of Alpines. When merely tinged with a little peat, cocoa refuse or loam, as the case requires, and kept moist artificially by filtration from above, this material exactly suits them and imparts a vigour that surprises the cultivator. Even river sand, unmixed with anything, often answers perfectly when the moisture is regular.'

With such knowledge it is not, perhaps, so surprising that the Backhouse nurseries were renowned for their alpines. Over a hundred years later there is nothing to add. Incidentally, in the same journal for May 1869 there is an article by a Mrs T. W. Webb describing her methods of collecting plants in the Alps. She took most of the earth from the roots, wrapped them in moss (which she took abroad with her), packed them in tin boxes, but exposed the plants to the air whenever possible during her travels. Once home, the plants were put in deep boxes which were lined with cinders and then filled with a compost of silver sand, peat and leafmould, in equal parts. The boxes were placed in a 'moderate hotbed', and sheltered from heavy rain and strong winds. During the following winters, gorse branches were laid across the plants. According to the authoress, the following rather difficult alpines flourished under these conditions, as well as the more easy plants: *Ranunculus glacialis*, *Viola biflora*, *Dianthus alpinus* and *glacialis*, *Campanula excisa*, *C. morettiana*, *Gentiana bavarica*, *G. imbricata* and *Soldanella alpina*. One always tends to think of the Alpine Garden as mainly a twentieth-century phenomenon, but this is evidently quite wrong.

Speaking of Alpine Houses, this is a good opportunity to mention my sole contribution to gardening, which I have called the Mediterranean House. I thought of this after collecting a large number of Mediterranean orchids and bulbous plants and it can be recommended for lazy gardeners. All it consists of is a house, glazed to the base. I personally used an aluminium frame, but I imagine any frame would do. If your local soil is suitable, leave it alone, but if it is very heavy it is probably best lightened with grit and peat to give a fairly open, quick draining medium. Leave a small path in the middle and plant up the beds on either side. I have a small electric fan heater to eliminate frost, but basically the house is unheated. The ground is kept moist from the end of August until mid-May, after which the bulbs are allowed to bake, provided there is sunshine to warm the soil up.

If you wish to turn one of the beds over to Oncocyclus iris, you should probably not water until late October and then only sparingly. Mediterranean bulbs seem to need not only drought during the summer, but also well-warmed soil, and so do better planted out in beds rather than in pots. The greenhouse also seems to warm the soil up more effectively than the bulb frame does, so this also is an advantage. The plan was devised for Mediterranean plants, but with suitable modifications it serves equally well for South African, Australian or Californian plants, although sometimes they can be mixed together. I find most South African bulbs enjoy the same treatment, and *Gladiolus tristis* increases to an excessive degree. Another plant which does very well with this treatment has been *Tropaeolum tricolorum*, which is usually seen as a rather restrained trailer, but planted out in beds can climb to eight feet and cover itself with scarlet flowers from February onwards.

My house starts in September with sternbergias and autumn crocuses and ends in May with *Gladiolus aleppicus, Serapias spp* and *Cyclamen persicum*, although this latter starts flowering in March. I also had, before I moved house, *Lilium chalcedonicum*, which was given the same treatment, but which did not flower until July; it appeared to thrive under drought conditions from May onwards and increased considerably. With the exception of *Iris planifolia*, I did not find that any of the junos flourished, and fritillarias certainly do not care for a summer baking. Possibly *Fritillarias graeca* might enjoy it, as it grows in fairly dry situations in the wild, but most of the eastern Mediterranean species come from near the snow line and have ample water while making their growth. Autumn crocus thrive under this treatment and *Crocus tournefortii* increases prodigiously. The various hermione narcissus also thrive well, and one can have them in flower from November until March. Of the autumn-flowering narcissus, *Narcissus serotinus* seems to flower fairly regularly once established, *N. viridiflorus* is very sporadic, while *N. elegans*, which looks to be the best, is apparently not in cultivation at all. The various ophrys all did well, although plants collected in Spain always seemed to do better than ones collected in the eastern Mediterranean; most Mediterranean orchis species did well, although *Orchis collina* was always a failure and *O. comperiana* lasted for only three years. All the tulips did well and most irises, other than junos. Indeed *Iris attica* did so well that I had to dispose of it, as it took up more space than was justified.

Since the house's main interest is at a time when other departments in the garden are rather lacking in interest, it is obviously attractive, and since it needs no attention after mid-May it does not interfere much with other gardening operations. One can also grow nerines under these conditions. The gorgeous *Ornithogalum arabicum* does far too well and make take over the whole Mediterranean House if not watched, as it both proliferates and seeds. Most Mediterranean plants will tolerate a little frost, but *Cyclamen persicum* seems to be very frost-tender and for this, at least, some slight heating apparatus is necessary.

There are a number of alpines which appear to be very difficult to grow or indeed impossible. First and foremost among these are the many handsome species of pedicularis, which live up only too well to their vernacular name of lousewort. These are known to be semi-parasitic, and so will require some root association, but this semi-parasitism seems to be rather a second string, as they produce perfectly adequate green leaves and roots, and quite often come readily enough from seed. I once brought back from the Alps a large clod containing *Pedicularis verticillata*, that marvellous crimson one of the higher meadows, and also, I hoped, sufficient of its hosts to make it unaware of the move. The result of this forethought was that the plant took three years to die in place of the more usual nine months; but it never looked as though it intended to do well. I once purchased a plant of *P. canadensis*, which actually flowered before retiring from the scene; naturally it was one of the less agreeable species. In the Alps there is a saxatile species, which cannot always find hosts to semi-parasitise in the wild, but I do not think it would prove any more amenable to cultivation (I think it is *P. asplenifolia*, but I cannot really identify most of them). The other semi-parasitic plant, the Indian paint brush of the North American meadows, *Castilleja spp*, seems to be slightly easier to keep for a short period. I had a plant of *Castilleja miniata* for quite a few years. Its chosen host was a forget-me-not, and, since this was only a biennial, it had to be replaced every other year; eventually the plant passed on to the happy hunting ground.

When I was young it was generally believed that the annual gentianellas were in this semi-parasitic class and, indeed, many of the species do have leaves that are deficient in chlorophyll, so there may have been some justification for this theory, although I do not think it is held nowadays. This might account for the complete inability of any gardener to grow *Gentiana* (*Gentianella*) *ciliata*, which is normally a biennial and so might be expected to come fairly briskly from seed; it is also found at varying heights, including quite low down, so it should not require any special climatic conditions. It was one of the plants brought back by Thomas Blaikie to Dr Fothergill, but we have no means of knowing if he was able to grow it. Miller apparently did grow it, and it is listed in the *Hortus Kewensis*, although this was not always so accurate as might have been expected, according to John

Smith, who worked at Kew while it was in preparation. Unless it needs some special root association, there is no apparent reason for this splendid plant's recalcitrance.

A plant that has no reputation for semi-parasitism, but which has proved remarkably loath to grow in cultivation, although it can be seen growing in the greatest profusion all over the Alps, is *Viola calcarata*, and its difficulty—one might almost say impossibility—of cultivation is not easily explained. In his *Himalayan Journals*, published in the early 1850s, J. D. Hooker wrote: 'It has long been surmised that an Alpine vegetation may owe some of its peculiarities to the diminished atmospheric pressure; and that the latter being a condition which the gardener cannot supply, he for this reason seldom successfully cultivates such plants. I know of no foundation for this hypothesis . . . The phenomena that accompany diminished pressure are the real obstacles to the cultivation of alpine plants; of which cold and the excessive climate are perhaps the most formidable . . . In our gardens we can neither imitate the conditions of an alpine climate, nor offer others suited to the plants of such climates.'

This must have sounded very plausible in the 1850s, but it will scarcely serve nowadays, when we can grow the majority of alpines with greater or less success. Most of the plants that grow in company with *V. calcarata* are easily enough accommodated; it is not a plant of the greatest heights, but on the other hand it never descends very low. Fournier, in his *Les Quatre Flores de France*, gives its lowest recorded level as 1,200 metres (about 4,000 feet) and it does seem to me just possible that there is some montane phenomenon which is essential to its well-being. I doubt whether it is atmospheric pressure, but it might well be increased ultra-violet radiation. It does occasionally flower in our gardens, but the flowers are never so ornamental as in the wild, and the plants survive for a very short time.

A similar phenomenon is observed with *Anemone baldensis*, which is found rather higher up, its range being from 1,800 to 2,700 metres. This will quite often survive at a low level, but it is loath to flower and when they do condescend to appear, they are miserable little horrors, with no visible relationship to the charming blooms that attracted us on high levels. There is yet another plant which may be found literally by the acre above 1,700 metres, which does not take readily to lowland cultivation, although it is not quite so difficult than the other two plants I have mentioned, and that is *Ranunculus pyrenaeus*. If it does consent to flower, the blooms are as good as in the mountains, but still it is not really happy. I am surprised to find that Farrer wrote: 'Give it a peaty crevice, and *A. baldensis* will be happy—and so will you.' Either plants were different in his day, or he was a better grower than anyone else, or perhaps he was exaggerating slightly. Listen to this: '*Viola calcarata* is a real robin-plant, a friend of man and delighted with his company. I have grown innumerable plants of him and they all smile at me as happily on the rockwork, even in autumn and early winter, as they do in July on the Alpine meadows.'

Of *Ranunculus pyrenaeus* he does not write with much precision, merely mentioning it as 'another of that delightful section headed by *amplexicaulis*, whose crowning merit is that they require no attention, but luxuriate in any cool light loam'. However, all his remarks about these ranunculus are inaccurate. He says that *R. gramineus* is one of the 'mountain Buttercups' that 'dwell only on the high pastures of the upper Alps', whereas it is found quite low down, even, according to Fournier, being recorded at sea-level. He also says that *R. pyrenaeus* is hardly distinguishable from *R. gramineus* except in flower colour, but *R. pyrenaeus* is confined to a single stem, while *R. gramineus* makes a great tuft.

Indeed, Farrer's claims about the ranunculus are surely inflated. Here he is writing about *R. glacialis*: 'And yet this plant, which looks as if it ought to be so exceedingly hard to cultivate, is the easiest and most robust of all the very high alpines. I give it a sticky, stony loam, and there *glacialis* thrives happily.' Has anyone ever seen *R. glacialis* thriving happily in an English garden?

But it is not only European alpines that have proved intractable, and it must be admitted that alpine plants are, by and large, more difficult to establish than any other form of plant. The scarlet *Meconopsis punicea* stayed for only a short time in cultivation; it did not set seed, so being monocarpic it was lost. *M. speciosa*, an inhabitant of high screes, with bright blue, deliciously perfumed flowers, was sent back on several occasions by Forrest and by Kingdon Ward, but no plant has ever flowered in this country. Occasionally failure appears inexplicable. The late R. D. Trotter could grow the purple-flowered *M. delavayi* with great success, but nobody else has ever been able to. *Incarvillea lutea* was often sent back by Forrest and was grown by many people with success, with the one essential proviso that nobody ever got it to flower. The number of Sino-Himalayan primulas which have made a very fleeting appearance in cultivation, owing to our inability to persuade them to set seed, is enormous. The seed of the cremanthodium species used to germinate readily, but the plants never reached flowering stage. Thomas Hay was of the opinion that this was due to the fact that they were completely intolerant of any root disturbance; he did, apparently, get some plants to the flowering stage, but they have all gone now, although no one would guess this from the article in the Royal Horticultural Society's *Dictionary*. Nor is it only the Sino-Himalaya which have provided so many plants that refuse to accommodate themselves to our gardens. The Andes are apparently full of the most fascinating-sounding plants: scarlet gentians, rosette-forming violets, scarlet gorse, brilliant blue oxalis, the list of tempting plants is long. Occasionally we hear of a solitary success, but no one has kept these plants for long. As for the mountains of Abyssinia and Kenya, they seem singularly intractable, with their extraordinary climate of very hot days and very cold nights. It would seem probable that the majority of herbaceous plants, trees and shrubs have been cultivated in this country at some time, either in the open air or in the glass house, but the number of montane plants that have never been seen growing and flowering in this country is still enormous.

18

LIGNEOUS PLANTS

What, I have no doubt you have asked yourself, is the difference between a shrub and a tree? In theory the tree has a central stem, which eventually becomes a trunk from which branches radiate, while a shrub will have a number of potential trunks rising from the base; but plants are liable to go their own sweet way and take very little notice of man-made definitions. Take for example the hawthorn. It can be trained up a single stem to make a tree, or it can be shoved into a hedge, where it will become bush-like. Acers are usually trees, but *Acer palmatum*, the Japanese maple, is usually seen as a bush. It may be only a matter of treatment.

On the other hand I cannot think of any treatment that would make the majority of berberis appear tree-like. The distinctions are, however, fairly fluid. One tends to think of a length of bare trunk as characteristic of the mature tree; but in that case what are you going to call a holly thirty feet high and a pyramid of verdure from the ground upwards. It is, of course, a perfectly good tree and the lower branches could all be sawn away to prove the point. The same can be said of the various cypress-like conifers, chamaecyparis and thuja. I suppose what it comes down to is that there are very few trees that could not be grown as bushes, but there are quite a few bushes that cannot be grown as trees. That is why I am labelling this section the ligneous department, rather than the more conventional trees and shrubs.

Have you observed how pejorative the suffix -ery has become? If you refer to the pride of the alpine gardener as a rockery, you will observe a pained look on the grower's face, while you might even risk physical assault if you spoke of a shrub garden as a shrubbery. No one has used the word treeery (and one can understand why), so it is still quite all right to speak of an arboretum. A century ago there was little distinction between a shrub garden and a shrubbery. Those curious amorphous clumps of evergreens that we now associate with the word were either more widely spaced then, and so less like a jungle, or they were inserted for a deliberate purpose. J. C. Loudon, the greatest garden theorist of the period, was wont to distinguish between the *picturesque* shrubbery, where an impression of bulk was required, and what he horribly termed the *gardenesque* shrubbery, where every plant was placed to be appreciated on its merits. The modern shrub garden is usually gardenesque.

Ligneous subjects have much to attract the practising capitalist. From a comparatively small capital outlay you can expect considerable appreciation, which should continue over a long period. It is not a coincidence that some investments are referred to as growth stocks, and shrubs and trees are certainly that. You cannot expect a rapid return on your investment, but it will gradually increase in size and beauty and by the time you are ready to die or to move house will probably be at its best.

This continued increase may sometimes be embarrassing, the more so if you do not know what the eventual size of your plant will be. I suppose one of the best shrubs of modern times is that cross between *Mahonia japonica* and *M. lomariifolia*, known either as 'Charity' or, correctly as *Mahonia × media* 'Charity'. *M. lomariifolia* is a rather gawky, tender shrub with deep yellow blooms in November and December; *M. japonica* has rather pale yellow flowers in February and March, while the hybrid will have deep yellow flowers at any time from January onwards. As I have said, *M. lomariifolia* is tall and gawky, and *M. japonica* eventually becomes a fairly spreading shrub, although it takes its time, but what will *M. × media* do? The only answer seems to be wait and see; but it is not easy, when one is designing one's shrub garden, if one does not know if a plant is going to be long and narrow or shorter and widely spreading. All the taller mahonias seem to start by elongating to some minimum height, usually around four feet, before they start to branch with much vigour, and if you attempt to encourage branching by the time-honoured method of removing the leading shoot, you are liable to find that this is just replaced, and that the plant has no intention of branching before it is ready. Most of the species have been in cultivation long enough for us to know their ultimate habit, but when new hybrids appear, this may well be a problem. Since even small plants are recalcitrant on being moved, you will probably not be able to move an established plant with much hope of success, if your first guess has proved incorrect, so you will have to take cuttings and start anew.

The same problem will arise with other hybrid plants, of which rhododendrons are likely to be the ones most often concerned, as well as any newly introduced plants you may be able to obtain. With the latter, you may get some idea of its ultimate size from the plant's behaviour in the wild, but this is not always a sure guide. Some plants do much better in cultivation, others do less well.

I am labouring this matter of dimensions, as it is crucial to designing the shrub or the tree garden. With herbaceous plants (with a few intolerant exceptions such as paeonies and hellebores) it is usually easy enough to shift plants which are unsuitably placed. With a fairly mature shrub or tree this is undesirable and may even be impossible, so it is important for the planter to have a mental picture of the ultimate size and shape of whatever woody subject he is inserting. I have mentioned this already, but the matter is so important that I make no excuse for harping on it, and I wish the compilers of catalogues would mention the probable dimensions of the plants they offer.

Here, however, we come up against a snag, as different plants reach different sizes in different districts. We think of the alder as a moderately sized tree of about forty feet when full grown, but near me is a monster some one hundred feet in height. Still, if the nurserymen would give the dimensions obtaining where they live, we could at least get some idea. I fear that sometimes the nurserymen have never seen a mature plant of some of the subjects they offer and might find it difficult to give the required information. Of course if there are well developed specimens in your neighbourhood, that is probably better than any other information.

With long-lived trees calculation may be impossible for a considerable period. The dawn redwood, matasequoia, has only been in cultivation for some twenty-five years, and no one can have the slightest idea as to its ultimate dimensions. It looks as though it will behave in much the same way as the swamp cypress, *Taxodium distichum*, in which case it may reach one hundred feet or more. On the other hand, it is growing so rapidly in cultivation that if it maintains its present rate it could be expected to get even taller. Still rapid growth in cultivation is not necessarily a good sign. Some of the nothofagus species grow very rapidly indeed, but as already pointed out have proved to be much shorter-lived in cultivation than in the wild, and the same may happen with the *Metasequoia*.

In the small gardens that most of us have to make do with nowadays, the question of dimensions has added importance, as there is probably only room for a single tree and a fairly small selection of shrubs. Not for such gardens are cedars, which may have a span of fifty feet at ground level. It is all very well saying plant a tree in seventy-three, but where are we to put it? There are, of course, a large selection of moderately sized trees that will do very satisfactorily in our small gardens and, indeed, it may well seem as though the genera *Crataegus*, *Malus*, *Sorbus* and *Prunus* were evolved entirely to furnish the small garden with attractive trees.

The disappearance of the potential market for trees and shrubs is the more regrettable as it is in this department that we can feel superior to our forebears. We certainly have a much larger selection from which to choose than they did, owing almost entirely to the exploration of the western Chinese flora in the early years of the century, mainly by E. H. Wilson and Georges Forrest; while in the field of rhododendrons F. Kingdon Ward must be bracketed with them. Moreover, not only did they find a lot of new plants, but they sent back plenty of seed. Discovering new plants is meritorious, but getting them into cultivation is even more so. Wilson felt slightly let down when he learned that he was not the first man to have introduced *Davidia involucrata* (the handkerchief tree) to cultivation, but he need not have been. The Abbé Farges had, it is true, sent back thirty-seven seeds before Wilson sent any, but only one of these had germinated and the bulk of plants in cultivation must have come originally from Wilson's gatherings, not from Paul Farges'.

The genus that was really transformed, from the garden point of view, from the exploration of the Sino-Himalaya is of course the rhododendron, which has become a great cult plant among many growers. Although in China and Tibet many of them seem to grow on calcareous soil, they all appear to require acid soil in this country, so that there are many districts where they cannot be grown. Where it is possible they are certainly very rewarding. They range in dimensions from prostrate shrubs to moderately sized trees and have a flowering season of at least nine months, so that the rhododendron-grower can have a very long display of flower, even though he grew nothing else. On top of that, many of the deciduous species produce brilliant autumn tints, so that the rhododendron garden is rarely dull. Admittedly, the foliage of many of them is rather monotonous, but on the credit side there are many with attractive glaucous blue-green leaves, while an even larger number have the young growths attractively coloured in red, purple, orange and silver. It would be quite possible to construct a bed of rhododendrons that was attractive solely through the foliage.

There are a very large number of species of hardy rhododendrons (and almost as many of greenhouse species) but this number has been topped by the quite fantastic number of hybrids that have been raised since about 1830. As a general rule, it might be argued that the hybrids are less attractive than the true species, though this is disputed, while it seems fairly certain that the hybrids tend to flower more reliably than the species, which are often somewhat irregular in their habits. The earlier hybrids were made to bring the colours of rather tender species, such as *Rhododendron arboreum* into the hardiness of species such as *R. ponticum*, *R. catawbiense* and *R. caucasicum*, and these so-called hardy hybrids are rather stereotyped in their appearance, with unattractive foliage and coarse semi-circular trusses of flower. As against this, they can be grown in almost any situation—the majority of species do best in dappled shade—and they start flowering when small, going on and on.

The one essential in growing rhododendrons is to discourage them from killing themselves by excessive seed production, so once the flowering is over you must go round and remove every truss of unripe capsules. This practice, known as dead-heading, is the only form of hard work that rhododendron-growing requires. Some of the species have very viscous stalks and dead-heading can be a thoroughly distasteful job. Oddly enough, this would seem to be a necessary chore even with sterile hybrids. There is a very attractive hybrid with tubular pink and white flowers early in the year called 'Seta'. This seems to be sterile, but when I left the capsules on a plant of mine, the resultant growth was unsatisfactory. It would seem that even if seed is not going to be set, the presence of capsules releases some chemical which inhibits growth. There is one plant which I always feel might set up problems, were it available. This is *R. cyanocarpum*. *Cyanocarpum* should mean that it has blue fruits and if the capsules really were blue, one might well wish to enjoy them. I believe the species is in cultivation, but it is not in commerce, so this temptation will not arise.

Some of the most impressive rhododendrons belong to the *Grande* series. These are said to be among the most primitive of the genus and make large trees with enormous evergreen leaves. In spite of their ultimate arborescent habit, they seem to require quite deep shade in their youthful stages and if this is lacking, the leaves will not attain the majestic dimensions that they might otherwise do. Unfortunately, these enormous leaves are very susceptible to wind damage, so that if your district is particularly liable to severe winds, it is probably as well to eschew them, even though the climate might otherwise be suitable. Most of them are, indeed, slightly tender and only really do well along the west coast, where the Gulf Stream tempers the winter cold and where the Atlantic will bring ample rain in the summer. Most of them are more decorative through their leaves than through their flowers, but an exception must be made for *R. macabeanum*, which has, in its best forms, butter-yellow flowers. Indeed one always tends to cherish yellow rhododendrons, as they seem to have a slightly luminous quality, in spite of the majority being a sulphur yellow rather than a rich yellow, such as found in the hybrid 'Crest'.

I have mentioned the various series into which the genus has been divided, so as to give some semblance of order to so many species, but the line of demarcation between the series is by no means clear-cut and

I suspect it would often be hard, even for an expert, when confronted with an unknown plant, to assign it correctly to its series. Some are reasonably simple. In the *triflorum* series, for example, the flowers do tend to be in bundles of three, although there may be more than one flower bud at the end of each growth, so that more than three flowers may be open at once. The *azalea* series is also fairly distinct, with its 5–10 stamens, besides the fact that many of them are deciduous. But the characteristics of the *irroratum* series seem to me to be nebulous in the extreme. I quote from *The Species of Rhododendron*, edited by R. J. Stevenson: 'The outstanding characters of the series are: the dominance of the shrub habit; the typical leaf is more or less lanceolate, although there are several exceptions . . . the indumentum is fugitive, and at maturity of foliage normally absent . . . the truss is rounded, recalling that of the series *Arboreum*, but much less compact; the calyx is usually very small, often a mere rim; the corolla is rarely other than tubular and rarely other than 5-partite.'

Now it may be that all these characters together do add up to something different from other series, but the only single character that seems worth anything to me is the very small calyx and, more doubtfully, the fact that the indumentum is absent at maturity. Even here it could in theory be confused with some of the *fortunei* series (*ss fortunei*) which also has glabrous leaves at maturity and a minute calyx, but usually has more than five lobes to the flower. It is a very artificial way of dividing up an appalling number of species, but nothing better has come along and we seem to be stuck with the series. Although it has been agreed for a long time that they are in need of revision, very little seems to have been done in this line. Not that it looks as though any revision will simplify matters much, but will probably increase the number of series and diminish the number of sub-series. There seems no reason why the various *argyrophyllum* should be regarded as a sub-series of the *arboreum* section, and the *cacucasicum* sub-series of *ponticum* appears to have nothing except the shape of the inflorescence in common with the *ponticum* sub-series, and so one might go on; apparently the *campanulatum* series is a complete ragbag of shrubs that will not fit comfortably into any series. The matter is probably of more interest to the botanist than to the gardener.

With a very large number of species to choose from, and a fantastic number of hybrids, how is the gardener who does not want to specialise in the genus to make a good selection? Well, there are various ways, but it will come as no surprise to anyone who has read anything else I have written to see that my suggestion would be to select those species and hybrids that have something more than attractive flowers to offer. For example, there is a very attractive early-flowering hybrid with pale yellow flowers called 'Bo Peep'. As an early-flowering shrub (and in a mild winter it may start to flower in February) it is certainly attractive, but later on it is also attractive when the chocolate-coloured young growth is emerging. R. *moupinense* is also liable to have attractive reddish young growth, which it has transmitted to its hybrid 'Tessa', and this may be more satisfactory in colder districts.

Another early-flowering plant, which can get very large in time, is R. *strigillosum*, which is often worth growing as a foliage plant alone; it tends to have long narrow leaves, which make a largish bush look like a green cascade. The red flowers, not always produced with the greatest freedom, may open in March. The trouble with these early-flowering species and hybrids is that they so often get damaged by frost, so that in some districts it is scarcely worth growing them. On the other hand, if room allows, the *barbatum* hybrids (or indeed *barbatum* itself) are so remarkably attractive, lighting up as they do the glum days of late winter with their glowing scarlet, that it seems worthwhile to resign oneself to only seeing the flowers irregularly. In mild locations R. *hookeri* (or, if it can be obtained, in cooler situations its hybrid with R. *barbatum*, 'Alix') not only has scarlet flowers in late February and March, but its new growths, which appear in May, have long scarlet scales between the leaves, giving a second season of attractiveness. The same brilliant scales can be found in the late-flowering R. *auriculatum* and some of its hybrids.

In April and May most of the azalea section come into flower, and among the deciduous ones are many with brilliant autumn tints. Although common, the pontic azalea, R. *luteum*, is still a smashing plant with its yellow, intensely fragrant flowers and its brilliant scarlets and yellows in the autumn. For sheer loveliness I suppose the awkwardly named *R. schlippenbachii* must always be in the top ten. This has large, open, soft-pink flowers, while the leaves, which open after the flowers are fully out, are attractively arranged in whorls and flushed with purple when young. They are said to colour well in the autumn, but I have never seen this happen. The plant is perfectly hardy so far as winter cold is concerned, but the young growths are susceptible to May frosts and if these are frequent in your district you should probably eschew this, as well as the almost equally attractive *R. albrechtii* with its plum-purple flowers.

For all but the coldest districts, *R. augustinii* has, in its best forms, bright blue flowers and purple-flushed young growth. The intensity of the blue seems to depend quite a long on climatic conditions and some years it may be a rather muddy blue-purple; there seems nothing to be done about this and the next year it may be back to its good colour again. In April or early May comes the enchanting *R. williamsianum*, which makes a low dome of neat heart-shaped leaves, copper-coloured when young, while the nodding pink flowers are very large for the size of the plant. It conveys the attractive leaf colour to its hybrids, of which 'Cowslip' with its ivory flowers, and 'Moonstone' with its pale-yellow flowers, are outstanding, while if a larger plant is required 'Arthur Ivens' can be recommended. 'Winsome', which is a second-generation hybrid from *williamsianum* (it contains the genes of RR. *griersonianum*, *haematodes* and *williamsianum*) still has the attractive colour in its young growth, although the leaf shape is quite distinct and it flowers in June.

Arguably—again in its best forms—the most attractive species is *R. thomsonii*, with its nearly circular leaves which are a vivid glaucous blue when young, while the flowers are deep crimson. The plant also has very attractive cinnamon-coloured bark. It is very sensitive to drought, nor does it flower until it is quite sizable, although you can enjoy its leaves immediately. Almost as attractive in its leaves, but a small plant with yellow flowers, is *R. litiense*, which is not very easy to obtain, although, owing to its glaucous leaves, it might be regarded as as more desirable than *R. campylocarpum* or *R. wardii*, two other yellow species, the first flowering in late April, the second in late May. A rare plant in this sub-series is *R. panteumorphum*, which is quite worth growing for its foliage alone, although its pale yellow flowers are certainly attractive.

If you want a smaller plant with red flowers and glaucous leaves, you can scarcely do better than the best forms of R. *cinnabarinum*, of which var. *roylei* is perhaps the most attractive. These have long drooping fuchsia-like flowers, quite unlike the majority of rhododendrons, and start to flower when comparatively small. In the same vein are R. *concatenans*, with orange flowers, and R. *xanthocodon*, which is a rather muddy yellow, so that there is a wide range of colour in this group. There are also hybrids with R. *maddenii*, which bring salmon and pink shades into this flower, but also a certain tenderness in the unopened flower buds which often seem to get frosted.

When we come to the June and July flowering plants it is not so easy to find any that can offer more than attractive flowers. There is a mysterious hardy hybrid known as 'Moser's Maroon', which has dark-crimson flowers and reddish young growth. There is that marvellous plant, R. *makinoi*, which has very narrow leaves, pink flowers in late May or early June, and very attractive silver young growth in August, when this is doubly welcome. I have already mentioned the red scales on the new growths of R. *auriculatum*, and these will also be found in its hybrids 'Argosy' and 'Isabella'. All these have large white fragrant flowers, 'Isabella' in late June, 'Argosy' in late July, and *auriculatum* itself in August. The snag about these late-flowering plants is that if it is hot and/or dry, the flowers at once flag, so that you have to water assiduously to enjoy the flowers. *Auriculatum* takes a long time to attain flowering size; although it grows rapidly it has to make a large plant before it starts to flower. Its hybrids take less time, but still tend to make large plants, so may not be suitable for small gardens. A smaller late-flowered plant is said to be R. *serotinum*, but I have never seen this, nor have any of my acquaintances.

The above selection is by no means exhaustive, but it does include plants that will be interesting over a longer period than the fortnight or so when the plant is in flower and it is this thought, I submit, which should guide us in selecting woody subjects for the garden. For far too long there has been a tendency to regard the shrub garden as a herbaceous border on stilts, but since we have to look at the shrubs all the year round we might well try to make them of some interest for most of that time. Of course, if you have plenty of space by all means plant such favourites as forsythias, lilacs and double cherries, but if space is limited you can almost certainly do better.

This seems an excellent point for me to introduce my King Charles's Head, *Koelreutera paniculata*, the Golden Rain Tree. This is a nice compact plant, quite suitable for the small garden; its leaves come out bright pink, then turn bronze and even when all colour has left them are of a graceful ferny shape. When the tree flowers in July and August, it has heads of bright-yellow flowers, at a time when any shrubs that do not have white flowers are particularly welcome. The seed capsules are also quite attractive, as they are inflated and bronzy in colour. The leaves will generally finally turn gold (or, apparently in some forms, scarlet) before they fall. The tree lacks attractive bark, but otherwise has every attraction a plant can have. It is hardy and not expensive, and why it is not in every garden I cannot think.

You may have observed that I have climbed on to my hobby horse, which is based on the assertion that you have to look at shrubs and trees for twelve months in the year, so they should be selected with a view to having as many attractions as possible. These can be listed in order of occurrence as attractive bark, coloured young wood, coloured young growth, attractive foliage, attractive flowers, decorative fruits and good autumn colour. We may as well realise at the outset that we are not going to get the whole list in a single plant. The koelreutera I have mentioned is not particularly attractive when there are no leaves on the tree. Glaucous-leaved evergreens such as *R. thomsonii* and the best forms of *R. cinnabarinum* are attractive at all seasons, but the main interest is when they are in flower and when the new growth is emerging. The point I would like to make is that the flowers should be only one consideration among many, not regarded as the sole *raison d'être* of the shrub garden.

In the case of trees, we might well add grace of habit to the list. It is this multiplicity of attractions that makes the woody department more interesting than the herbaceous or the alpine section of the garden. Admittedly in both departments there are some plants that are grown principally for their foliage; one thinks immediately of various artemisia species from the prostrate *Artemisia glacialis* to the shrubby *A. absinthium* and *A. splendens,* where the combination of silver with a ferny shape is not only equal to most flowers, but persists for much longer. But with a plant like the forsythia, you have your fortnight of beauty in early spring, at a time when it is most welcome, but once you have had that there is nothing for the other fifty weeks of the year.

Now let us suppose that instead of forsythia you plant *Hamamelis mollis.* It will grow more slowly, so that you do not get your grand effect so quickly, but it will give a brilliant display in late winter, any time between December and February, depending on the season, while the leaves will turn golden in the autumn, so that you have at least two seasons of interest. Take again those great double Japanese cherries. In May they will cover themselves with blossom (too thickly to be really attractive in my view, one might as well cover the trees with pink cotton wool, but few people will agree with me there) but again once it has flowered you have had all that the plant has to offer. If, instead, you plant the single *Prunus sargentii,* you still have a magnificent display of pink flowers in late April or early May, and, in addition, the leaves will turn crimson in the autumn, so again you are better off.

Again let us suppose that you require a small specimen tree for your garden. Most of the ornamental conifers, cedars, spruces and the like, are eventually too large for the small garden, so you have to look elsewhere. Consider one of the snakebark maples. If you can get it, try *Acer pennsylvanicum* 'Erythrocladum'. This has the same striped bark as the normal species, the leaves also emerge pink, again as in the species and may well turn golden before falling, but in this cv the year-old wood is bright red, so that a mature tree in the winter is a very brilliant sight. If you can't get this, there are other snakebarks, of which *A. capillipes* and *A. rufinerve* seem to be the most reliable. In *A. capillipes* the emerging leaves are mahogany red, while the autumn coloration is brilliant crimson. In *A. rufinerve* the young growths are a lovely glaucous blue, and the leaves often turn crimson before they fall.

Of course, with all these trees you have to wait a while before the trunk is sufficiently large to be really impressive, but once this has occurred you have a plant which is a joy to look at the whole year round. It is true that the floral display is negligible, so if you want

230

flowers perhaps you should consider some of the hawthorns. Apart from the pink and red forms of *Crataegus oxyacantha*, the flowers are always white, but they are produced in great quantity and are followed by brilliant fruits and, in many species, with brilliant autumn tints. One of the most distinctive is *C. phaenopyrum*, the Washington Thorn, which does not open its flowers until July, which is a time when tree and shrub flowers are becoming rather hard to find. These flowers are followed by haws that look as though they have been dipped in scarlet sealing wax, while the leaves will turn gold and crimson before falling. It has, also, a graceful habit.

However, with berries we must face up to the risk of bird damage. So far as I can make out, if you live in town, or if your garden adjoins a fairly busy road, bird damage is often negligible, but if you are in the country you may well find that you never see your berries at all, or that they persist for only a day or so. With sizable trees there seems little you can do about this. Birds-repellent sprays may work with smallish bushes, but it is quite a major operation to spray a well grown tree and it may be better in this case for you to eschew berrying plants altogether. You can, of course, grow the Sea Buckthorn, *Hippophae rhamnoides*, which the birds will ignore, but you have to have plants of each sex, so it may cause a space problem, although the plants are attractive with their silver leaves and orange berries if space can be found.

Otherwise if you want brilliant fruits you will do better to look at the various species of *Rosa*. I suppose the best value in this line is *Rosa moyesii*, with its deep crimson flowers and its huge flask-shaped heps, and these have been inherited by many of its hybrids, such as 'Sealing Wax', 'Highdownensis', 'Pruhoniciana' and 'Wintoniensis', while species with less brilliant flowers but equally good heps and slightly more attractive habit are *RR. macrophylla* and *setipoda*; *R. moyesii* is often a rather gaunt shrub. Less brilliant florally, but with the attraction of grey foliage as well as attractive heps, are *R. fedtschenkoana*, which has a very extended flowering season, so that the early heps are coloured before the last of the white flowers have opened, *R. murielae*, with rather small white flowers, and *R. soulieana*, with large heads of white flowers and orange heps; a magnificent plant, but a very large one, often growing ten feet high and wide and so a problem where space is limited. If that is the case the western American *R. woodsii* var *fendleri* can be recommended for its grey leaves, pinky-mauve flowers and long-lasting heps.

I rather resent my birds, as I have a great love of the various sorbus species. I do find, however, that *Sorbus cashmeriana*, with its ferny leaves, pink flowers (unusual in sorbus) and large white fruits, remains untouched for quite a time. This is a slow-growing tree, and never very large, so in many ways it is ideal for a small garden. The larger *S. hupehensis* with glaucous leaves and pale-pink fruits, is less dependable, but the small *S. gracilis*, even if the red fruits do not persist for long, has bronze young leaves which turn scarlet before falling. This plant, however, is more of a shrub than a tree.

Once one has a substantially sized tree, one can add a season of attraction by training a flowering climber into it. Climbers are, after all, intended to grow through shrubs and trees by nature and they will usually both look and grow better that way than pinned against walls. The main thing is to match your climber with the size of the tree. It is not much use putting *Clematis montana* up a small tree, as it will soon smother it, unless pruned regularly, and it is better to keep that species for a larger tree. Honeysuckles tend to do much better if much of their foliage is in the shade; they seem less liable to aphis attack, and not only do they flower but most of them have remarkably attractive fruits. *Schizandra rubrifolia* is a slow starter, but once away it will cover its host with rubies in May, while if both sexes can be obtained the female will later bear little coral necklaces. *Clematis tangutica* is always good value, with its yellow flowers and later its shaggy iridescent seed-heads, but almost any clematis is worth growing among trees or shrubs, although it must be remembered that they tend to grow with much greater vigour under these circumstances than they do on walls or fences.

To return to our fruits, some of the larger crabs are left by voracious birds, and plants such as 'Robusta' are very good value, with their abundant white flowers in the spring and their large red or yellow fruits in the autumn. The purple-leaved, red-flowered and red-fruited *Malus niedzwetzkyana* may be rather a large tree in itself, and it is

more often found in the purple-leaved hybrids which are so popular. I
have already mentioned one of the most exceptional, malus but as it is
still a rarish plant I will mention it again. This is the unfortunately
named *Malus tchonoskii*, with silvery leaves in the spring which colour
with great brilliance in the autumn. The flowers look like ordinary
apple-blossom, and are not easily distinguished against the silver leaves,
while the fruits are said to be unattractive, although I have never seen
them and can only report at second-hand. It has an upright, poplar-like
habit, so it is admirably suited for small gardens, where it looks quite
outstanding with its silver spire in the spring and crimson in the
autumn.

If the garden is almost entirely composed of woody plants, there
must, perforce, be other considerations than a multiplicity of charms,
and one of these is the paucity of subjects that flower after July. If one
starts to rout around, there are in fact quite a number of subjects, but
most of them are white-flowered, and in order to get colour other than
white into the garden in late summer and early autumn some ingenuity
has to be employed. There are a group of Burmese rhododendrons
which flower in July and early August with very showy red flowers,
but since they are tender and also generally unobtainable, one has to
search rather for their hybrids, which may have inherited their late-
flowering propensity. The only one of these that I know is called
'Firetail', which much resembles its pollen parent, *Rhododendron
eriogynum* and waits until July before it flowers. 'Europa' (*kyawi* ×
ungernii) should be a late flowerer from its parentage, but I have never
knowingly seen it. The various pink and red forms of *Hydrangea
macrophylla* always give the impression of florists' flowers and seem
rather out of place among other shrubs, although they are certainly
decorative, and the mauve-flowered *H. villosa* will blend in quite
happily with other plants. In the right districts fuchsia and escallonia
can bring reds and pinks into the late shrubs, while the various large
hypericums, formerly all known as patulum, will contribute yellow
over a long period. *Sophora japonica* has mauve flowers, but since it only
starts to flower when it has made a sizable tree one might feel that it is
grown more for its delicate foliage and attractive habit than for its
flowers.

The various indigoferas tend to behave like herbaceous plants in most parts of Great Britain, but they are shrubs and they do have late flowers in various shades of pink and purple, while among the climbers we have a large selection of clematis, both species and hybrids. Who has seen *Hedysarum multijugum*? Apparently it makes a shrub up to five foot high with from June to September erect racemes of rosy-magenta flowers. One can see that it may have been unpopular when magenta was regarded as an unpleasing colour, but that is not the general feeling nowadays, so perhaps we should be looking this mystery plant up. It sounds as though it might be rather attractive.

Among whites there is a fairly large selection from trees such as *Cladrastis sinensis* and *Maackia amurensis* (which has also very attractive metallic-blue young growth) to large shrubs among which the hoherias and ligustrums are probably pre-eminent. The hoherias tend to be rapid growers and very floriferous, although only *Hoheria sexstylosa* is reliably hardy, and even that can be damaged in the severest winters. Among the privets, *Ligustrum sinense* is probably the most graceful and spectacular, although *L. quihoui* is worth growing, not only for the sake of exhibiting its label, which must always have some value in one-upmanship, but also because it makes a very graceful, fountain-like shrub and since it does not open its flowers before October it prolongs the flowering season to some degree.

Earlier flowering, but in some ways more ornamental, is *Clerodendrum trichotomum*, with its fragrant white flowers, which may be followed by blue berries set in red calices, but this desirable effect is usual only in hot summers. *C. bungei* (*foetidum*) has handsome pink flowers, but tends to behave like a herbaceous plant and never gets very tall. Of course, if you are in a district where berries are not immediately devoured by our feathered songsters of the grove, by September the first sorbus are starting to introduce scarlet into the scene, and the latter part of the year can get progressively brighter as fruits ripen and leaves change colour.

Winter is when the ornamental barks and young woods make their strongest appeal. The Japanese maple known as 'Senkaki' has branchlets that are a coral pink. The red wood of *Cornus sibirica* is brilliant during the fitful sunlight of January, while the various willows with attractive branchlets, *Salix irrorata, daphnoides, purpurea, alba vitellina, alba britzensis* and the rest, now come into their full glory after having looked somewhat undistinguished during the summer. There is a tendency to pollard these, in order to get plenty of the brilliantly coloured year-old wood, but they are also very attractive if allowed to assume their natural tree habit. The display is not so concentrated, but it sometimes gains from this; a gracefully habited tree with coloured branchlets disposed over the whole surface has, for me, more attraction than the besom of coloured twigs which results from pollarding.

During the winter the birches really come into their own. They are probably not very suitable for small gardens, owing to their prodigious root growth, which exhausts the soil for a large area all around them, but the best species with their dazzling white bark (I think I am talking about *Betula ermanii*, but trying to identify *Betula* species is not an occupation for the amateur) are spectacular at all seasons, once they are sufficiently large, but particularly so in the winter. *Prunus serrula* (as opposed to *P. serrulata*) has a trunk which exfoliates to reveal a polished mahogany-like shining trunk below, and this looks splendid in the winter. Unfortunately the flowers are a rather dirty white and not very conspicuous, so clever nurserymen are now budding more attractive cherries on *P. serrulata* trunks, in the hope that we will get the best of both worlds.

It is in winter too that the evergreens really establish their true worth. Those that are variegated or golden in colour lighten the garden in winter, but almost any evergreen is welcome, although the very dark-leaved plants like many hollies, yews and various other conifers, need placing with care, as although they are a joy in the winter, they may look rather heavy in the summer. Some forms of *Cryptomeria japonica* turn bronze-coloured in the winter, but I am never sure if that is an advantage or no, unless you have room to grow a selection. I feel that an evergreen should look fresh in the winter and an autumnal tinge is apt to look rather lurid.

If your garden is too small to have some of these large, or potentially large, evergreens, you can scarcely do better than the various evergreen eleagnus. The variegated forms of *Eleagnus pungens*, particularly the golden-leaved forms, radiate cheerfulness at all times, but even the

P*

unvariaged *E. macrophylla*, with its rounded leaves and silvery reflexions, is attractive and this has the advantage of producing small but very fragrant flowers in October. Generally, if evergreens have attractive leaves, they will not contribute much to the floral display, although we should except the various mahonias from this generalisation, as their leaves may well be regarded as ornamental, while the flowers have the advantage of beauty and fragrance. The evergreen berberis from South America are not, perhaps, particularly striking in the winter, while the evergreen Asian species are less ornamental when in flower.

It is such an old inhabitant of our gardens, and has such dreadful connotations of old overgrown shrubberies, that it needs a bit of courage nowadays to suggest that the cherry laurel, *Prunus laurocerasus*, is an excellent garden plant. It has large evergreen leaves of a cheerful bright green; it has racemes of white flowers which are quite conspicuous, and after these it has red, cherry-like fruits, which the birds tend to disregard for a long period. I feel slightly touchy about this plant as I wrote a book about shrubs with their various attractions and omitted the cherry laurel, which is a good example of how one can miss something that is directly under one's nose and how familiarity can breed not only contempt but also unawareness. We are only too apt to disregard reliable and attractive plants because they are too common and too easy. Just think what a fuss we would make of *Laburnum* × *vossii* if it had to be grown against a south wall and only flowered at rare intervals. The fact that a plant is widely grown is usually a fairly safe guarantee that it is a good plant.

I must confess that the charms of *Aucuba japonica* have always eluded me, but that is probably because the heavy blotched leaves always seem particularly unattractive, while the red berries tend to be concealed from view. The plant is dioecious, and the female had been grown in gardens for its variegated foliage since 1783, but it was only after Fortune visited Japan in 1860 that the male plant became available and it was realised that the plant bore these large red fruits, so its popularity probably dates from the late 1860s and early 1870s. To get back to the cherry laurel, it is usually grown as a large, spreading shrub, where it is handsome but looks rather heavy; I wonder if it were grown as a tree, with the lower branches removed, it might appear more attractive. It might well be worth trying.

The beauty of woody subjects in the garden is that they can provide something of interest at any time of the year. The disadvantage is that most of them are eventually quite large, so that if your space is limited you cannot indulge in very many. I suppose that the aims of the garden are twofold: you want to grow the plants that interest you, but you must cut your suit according to your cloth and, for most of us, some compromise is forced upon us between what we want to grow and what we can.

BIBLIOGRAPHY

BOOKS

Bartram, William. *Travels* (1792)

Bean, W. J. *Trees and Shrubs Hardy in the British Isles* (1921)

Bowles, E. A. *Crocus and Colchicum* (1951)

——. *My Garden in Spring* (1914)

Farrer, Reginald. *My Rock Garden* (1907)

Hibberd, Shirley. *The Amateur's Flower Garden* (1871)

——. *Rustic Adornments for Homes of Taste* (1856)

Hooker, J. *Himalayan Journals* (early 1850s)

Li, H. L. *The Garden Flowers of China* (1959)

Lloyd, Christopher. *The Well-tempered Garden* (1970)

Loudon. *Hortus Britannicus* (1840)

Miller, Philip. *Gardener's Dictionary* (1768)

Philips, Henry. *Flora Historica* (1830)

Rehder, Alfred. *Manual of Cultivated Trees and Shrubs* (1949)

Robinson, William. *Alpine Plants for Gardens* (1870)

——. *The English Flower Garden* (1883)

Royal Horticultural Society. *Dictionary of Gardening* (1951)

Stevenson, R. J. (ed). *The Species of Rhododendrons* (1930)

Sweet, R. *Hortus Britannicus* (1833)

NINETEENTH- AND TWENTIETH-CENTURY PERIODICALS

Alpine Garden Society Bulletin
Asiatic Journal
Botanical Magazine

Edinburgh Journal
Floral World
Floricultural Cabinet
The Garden
Gardener's Chronicle
Gardening Illustrated
Horticultural Magazine
Transactions of the Horticultural Society

INDEX

240